PLACING HISTORY

How Maps, Spatial Data, and GIS Are Changing Historical Scholarship

Edited by Anne Kelly Knowles
Digital supplement edited by Amy Hillier

ESRI PRESS
REDLANDS, CALIFORNIA

ESRI Press, 380 New York Street, Redlands, California 92373-8100

Copyright © 2008 ESRI

All rights reserved. First edition 2008
10 09 08   1 2 3 4 5 6 7 8 9 10

Printed in the United States of America

Library of Congress Cataloging-in-Publication Data
    Placing history : how maps, spatial data, and GIS are changing historical scholarship / edited by Anne Kelly Knowles ;
    digital supplement by Amy Hillier.—1st ed.
        p.   cm.
    Papers presented at a conference held at the Newberry Library in Chicago in March 2004.
    ISBN 978-1-58948-013-1 (pbk. : alk. paper)
    1. Historical geographic information systems—Congresses. 2. Historical geography—Methodology—Congresses.
    I. Knowles, Anne Kelly. II. Hillier, Amy, 1970–
    G70.212.P55   2007
    902.85—dc22   2007038445

Ask for ESRI Press titles at your local bookstore or order by calling 1-800-447-9778. You can also shop online at www.esri.com/esripress. Outside the United States, contact your local ESRI distributor.

ESRI Press titles are distributed to the trade by the following:

In North America, South America, Asia, and Australia:
Ingram Publisher Services
Toll-free telephone: (800) 648-3104
Toll-free fax: (800) 838-1149
E-mail: customerservice@ingrampublisherservices.com

In the United Kingdom, Europe, and the Middle East:
Transatlantic Publishers Group Ltd.
Telephone: 44 20 7373 2515
Fax: 44 20 7244 1018
E-mail: richard@tpgltd.co.uk

Cover and interior design
by Jennifer Jennings
Cover image is a detail from the
Peutinger Map, by permission of the
Austrian National Library, picture
archive, Vienna: Cod. 324, Segm. IV.

The concept for *Placing History* and the various contributions to this volume originated in "History and Geography: Assessing the Role of Geographical Information in Historical Scholarship," a conference held at the Newberry Library in Chicago in March 2004. The conference was organized by Anne Kelly Knowles in collaboration with the Newberry's Hermon Dunlap Smith Center for the History of Cartography under the direction of James R. Akerman. "History and Geography" was made possible in part by a major grant from the National Endowment for the Humanities: great ideas brought to life. Additional support was provided by Jack and Laura Dangermond.

CONTENTS

CONTENTS OF DIGITAL SUPPLEMENT

FOREWORD

Scholars have claimed to write "new histories" that broaden the scope and techniques of the discipline for more than a century. Those efforts, however, have rarely involved new ways of doing history. Virtually all have been new varieties of narrative histories, and their format has been the printed book or article. Quantitative history was a new history that claimed to go beyond narrative. But as Ian Gregory writes in his essay in this volume, the crude positivism, narrow questions, and restricted evidence of quantitative history cost it an audience among historians. It ultimately promised far too much and delivered far too little. Historians would therefore have good reason to approach this collection and its claim of doing history in a new way with considerable skepticism and suspicion. These are, after all, the major virtues of historians.

I think, however, that the comparative modesty and good sense of these essays, as well as the real excitement they generate, will impress historians. The authors do not claim, as quantitative historians once did, that narrative histories are henceforth obsolete and that calculus will be the new language of historical discourse. They do not claim that the book is dead; indeed, one of the ironies of this collection is that by offering representations of space that are, in their original form, digitalized data accessible on the Internet or in other ways, the authors offer alternatives to the book in a book. This is a little embarrassing, but it is more than a little necessary. The formats for the kind of histories called for here are only now being established.

The histories proposed and outlined in these essays are in the broadest sense spatial histories. Historians have concentrated on developments over time. Geographers have tended to concentrate on developments across space. There have, of course, been historical geographers, and historians are no longer as guilty of ignoring space as they were twenty years ago when Edward Soja in his *Postmodern Geographies* accused them of writing history as if it was "packed solidly on the head of a pin." Historians today do not ignore space, and geographers are hardly unaware of time.

The problem is not one of awareness. The problem is not having available, first, the techniques to analyze the historical construction of space and its representations and, second, the present inadequacy of forms in which to present such research. The major geographical form—the map—is good at representing some kinds of space but not very good at tracing relationships through time. The historical form—the narrative—is not very good at expressing spatial relationships.

Relationships that jump out when presented in a spatial format such as a map tend to clog a narrative, choking its arteries, until—even if the narrative does not expire—the reader, overwhelmed by detail, is ready to die of tedium and confusion.

Recent advances in geographical information system technologies promise a way out of the problems that historians have faced in tackling the historical construction of space. These new techniques allow scholars to explore spatial variation without getting boxed in by a single cartographic representation. GIS, as Peter K. Bol writes in his essay, presents a "platform for organizing data with temporal and spatial attributes—population, tax quotas, military garrisons, religious networks, regional economic systems, family history, and so on—representing them graphically and analyzing their relationships." Some of the essays in this volume offer a clear and critical account of what GIS does, stressing both its possibilities and its limits. Other essays give examples of spatial research, and some, like Bol's essay, do both.

In reading these essays, I would caution, as several of the authors do, against reducing GIS to mapping, even if it does enable one to create more accurate and more sophisticated maps. As Richard Talbert's and Tom Elliott's account of the Peutinger Map demonstrates, GIS also allows a more sophisticated understanding and analysis of existing maps. One of the great promises of historical GIS is the possibility of organizing and presenting knowledge visually in new ways that go beyond maps and mapping.

GIS offers the ability to experiment with different ways of organizing historical data. Historians already organize material by location, but they usually do so on the local scale. Essays such as Brian Donahue's can be read as simply more sophisticated, detailed, and nuanced ways of doing what historians and historical geographers already do, but the kind of detail Donahue musters can usually only be presented on the local scale. When historians move to the regional, national, and transnational scales, not only does the detail usually fall away, but the region and nation often become mere containers. Spatial analysis matters less and less as the scale increases. GIS creates the possibility of extending spatial analysis beyond the local scale. It allows us to move up and down scales in a single study instead of concentrating on a single scale. We can tell more complex stories more clearly and coherently.

Both Michael Goodchild's and Ian Gregory's essays should be required reading for anyone interested in an intelligent discussion of the new technologies. Goodchild explains that the real breakthrough with GIS databases is their ability "to store things that were fundamentally not mappable. Classes could be time-dependent, with attributes and locations that changed through time. Areas could overlap, and lines could cross without forming nodes." He argues that "GIS has moved from a technology heavily dominated by the map metaphor to one that provides a comprehensive, efficient, and flexible approach to the representation of phenomena in space and time." To see what he means, read his essay and look at his examples.

Today, as Goodchild notes, GIS databases can readily deal with "objects that move, objects that change shape, and other phenomena that cannot be portrayed on paper maps." With these changes, the possibilities of interesting convergences of narrative histories and visual histories increase. Changes that are hard to express or even comprehend through conventional historical research and narrative become visible and comprehensible through the new technologies and visual presentations.

Because GIS databases are costly to create and use, they are going to change the practice of history in a second, related way. Spatial history not only creates the possibility of history becoming more collaborative, it virtually necessitates it. The individualism of history has always been overstated. All history is collaborative in the sense that no historian begins anew. We build on, quarrel with, and reinterpret existing history; and we always, using footnotes, plunder the sources that others have assembled. All history depends on earlier histories. The extension of this collaboration means that we will not only depend on prior histories but on contemporary historians. If we are going to build these databases, we need to make them as flexible, accessible, and functional as possible. They need to be open to the contributions of many researchers. We may all make different sense of the results, but we need to make sure that the database itself is coherent and as broad as possible. This means that we must try to reach some consensus on what we imagine a broad spatial history would be and try to build databases that will allow us to construct it. As we build such projects, we will be able to imagine even greater possibilities. There is great potential here. Whether we will achieve it or simply spend what for historians is an awful lot of money remains to be seen.

—Richard White
Stanford University

PREFACE

Over the past twelve years or so, what is coming to be called "historical GIS" has emerged as a promising new approach for studying the past. Historical GIS is an umbrella term covering the many ways researchers are using geospatial technologies and analytical techniques for historical research and teaching. The core technology is usually GIS (geographic information systems) software, which enables one to display and analyze any kind of information that can be located on the face of the earth, or any other place with known location. Because almost every kind of information is located someplace, the potential applications of GIS are limitless. As a research method for history, GIS offers an unprecedented range of tools to visualize historical information in its geographic context, examine it at different scales, interrogate its spatial patterns, and integrate material from many sources on the basis of shared location.

Historical GIS is still something of a maverick method in the study of history, as yet unheard of in some quarters. While only a small proportion of historical scholars are using GIS for mapmaking or as a core database architecture for large projects, the number of scholars applying GIS to historical questions seems to be growing exponentially. The excitement generated wherever scholars present GIS-based research seems a clear indication that this dynamic method is bound to be more widely adopted in coming years. At the same time, historical GIS also raises skeptical eyebrows, as some question whether the results of geospatial historical analysis are entirely new or warrant the tremendous labor the method can require.

This book and accompanying digital supplement originated in an interdisciplinary conference intended to examine the promise of historical GIS and the problems it poses for historical scholars. The conference, titled "History and Geography: Assessing the Role of Geographic Information in Historical Scholarship," was held at the Newberry Library in Chicago in March 2004. Given the growing interest in the use of GIS and other geospatial methods in historical research, the time was ripe to bring together leading practitioners from across the humanities and social sciences for focused intellectual exchange and to assess the state of the field. The field was also sufficiently mature to be ready for serious critique. With the first generation of historical GIS projects around the world coming to fruition in the form of books and digital infrastructure projects, it was time for those engaged in the enterprise to pause to consider whatever assumptions were embedded in their work and identify issues that should be addressed in future research. The conference proved to be a landmark event, thanks to the generosity of the twenty-eight scholars who presented outstanding papers and offered insightful critiques, as well as the energetic participation of more than one hundred other attendees.

The alternation between case studies and critical reflection that structured the conference also serves as the organizing principle for *Placing History: How Maps, Spatial Data, and GIS Are Changing Historical Scholarship.* Because one book could not contain all the conference papers, Anne Kelly Knowles and James R. Akerman, as the conference organizers, were compelled to choose. The case studies selected for this book address important questions of historical interpretation and collectively give a good sense of the great variety of GIS techniques now being used in history. The issues-oriented essays stem from papers that provided essential background information for understanding the development of historical GIS or that articulated methodological and philosophical problems historical scholars commonly encounter when they incorporate geographic information and geospatial methods into their historical research and teaching.

When *Past Time, Past Place: GIS for History* was published in 2002, the field was still very new, and few major projects had been completed. Like that book, *Placing History* aims to inspire professors, students, and professionals in history-related fields to think geographically about the past and to imagine how GIS might help them pursue interesting questions. Where *Past Time, Past Place* was a sampler of ideas, *Placing History* presents mature scholarship, the final fruit of projects that took many years to complete. In the opening essay, "GIS and History," Anne Kelly Knowles gives a comprehensive overview of the intellectual roots of historical GIS and how it has developed over the past decade. Award-winning environmental historian Geoff Cunfer offers new evidence to support his regional analysis of the Dust Bowl, which was featured in *Past Time, Past Place.* Ian N. Gregory, a historical geographer who sketched the problem of administrative boundary changes in the earlier volume, here examines the much broader issue of the inherent limitations of conventional thematic maps and argues for probing geographic data further with geostatistical methods. Deconstruction takes on new meaning in the creative digital surgery performed by classics scholars Richard J. A. Talbert and Tom Elliott as they reveal the genesis and accuracy of the Peutinger Map of the Roman Empire. Their GIS analysis of the ancient map goes far beyond the essentially cartographic use of GIS described in their *Past Time, Past Place* contribution. Historian David J. Bodenhamer, who previously introduced the *Atlas of American Religion* project, here takes the position of devil's advocate, asking why historians have been slow to adopt GIS. He argues that the technology's basis in mathematics and geographic location is in many ways foreign to the traditions of historical inquiry.

Other authors are new to this volume. East Asia scholar Peter K. Bol explains the fundamental differences between Western and Chinese conceptions of space and place and their implications for structuring the ambitious China Historical GIS project, which offers a geographical window on two thousand years of Chinese history. His use of nodes and networks rather than administrative areas offers an alternative model that will intrigue all historians who study cultures and periods whose spatial and cartographic traditions differ from those of Western nation-states. Robert Churchill and Amy Hillier show in their essay on GIS in liberal arts education how GIS-based instruction enriches students' education by giving them a flexible tool for understanding the world around them. Brian Donahue explains how he constructed the historical GIS of landownership and land use that stands behind his prize-winning study of colonial farming in Concord, Massachusetts—an approach that solves a basic methodological problem in agricultural and environmental history. Michael F. Goodchild, the leading scholar of GIScience, encapsulates the historical evolution of GIS database design, arguing that the new generation of object-oriented GIS offers the best model for historical applications. And lastly, Anne Kelly Knowles and a team of student researchers explore the potential of using GIS terrain analysis to investigate the meaning of "good ground" and the importance of visual reconnaissance in military history.

Placing History also includes a CD-ROM digital supplement that contains four Microsoft PowerPoint presentations and interactive mapping exercises, some of which extend the scholarly material in the book and others that address new issues. This is our invitation to students and scholars to join us in discovering new interpretations and new ways to apply GIS and geographic inquiry to the study of history. The CD is designed to assist teachers and students by providing ready-to-use resources about maps and GIS, including hands-on material for those ready to try GIS for themselves. We encourage readers to pick and choose what is most useful. Each of the PowerPoint presentations includes extensive notes that provide context and explain the slides so that instructors can use them confidently in class. Because the notes explain spatial analysis techniques and concepts as well, they may also be helpful to students and scholars who are learning GIS on their own.

The first presentation, created by Anne Kelly Knowles, walks through the process of reading historical maps. It features images of historical maps representing a wide range of places and themes, from a chart of whaling grounds published in 1851, the same year as *Moby Dick,* to a Civil War map of New Orleans. Using her background as a historical geographer, Knowles explains what historical maps can tell us about the past and what kinds of information they include. She uses a series of maps created by her Middlebury College students to show what novice mappers can achieve in historical–geographic research.

Peter K. Bol offers an overview of the data included in the China Historical GIS (CHGIS) in his presentation. He describes the different types of GIS data he and his team created and how they recorded changes in place names between 222 BC and AD 1911, the years that the CHGIS covers. He then shows how the different map layers can be symbolized to address specific questions, such as how commerce developed in particular regions and how population changed over time, as well as what further information is available on the CHGIS Web site.

Geoff Cunfer's digital presentation reveals how photography and film have helped shape our understanding of history, in particular the causes and consequences of the Dust Bowl in the 1930s. His slides feature dramatic photographs from the Farm Security Administration and clips from Pare Lorentz's film *The Plow that Broke the Plains.* Amy Hillier's presentation uses examples from her research on mortgage redlining in Philadelphia from the 1930s to the 1950s to show how different research questions require different GIS techniques. She shows how paper documents of various kinds can be transformed into GIS layers and how GIS and spatial statistical techniques can help answer long-standing questions about how mortgage lending created and reinforced inequality in cities like Philadelphia.

In addition to the presentations, the authors have provided scanned maps and GIS layers from their research. These include many of the GIS layers from the China Historical GIS, county-level data relating to the Dust Bowl, and census-tract and address-level data on mortgage lending in Philadelphia. We have bundled these into three different GIS projects for viewing and manipulation using ArcExplorer Java Edition for Education software. We hope that teachers without the resources to design their own GIS lessons will take advantage of this option. This data can also be used with ArcGIS software. Using GIS to create and analyze maps can be fun and rewarding.

The accessible writing and striking graphics in the book and CD make *Placing History* a stimulating source of readings and classroom exercises for survey courses in U.S. history (see particularly the Dust Bowl, Concord, and Gettysburg chapters) and world history (the China and Peutinger Map chapters). As a rich survey of the emerging field of historical GIS, *Placing History* offers a compelling core text for upper-level courses in research methods and specific topical areas in history, geography, GIScience, sociology, anthropology, and many other disciplines. The book and CD are also an excellent resource for teachers and researchers in information technology, humanities computing, and public history, where the need to understand GIS and geographic information is increasingly important.

—Anne Kelly Knowles and Amy Hillier
Middlebury / Philadelphia, January 2008

ACKNOWLEDGMENTS

We are indebted to many fellow scholars and friends for the support, enthusiasm, and helpful criticism they have given this project. Our greatest debt of gratitude goes to the people in the Newberry Library's Research and Education division who made the "History and Geography" conference possible. James R. Akerman, director of the Hermon Dunlap Smith Center for the History of Cartography, organized the conference seamlessly with the able assistance of Susan Hanf. James R. Grossman, vice president for research and education, warmly encouraged the idea of holding such a conference when it first came up in 1998 and throughout its long gestation. The conference was funded by a collaborative research grant from the National Endowment for the Humanities, with additional support from Jack and Laura Dangermond.

We also thank the many scholars whose reviews significantly improved the book manuscript: Ralph E. Ehrenberg, former chief of the Geography and Maps Division, Library of Congress; Michael Haines, Department of Economics, Colgate University; Stephen J. Hornsby, director of the Canadian-America Center, University of Maine, Orono; Mark Monmonier, Department of Geography, Syracuse University; Penny L. Richards, research scholar, UCLA Center for the Study of Women; Richard H. Steckel, Departments of Anthropology, Ohio State University; Jennifer Trimble, Classics Department, Stanford University; Joseph S. Wood, provost, University of Maine, Portland; Cordell D. K. Yee, St. John's College, Annapolis; and May Yuan, Department of Geography, University of Oklahoma. Special thanks to Graeme Wynn, Department of Geography, University of British Columbia, who reviewed the entire manuscript.

We deeply appreciate all the creative energy and care this project has received from the staff of ESRI Press. Thanks to Mark Henry for editing the text and shepherding it through production, Jennifer Jennings for her lovely cover design and interior layout, Tiffany Wilkerson for her conscientious copyedit, Jay Loteria for his development of the digital supplement, Michael Law for his cartographic review, David Boyles for his editorial oversight, Kelley Heider for administrative assistance, and Cliff Crabbe for overseeing production. Thanks also to Jennifer Hasselbeck for design assistance and to Bernard Szukalski and Charlie Frye for their GIS expertise. Mike Hyatt gave us his design wisdom and his wit. Kathleen Morgan kept her humor throughout the permissions process. We particularly thank Judy Hawkins for her strong support for this project.

Lastly, we note with great sadness that Robert Churchill, who authored part I of chapter 3, died while this book was in preparation. Bob was an enthusiastic supporter of this project and of using GIS in history and across the curriculum. He was an inspiring teacher and an unforgettable colleague.

GIS AND HISTORY

By Anne Kelly Knowles

This book argues that scholars' use of geographic information systems (GIS) is changing the practice of history. Time will tell whether the argument is prophetic or premature. The number of historians using GIS and allied geospatial methods is growing so rapidly that many of us in the field expect to see an exponential increase in GIS-based historical studies over the next decade. At the same time, some of the fundamental characteristics of GIS can make it difficult to apply to historical problems. As a kind of computer software designed to facilitate the mapping of very large quantitative datasets, GIS has been embraced most readily by social science historians. It is a superb tool for mapping and geographically analyzing census data, social surveys, and other kinds of systematically collected information linked to known geographical units and locations. It allows one to visualize the geographic patterns embedded in historical evidence, examine evidence at different scales, aggregate data from smaller to larger units, and integrate material from textual, tabular, cartographic, and visual sources, provided that they share common geographic location. The precision that makes GIS so useful in many kinds of scientific and statistical analysis, however, can make it an awkward instrument for historical research when sources cannot easily be reduced to entries in a tabular database.

GIS is also problematic for history because it is an emphatically visual medium and its internal architecture and many of its analytical functions are based in mathematics, beginning with the geometry of map projections and geographic coordinates. The visual and mathematical characteristics of GIS count as strikes against the technology for many historians. Art historian Barbara Maria Stafford argues that since the late nineteenth century, history has been a logocentric profession that privileges words and linear logic over images and our more synoptic apprehension of their content and meaning.[1] Historical research usually focuses on the study and interpretation of verbal texts. Quantitative history has never attracted a huge following, and the proportion of statistically inclined historians appears to be dwindling. Historians use images more freely than numbers. Fine art, photography, and historical maps are subjects of historical study in and of themselves. But historians generally do not regard images as sources of historical evidence,[2] which is their primary purpose in historical GIS. It is a telling indication of the gulf between the conventions of GIS and history that in GIS parlance the word "image" means both pictures in the usual sense, such as photographs, and data stored in grids of pixels, such as satellite images that record thermal radiation from the earth's surface. The form of information in GIS can seem quite alien to humanists upon first encounter.

A third basic impediment to the adoption of geospatial methods in historical research is the epistemological divide between geography and history.[3] Scholars in the two disciplines are fond of saying that history is the study of when, geography the study of where. This truism applies to historians' attachment to periodization as an organizing principle and geographers' interest in explaining spatial differentiation, but it obscures a number of other equally important epistemological differences. I have already mentioned one of them—that history's classic mode of communication is narrative, while geography finds its most distinctive expression in the visual, synoptic presentation of evidence in maps. Historians seek causal explanations by establishing the temporal sequence of events. Geographers find causation in the spatial proximity or distance of conditions. Geographic training inculcates acute awareness of scale as a limiting factor on interpretation, for the results of geographic analysis at one scale may not hold at another scale. Historians have a comparable but quite different sensitivity to social context as a critical factor for understanding the limits of historical evidence and one's interpretation of it. Members of the two disciplines also practice their craft quite differently. While historians valorize books, the majority of geographers publish research articles. Most historians work alone; many geographers conduct research in teams. Professional training in each discipline reinforces the differences between them. Geographers typically receive little training in writing, textual analysis, or understanding the social bias inherent in their sources. Not many read history. Few historians learn technical skills in the visual arts such as drawing, graphic design, or cartography, skills that help one interpret maps and other forms of visual evidence and enable one to present research findings effectively in graphic form. Exposure to geographical principles is just as rare.

Historical GIS calls for all of these skills, kinds of awareness, and intellectual training. It compels writers to think graphically and forces spatial thinkers to come to grips with the subtlety of historical texts. Every contributor to this book has found historical GIS to be challenging, which is no doubt part of its attraction. The interdisciplinary nature of historical GIS is reflected in its practitioners, who include scholars of every discipline in the social sciences and humanities. Despite its diversity, historical GIS is animated by a common interest in situating history in its geographical context and using geographic information to illuminate the past. In the remainder of this essay I will explain the intellectual contexts from which historical GIS has arisen and the thematic areas where GIS-based history has developed most strongly. I will conclude with reflections on several conceptual and technical challenges that historical GIS poses for historians and for GIS experts.

INTELLECTUAL CONTEXT OF HISTORICAL GIS

Historical GIS follows several antecedent genres of scholarship whose practitioners have examined history from a geographical perspective. One was the French *Annales* school. Historian Fernand Braudel's idea of *geohistoire* was, as Alan Baker writes, "a historical understanding of the spatial and environmental contexts of human activities," which would involve mapping them where possible.[4] Although the *Annales* approach has been called "the cartographic method in history,"[5] its French adherents and their followers elsewhere made little use of maps or geographic information. Their method mapped history in a metaphorical sense by combining cultural, economic, and political history like the layers of information in a complex map. They also more deeply considered the significance of the physical environment than had most historians. The most geographical characteristic of the *Annales* school was its treatment of place and region as historical subjects, as in Braudel's expansive study of the Mediterranean world and Emmanuel Le Roy Ladurie's exhaustive recreations of medieval Pays d'Oc and Languedoc.[6]

The idea of *geohistoire* and the writings of the *Annales* school made an impression on historians but did not convince many to adopt its underlying precepts. In much the same way, historians are aware of historical geography, notably the writings of Donald Meinig, without being strongly influenced by geographers' work, at least in the United States.[7] Anglophone historical geography differs from *geohistoire* in several ways. Although both value the descriptive art of capturing the uniqueness of places, historical geography has traditionally been more concerned with discovering the underlying social and economic processes that shaped the development of rural and urban landscapes over time, and how localized circumstances modified the outcomes of larger structural forces as they played out in particular places. Beneath the topical diversity of historical geography are three common practices: testing historical explanation with empirical geographical evidence; using maps and spatial diagrams to visualize spatial processes and make visual arguments; and a proclivity to develop typologies that pin the stages of historical-geographical change to characteristic manifestation in the built environment or the movement of people, goods, and ideas through space.

"Spatial history," a term coined by Paul Carter in *The Road to Botany Bay: An Essay in Spatial History* (1987), has become a broad umbrella term for scholarship that examines human experience of social and physical space. Much of this work focuses on the exercise of power over territory. Carter chronicled the imposition of

British place-names in Australia as the symbolic erasure of aboriginal land claims and knowledge. The application of British force followed just as surely as a hand applies pressure to make the pen draw. In geography, historian of cartography J. Brian Harley inspired a generation of scholars to critique colonial maps and mapping projects as the instruments of imperial conquest, which intellectual historians and literary scholars came to view as an inherently spatial process.[8] Spatial history also treats mapping more metaphorically, as the process of ascribing meaning according to hierarchies that structure social relationships by regulating who is allowed or denied access to particular places. This has become a dominant theme in cultural geography and mobility studies, which have interpreted the experience of the poor, homeless, and most mobile in society as a history of spatial exclusion.[9] Baker applies spatial history in yet another way, to scholarship that focuses on spatial concepts and spatial relationships.[10] His definition embraces many historical geographers' studies of urban morphology (the form of cities and how it changed over time) and the relationship of transportation to settlement and economic development.

Most spatial history has been published in books and academic journals. As Richard White points out in the foreword to this volume, however, studies of spatial phenomena and experience are gravitating to more fluid Web-based media. "Visual history" and "digital history" refer mainly to electronic publications that typically allocate as much or more space to images as to text.[11] Many of these projects use a search-tree structure that reflects the authors' desire not to assert the authority of written history, whose aim has traditionally been to argue for particular interpretations of events. Instead, digital historians want to encourage readers to engage with evidence as they see fit and draw their own conclusions. Two influential projects mounted by the University of Virginia's Center for Digital History provide digital compilations of manuscript sources through Web interfaces to facilitate research and teaching based on primary documents. The *Salem Witch Trials Archive* presents court documents from the infamous proceedings in Massachusetts Bay Colony in the form of scanned manuscripts, transcriptions, and a GIS that links biographical information about the individuals mentioned in the documents to the locations of their homes. *The Valley of the Shadow Project* was built to allow scholars and students to compare two counties on either side of the Mason-Dixon line in the decades leading up to the Civil War. It provides a wealth of scanned manuscripts, newspaper articles, graphic images, information about individuals from the manuscript census and city directories, and a GIS for mapping social and economic data.[12]

Both of these projects began as efforts to make primary documents more accessible for research and teaching. Along the way, their creators realized that they could learn much more from the data they were amassing if they could organize it geographically and map it, functions for which GIS is ideally suited.[13] Much of the information they were gathering was place-based (city directories and census data in the *Valley of the Shadow,* town tax records and church records in the *Witch Trials*). The process of transcribing that information while working with historical maps heightened researchers' awareness of geographical patterns embedded in the data. Both projects incorporated GIS midstream. Since then, researchers building projects of this kind have more often incorporated GIS from the outset and commonly use it as the organizing framework.

Geographical inquiry became central to interpretive work stemming from the digital archives' construction. Benjamin C. Ray, creator of the *Witch Trials Archive,* has used maps generated from the GIS to argue that witchcraft accusations did not reflect clear geographical and social divides between Salem's merchant class and less wealthy farm families, as the prevailing view has long contended.[14] In "The Differences Slavery Made," an electronic article based on the *Valley of the Shadow,* William G. Thomas III and Edward L. Ayers used geographical evidence and GIS methods to argue that although slavery was "the defining difference" between the antebellum North and South, it was "not intrinsically opposed to modernity."[15] Their purpose was not to assert a definitive argument, however, but to demonstrate how one can use the digital resource they had created. Thomas and Ayers explain that they employed the medium of electronic publishing "to open the process of scholarly inquiry, to allow readers not only to confront our argument but also to work with its evidence and its constituent parts."[16]

Some scholars are frustrated by the inconclusiveness of this approach. The fragmentation of argument between Web pages, like the nonsequential storytelling of postmodern novelists, leaves the work of final synthesis to the reader. Digital history also raises the question of the value of creating intermediate resources that provide compendia of primary sources or partially digested, digitally organized information in the form of user-ready databases. Making historical materials more conveniently available saves researchers time and effort, but if one does not grapple with raw data, can one know a source well enough to use it creatively? Federal and private funding agencies think so. In recent years, the National Endowment for the Humanities, the National Science Foundation, the Mellon Foundation, and other agencies have launched major funding initiatives for work in digital humanities and social science research and teaching. The proliferation of GIS-based history projects on the Internet testifies to how powerfully this mode of presentation appeals to the imagination.

One can also trace significant connections between historical GIS and work in disciplines other than history. Archaeologists were among the first scholars in the humanities to use GIS and global positioning system (GPS) methods, beginning in the early 1980s. Their familiarity with field methods and long-standing interest in the relationship between terrain and human settlement drew archaeologists to digital tools that could improve the accuracy of site measurements and locate artifacts more precisely. Today, archaeologists routinely use GIS visibility analysis to model and predict the location of topographically prominent features and settlements, such as tumuli and hill forts. Archaeologists' analysis of aerial photography and satellite imagery rivals that of remote sensing experts in geography and environmental science. Archaeology textbooks include extensive discussion of GIS-based methods.[17] Urban planners and architectural historians have also readily adopted GIS and computer cartography as tools that extend the skills of place rendering considered essential to those fields.

Historical GIS combines elements of *geohistoire,* historical geography, and spatial and digital history. At this point in its development, if one needs a firm definition, historical GIS scholarship has the following characteristics:

1. Geographical questions drive a significant part of the historical inquiry.
2. Geographical information provides a good share of the historical evidence.
3. The bulk of evidence, or the evidence that provides the study's key analytical framework, is structured and analyzed within one or more databases that record both location and time.
4. Historical arguments are presented in maps as well as in text, graphs, tables, and pictorial images; maps serve in particular to show patterns of change over time.

Historical GIS and its kindred approaches are more than methods; they are becoming a scholarly practice increasingly recognized as an interdisciplinary subfield within historical studies. The distinction between method and practice may seem like splitting hairs, but among geographers, the question of whether GIS is a tool or constitutes a proper field of study has at times been a burning issue.[18] I use the word "practice" with its social theoretical meaning in mind as well, for historical scholarship anchored in GIS is being deeply shaped by the technology's inherent capacities and constraints.

HISTORICAL GIS AS A SCHOLARLY PRACTICE

Although historians are using GIS to study a tremendous variety of subjects, periods, and places, most research and resource creation during the past decade has been concentrated in three areas. One is empirical research on the history of land use and the development of spatial economies. The second is using GIS to visualize past landscapes and the changing morphology of built environments over time. The third consists of infrastructure projects that aim to make historical source materials available to scholars and the general public for mapping and other kinds of analysis.

History of land use and spatial economy

Environmental historians and historical geographers interested in land use were among the first to recognize the potential that GIS held for "rendering intelligible those territorially comprehensive historical sources which contain a mass of detailed and place-specific data."[19] Geographer Bruce M. S. Campbell, quoted here, began using GIS in the early 1990s to map agriculture and land tenure in medieval Britain. Manorial and ecclesiastical records had long been standard sources for medieval history, but Campbell revealed their geographical content by translating the land records into geospatial databases whose contents could be mapped with GIS. His atlas of medieval agriculture resembles H. Clifford Darby's *Domesday England*, a classic in historical geography, which presents the story of English agriculture in 1086 in more than eight hundred maps. Using GIS, Campbell combined variables in more complex maps than were possible in Darby's day. More importantly, the mathematical functions of GIS (what is called *map algebra*) enabled Campbell to calculate sums, averages, proportions, and thus the relative significance of various crop and tenure configurations across the medieval landscape.[20]

Detailed mapping of land use underlies two recent landmark books in U.S. environmental history.[21] Brian Donahue's study of agriculture and inheritance in colonial Concord, Massachusetts, and Geoff Cunfer's history of Great Plains agriculture examine land use at very different scales. Donahue counts every fence post in his exacting reconstruction of field patterns, pasture and arable, and animal husbandry in one small New England town. Cunfer's canvas is a huge region that stretches across millions of acres from Texas to the Canadian border. Their time scales differ, as Donahue follows four generations of farm families while Cunfer focuses on a few decades. Their core sources are also poles apart. Donahue built his GIS of landholdings from records of individual estates, farm inventories, and tax records, while Cunfer tapped computerized datasets of the U.S. agricultural census for hundreds of counties.

Both studies are based on systematically gathered land-use data covering enough time to register significant change. In cartographic terms, both Donahue and Cunfer's choropleth maps (maps that show information by area, such as land use by parcel or precipitation by county) are conceptually simple. What makes them powerful is that they "visualize the data landscape."[22] They show geographical patterns and reveal changes over time that we have not seen before and that do not fit standing interpretations. Lynne Heasley, another environmental historian, writes in a similar vein that mapping land use in detail made it possible for her to answer "basic questions about property regimes and ecological change" in Wisconsin's Kickapoo Valley. GIS enabled her to tell "a more complicated story" than could methods that did not first establish what existed, quite literally, on the ground.[23]

Mapping the mosaic of economic activity and ways of life gives us a portrait of the spatial economy within a given region or locality. Spatial economy also refers to the interactions between places—the dynamic links created by trade, migration, and war. Geographer Richard G. Healey argues that GIS provides an ideal tool for studying conditions at particular moments in time as well as shifting spatial relationships, provided that one can assemble fine-grained microdata (locally specific information collected over many years) that can then be aggregated for analysis at a variety of geographical and temporal scales. His regional studies of the development of heavy industry in Pennsylvania show how GIS analysis of firm-level manuscript data can provide a much more nuanced picture of the dynamics of change than can conventional statistical analysis of published aggregate data, on which so much economic history has been based.[24]

Historian Michael McCormick used GIS to trace the emerging connections between places and peoples in Europe from AD 300 to 900. In his pathbreaking book, *Origins of the European Economy,* McCormick combined and compared a great many layers of data that previous scholars had studied in isolation, including the distributions of Mediterranean shipwrecks, relics, and coins; pilgrimage narratives; diplomatic missions; and the life paths of hundreds of slaves and slave traders. Visualizing the confluence and movement of historical patterns within and between these layers provided the basis for McCormick's argument that the European economy took shape in the final decades of the eighth century, much earlier than previous scholarship had recognized such coherence in communication and trade networks.[25] As often happens in geographical research, seeing geographical distributions (what historian Bernard Bailyn once called "the merely illustrative" use of GIS[26]) can generate new research hypotheses and interpretations and provide layers of data for more complex spatial analysis.

Reconstructing past landscapes

Much of the historical GIS being done today involves visualizing places themselves—the digital reconstruction of past landscapes. Some "geovisualization" strives for verisimilitude for its own sake, inspired by the beguiling realism of computer animation in cinema and gaming. But the digital reconstruction of historical landscapes can also serve scholarly purposes.

Scholars in a variety of disciplines are using GIS to create digital landscapes to study urban morphology over time. An outstanding example of collaboration between architectural historians and geographers is the Nolli Map project (figure 1.1). The project's interactive Web site combines a georectified version of Giambattista Nolli's superb 1748 *Map of Rome* with layers of archaeological data and satellite imagery of present-day Rome. Keith Lilley leads a group of researchers at Queen's University Belfast who are using quasi-3D renderings of medieval towns in Wales to determine whether the towns' construction was adjusted to suit local topography or rigidly followed ideal forms. Roy Bradshaw and Robert Abrahart are building a "digital Derby" whose ultimate goal is to capture, map, and make accessible the detailed geography of that English city as it was at the height of the industrial revolution.[27]

Loren Seibert's GIS spatial history of Edo-Tokyo is even more ambitious, as it includes physical features, the history of urban boundaries and administrative consolidation, the development of the rail network, and population change since 1900.[28] An approach to local history that many college teachers have adopted links historical plat maps, fire insurance maps, landownership data, scans of newspaper clippings, and historic photographs to a digital basemap of city streets.[29] Not all virtual cities are built with GIS. Digital London, Digital Prague, and other virtual urban Web sites have been created by architects and graphic designers using software that more effectively simulates the dimensionality of streetscapes and texture of building materials, or that models certain kinds of urban functions. Architectural historian Diane Favro has created a strikingly realistic rendering of the Temple of

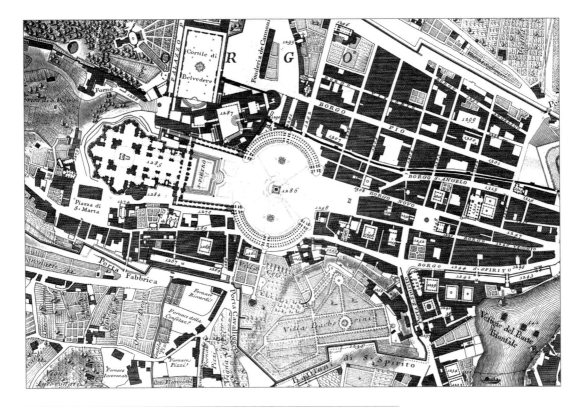

FIGURE 1.1

Detail of the georectified Nolli Map showing the Vatican. The University of Oregon team found it relatively easy to georectify Nolli's 1748 map because the large-scale map was remarkably accurate planimetrically. The map's exceptionally clear rendering of the Roman landscape demonstrates what a master cartographer could achieve in black and white.

University of Oregon Nolli Map (detail). Copyright 2006. Reprinted by permission of the University of Oregon Nolli Map Project http://nolli.uoregon.edu/. Digitally prepared by James Tice and Erik Steiner.

Saturn and other monumental buildings in ancient Rome as a virtual learning environment.[30] Differences between GIS-based projects and projects built on other platforms are blurring as GIS users become more interested in visualization techniques and strive for more realistic effects in the historical landscapes they render, even as they continue to exploit the metric capacities of GIS—its ability to measure distance, concentration and dispersal, coincidence in space, area, elevation, and so forth.[31]

Cities lend themselves to historical geovisualization. Large-scale urban maps and street plans can provide rich historical information as well as handsome backdrops for visual history. Technically speaking, urban maps from the United States and many other countries that were influenced by European cartographic traditions are the easiest historical maps to georectify because they have many stable landmarks and were often carefully surveyed. (Georectification is a process that assigns geographical coordinates to the map's digital image so it can be aligned with other data in GIS.) David Rumsey has done more than anyone to introduce the seeming wizardry of georectifying maps from different eras so that they can be superimposed to show change over time. One need only adjust the transparency of the layers for the maps' evidence of urban change to materialize on the screen.[32] Once historical maps are brought into GIS, the information they contain can be extracted, analyzed, and compared with more recent data. An effective teaching exercise has students go out in the field to record the GPS locations of extant historic buildings and then compare their findings to the urban fabric as it was recorded in historical maps.[33]

Programs like Google Earth and ArcGIS Explorer make it possible to visualize change over time in an approximate way, as one can roughly align historical photographs with their location on the earth using online GIS-based overlay tools. Images will register nearly perfectly if they have been georectified or were created with high-quality photogrammetric techniques. It can be revealing to compare historical maps to satellite views of the present-day landscape. Although georectifying historical maps can be difficult, the example of the Gettysburg project (chapter 10) indicates why it can be worthwhile.

Georectification was crucial to answering the question of what Robert E. Lee could and could not see at the battle of Gettysburg. A GIS method called *visibility analysis* enabled us to investigate how lines of sight may have influenced command decisions during the battle. Modern-day digital data, however, was not ideal for representing the battlefield topography. The alternative was a superb topographic map made shortly after the Civil War. Its remarkable four-foot elevation contours promised a better base for the digital landscape, if the contours could be extracted from the welter of other details on the map and then georectified to create a landscape surface that would return reasonably accurate results for the visibility analysis. The struggle to accomplish this revealed the limitations of both modern digital data and historical maps, even as the results suggest what GIS terrain analysis offers to military history.

Because of the state of geographic knowledge, the limitations of surveying instruments, and the cartographic conventions of earlier times, georectification can sometimes be a pointless exercise for small-scale maps produced in the West before about 1750 or for Asian maps well into the nineteenth century. But georectification is just one of many GIS techniques that one can fruitfully apply to historical maps, as Richard J. A. Talbert and Tom Elliott argue in their essay here. The Peutinger Map is a uniquely valuable document of the geography of the Roman Empire. It has been studied by generations of scholars. But as Talbert and Elliott demonstrate, using GIS methods to extract and analyze the map's physical and cultural iconography reveals surprising insights into why the map was probably made, what purposes it served, and just how good a record it may be of the imperial system.

The projects mentioned thus far illustrate that the process of translating historical sources for use in GIS can itself be a complex, taxing work of scholarship. It can take years to develop a historical GIS database to the point of producing results. Extracting geographical data from historical sources is analogous to data mining, but it is mining done with pickax and shovel at the rock face; it is difficult to automate, though the automation of georeferencing so that information can be quickly located and mapped is a rapidly growing field of research and software development.[34] For historians, it remains important to understand a source's provenance, the mentality that produced it, its inherent biases, and the points on which the information is most and least reliable. Determining the location of named historical sites can require extensive archival research. The great benefit of all the preparatory work that goes into creating a historical GIS is that one gains intimate knowledge of one's sources and study area. Such deep engagement with historical sources and their geographical context can lead to remarkable discoveries and exciting, creative scholarship.

Infrastructure projects

The third major area of historical GIS development is infrastructure projects that generally aim to facilitate the use of GIS in historical research. National historical GIS projects lead this part of the field (table 1.1).[35] The Great Britain Historical GIS (GBHGIS) was the first to be completed. Like most such projects, the GBHGIS consists of historical administrative boundaries (the spatial component of the database), which are linked to demographic information derived mainly from published census reports (the attribute data). In most countries, administrative boundaries have been mapped carefully, if at all, only since the late eighteenth or early nineteenth century. Reconstructing historical boundaries requires painstaking research, but it is work that social science historians in particular feel is worthwhile, for only with historically accurate boundaries can one derive accurate demographic analyses. Knowing to which administrative unit or units a place has belonged also facilitates research in local archives.[36]

One outstanding example of an infrastructure project, the China Historical GIS, offers a model for GIS data structure that may be useful for nonwestern history and for periods of history before the rise of nation states. Peter K. Bol suggests that nodes and networks, rather than polygons, best describe the hierarchical relationships that shaped most of Chinese administrative and religious history.[37] Nodes and networks also more accurately reflect Chinese conceptions of space and place. Locating places as points, however, is not necessarily a simple task. Much of the spadework in creating the China Historical GIS involved determining the location of villages, temples, and other features of the cultural–historical landscape—features whose names changed over the course of two thousand years. To be useful to scholars working in many different languages, the project also had to account for alternate names for physical and cultural features in China. The creation of a geographical concordance, or gazetteer, proved essential for the project, as it has for many other national historical GIS that embrace centuries of historical space.[38]

Because of their focus on administrative units and demographic data, national historical GIS projects to date have been best suited to social science research. International projects include more humanistic ventures and some developed by physical scientists. For example, historians of Euro-American print culture have embraced GIS as a means of linking their diverse datasets and visualizing the movement of books, printing technology, and ideas over space and time.[39] The Pleiades Project is a GIS-based, collaborative digital resource for research on the ancient

Table 1.1   Selected national and international historical GIS projects, 2005

Region and project	Host institution(s)	Host Web site(s)
Asia		
China Historical GIS	Harvard University, Fudan University	www.fas.harvard.edu/~chgis
South Korean HGIS	University of Korea	ikc.korea.ac.kr/culture/ culture_start.htm
Europe and Eurasia		
HGIS Germany	Institute of European History Mainz, University of Applied Sciences Mainz	www.ieg-mainz.de; www.hgis-germany.de
Great Britain Historical GIS	University of Portsmouth Edinburgh University, University of Essex	www.edina.ac.uk/ukborders; hds.essex.ac.uk
Historical GIS of Russia	Institute of Geography, Russian Academy of Sciences	www.ihst.ru/personal/imerz/ bound/bounds.htm
North America		
Canadian Century Research Infrastructure	University of Ottawa	www.canada.uottawa.ca/ccri
Atlas of Historical County Boundaries	Newberry Library	www.newberry.org/ahcbp/
U.S. National Historical GIS	University of Minnesota	www.nhgis.org
International		
History of Print Culture	Dalhousie University, University of Birmingham	www.dal.ca/hbic-hlic; www.bbti.bham.ac.uk
Electronic Cultural Atlas Initiative	University of California at Berkeley	www.ecai.org

Source: *Based on Anne Kelly Knowles, "Reports on National Historical GIS Projects," in "Emerging Trends in Historical GIS,"* Historical Geography 33 (2005), 134–58.

world. It stemmed from the *Barrington Atlas of the Greek and Roman World,* the first comprehensive cartographic representation of the ancient world since William Smith's atlas of 1874 (figure 1.2). Atlas editor Richard J. A. Talbert declared in his introduction that ancient historians are reconceiving their field as intrinsically geographical, which makes cartography an essential tool for representing what we know about the Greek and Roman worlds. Pleiades extends this conception to the core of scholarly practice by providing an online "work space" where scholars can deposit data and review, edit, and comment on one another's work. A similar spirit animates the Electronic Cultural Atlas Initiative (ECAI), a truly global project whose overarching goal is "to facilitate digital research by collecting, standardizing, and cataloging online databases and projects." ECAI sponsored the creation of a GIS software program specifically designed for historians, called TimeMap, and its clearinghouse makes GIS-compatible historical data available to hundreds of affiliate scholars.[40]

Scientists concerned with global warming and other aspects of environmental change have created historical datasets of land use and land cover that could be very useful in social science and humanities research. One notable example is the Global Historical Croplands Cover dataset created under a NASA initiative. It estimates land use and land cover for 1700 to 1992 from satellite imagery for recent years and from a variety of historical sources and scholarship for earlier periods. Researchers at Harvard Forest have created a series of datasets on ecological and population change for New England from 1600 to the present.[41] The number, size, and complexity of geospatial datasets related to the natural environment currently dwarfs historical GIS data. The time is ripe for historians and earth scientists to collaborate on projects that situate human history in its environmental context.

FIGURES 1.2A and B ▶

Historical cartography in the Smith and Barrington atlases of the ancient world. These two maps compare the representation of Lycia, a region on the southern coast of Turkey, in Smith's atlas (1.2A) and the *Barrington Atlas of the Greek and Roman World* (1.2B). Cartographic style changed greatly between 1874 and 2000, as indicated in the two maps' symbolization of topography. Notions of locational certainty also changed. While Smith drew firm lines around Lycia and neighboring regions, today's scholars acknowledge the uncertainty of ancient territorial divisions by suggesting their location more generally. The coastline and many settlement locations on the Barrington map, however, reflect research that permits much more precise mapping of the physical and cultural landscape than was possible in Smith's day.

(A) From William Smith, An Atlas of Ancient Geography, Biblical and Classical: To Illustrate the Dictionary of the Bible and the Classical Dictionaries (London: John Murray, 1874). (B) Detail from map of Lycia, in Richard J. A. Talbert, editor, The Barrington Atlas of the Greek and Roman World. © 2000 Princeton University Press. Reprinted by permission of Princeton University Press.

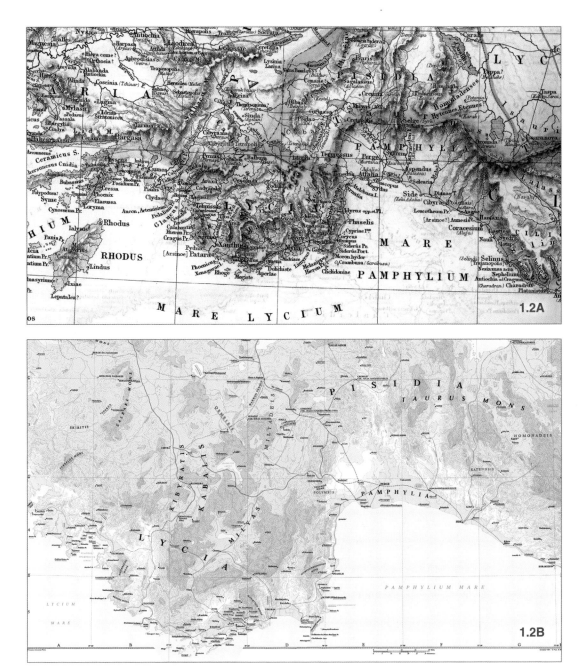

CONCEPTUAL AND TECHNICAL CHALLENGES

Some of today's historical GIS projects are the first scholarly efforts to map important historical events or to capture and explore the geographical information contained in a major primary source. The most exciting thing about historical GIS is often the "eureka" moment when someone sees data mapped for the first time.[42] Relatively few historical scholars have experienced such moments because few have been trained to work with maps or to use visual analysis and graphic representation in their work. As this book goes to press, only three graduate programs in history in the United States allow PhD students to satisfy the degree skills requirement with GIS.[43] In fall 2006, the history department at Idaho State University inaugurated a new masters program in geographically integrated history, the first of its kind in the country.[44] For all practical purposes, historical GIS remains an ad hoc subfield that scholars discover serendipitously. While this gives historical GIS a certain maverick excitement, it also means that many people are reinventing the wheel or struggle to learn GIS on their own without much technical support or theoretical background. It can be difficult to find peers with whom to discuss one's work until one happens to make contact with the informal network of historical GIS practitioners.

A more conceptual challenge is learning to recognize the geographic information embedded in historical sources and to imagine how it can inform historical research. I once had a telling conversation with an anthropologist at a leading liberal arts college that had eliminated its geography department in the 1960s.[45] For years, her ethnographic research had focused on incidents of domestic violence on an island in the South Pacific. She had collected exhaustive information about what kinds of attacks had taken place over a long period of time—which had come to trial, how the decisions fell, and what happened to the women afterward. I asked her if she had recorded where the attacks took place, or where the women fled, or the home communities of the women and their violent partners. "Well," she said, "all of those things would have been interesting, I suppose, and I know I saw information like that in the documents, but it never occurred to me to write it down." Almost every historical document contains some kind of geographic information—where something took place, where someone was at a certain time, what life was like in a particular place, the spatial extent of an event or phenomenon, and so on. Only if one captures geographic information is geographic analysis possible. Whether one works with texts, historical maps, or any other kind of source, cultivating a spatial and visual imagination makes it easier to recognize the place-based information and spatial relationships embedded in historical evidence.

Another conceptual challenge stems from the common perception that mapping in general, and GIS in particular, demands a level of accuracy and certainty that much historical data cannot support. This issue combines two problems, the erroneous perception of maps as authoritative, complete statements of fact and the difficulty of representing error, uncertainty, and vagueness cartographically. Many scholars outside geography are unaware of the recent spate of critical analysis of maps as unavoidably partial, biased representations of reality by historians of cartography and cultural geographers.[46] GIS tends to reinforce the naïve acceptance of maps as authoritative statements because the software so swiftly produces maps behind whose veneer of professionalism may lie all manner of unseemliness.[47] Cartographers have suggested a variety of methods for representing data quality in maps, such as using fuzzy edges to indicate uncertainty about the location of boundaries.[48] Symbolic representations of uncertainty look so odd and unattractive that they are almost never used, though the editors of the *Barrington Atlas* demonstrate that a simple scheme of solid, hollow, and dashed symbols can quite effectively suggest degrees of uncertainty about the location of historical sites.[49] GIS scholars are increasingly interested in the problems associated with uncertainty, which constitutes a growing field of research within GIScience.[50]

Geographers are becoming interested in temporal uncertainty as part of the broader interest in developing a form of GIS that can analyze and represent change over time as effectively as current systems handle change over space. For example, Brandon Plewe argues that the processes of conceptualizing and measuring spatio-temporal phenomena generate uncertainty that can be modeled and should be taken into account in one's analysis.[51] Historians have a great deal to offer the development of truly temporal GIS. Rather than entering time as crude start and end dates in tables with other kinds of information, as it is now done, we should be able to specify subdivisions of time or analyze probabilities of windows of time within which something probably happened (a temporal version of spatial "fuzzy logic"). The elusive goal is to modify the rigid, Cartesian logic of GIS so that computer-based geographic analysis can more closely mimic the vagaries of human experience.

Lastly, GIS challenges historians' conventional modes of documentation and even their understanding of what constitutes a unit of historical information. A geographic information system of any significant size includes dozens if not hundreds of layers of spatial data and its associated attribute data. In creating a historical GIS, placing each point, line, or polygon may require consulting a number of sources. An example from my research on the iron industry illuminates the difficulty. The location of a nineteenth-century iron works in Litchfield County, Connecticut, is described in the leading contemporary source as "four miles south of Kent Station, on the Housatonic Railroad." Having worked with the source for years, I knew the distance was approximate and required verification. That involved consulting an 1859 county map, three U.S. Geological Survey topographic maps, and a history of the region's iron industry. Were I merely describing the location in words, I could footnote the sources at the appropriate place in the text. But because the research resulted in the placement of one point on a map that includes nearly two thousand iron works, each of whose location required research, source documentation was not straightforward. One solution would be to list all sources for mapped data in an appendix. The historian's urge to account for the sources behind every act of interpretation has led some researchers to incorporate source information directly in GIS databases.[52] Current GIS packages were not designed to accommodate the detailed source documentation historians think necessary. At the same time, the kinds of information routinely included in GIS metadata, which documents the spatial characteristics of a dataset, can be bewildering to those unfamiliar with the technology's highly specialized vocabulary. It may not be the job of historians to devise more sensible forms for documenting the information that goes into a historical GIS, but if they teamed up with GIS specialists, the result could be useful for many branches of scholarship.

The essays contained in this book address these issues in a variety of ways. The case studies by Bol, Cunfer, Donahue, Talbert and Elliott, and Knowles highlight the analytical insight GIS methods can bring to familiar historical problems. These essays exemplify the great diversity of historical GIS methods and the potential GIS holds to challenge long-standing interpretations while opening new veins of inquiry. The issues-oriented essays by Churchill and Hillier, Gregory, Goodchild, and Bodenhamer address the challenges GIS poses for historians while also suggesting the opportunities it offers for new scholarship. Everyone involved in this book aims to be encouraging and critical. This spirit mirrors the intent of the specialist conference on the role of geographic information in historical scholarship at the Newberry Library in Chicago in March 2004, where the first versions of these essays were presented along with many other fine papers on historical GIS. We hope that *Placing History* will inspire many more researchers to interrogate the past from a geographical perspective.

ACKNOWLEDGMENTS

Special thanks to Stephen J. Hornsby for his comments.

NOTES

1. Barbara Maria Stafford, "The Visualization of Knowledge from Enlightenment to Postmodernism," in *Good Looking: Essays on the Virtues of Images* (Cambridge, Mass.: MIT Press, 1996), 20–40. See also John B. Krygier, "Envisioning the American West: Maps, the Representational Barage of 19th Century Expedition Reports, and the Production of Scientific Knowledge," *Cartography and Geographic Information Systems* 24:1 (1997), 27–50; and Anne Kelly Knowles, "A Case for Teaching Geographic Visualization without GIS," *Cartographic Perspectives* 36 (Spring 2000), 24–37.

2. Ronald E. Doel and Pamela M. Henson, "Reading Photographs: Photographs as Evidence in Writing the History of Recent Science," in *Writing Recent Science,* ed. Ronald E. Doel and Thomas Söderqvist (London: Routledge, 2006), 201–36.

3. The best study of the two disciplines' shifting historical relationship is Alan R. H. Baker, *Geography and History: Bridging the Divide* (Cambridge: Cambridge University Press, 2003).

4. Baker, *Geography and History,* 22.

5. Baker, *Geography and History,* quoting Charles Higounet, 22.

6. Fernand Braudel, *The Mediterranean and the Mediterranean World in the Age of Philip II*, trans. Siân Reynolds (Berkeley, Calif.: University of California Press, 1992); Emmanuel Le Roy Ladurie, *Love, Death, and Money in the Pays d'Oc,* trans. Alan Sheridan (New York: Braziller, 1982); Ladurie, *The Peasants of Languedoc,* trans. John Day (Urbana: University of Illinois Press, 1974). The original French edition of the latter contained a lengthy geographical introduction modeled on Braudel's *Mediterranean,* which was dropped in the American translation, a reflection of Americans' lesser interest in the geographical context of *geohistoire,* at least as perceived by the publisher. My thanks to Stephen J. Hornsby for this insight.

7. Best known is Meinig's four-volume work, *The Shaping of America: A Geographical Perspective on 500 Years of History* (New Haven: Yale University Press, 1986–2004). Carville Earle's work more directly engaged historiographic issues; see *Geographical Inquiry and American Historical Problems* (Stanford: Stanford University Press, 1992).

8. Paul Carter, *The Road to Botany Bay: An Essay in Spatial History* (London: Faber & Faber, 1987); J. Brian Harley, *The New Nature of Maps,* ed. Paul Laxton (Baltimore: Johns Hopkins University Press, 2001). See also Ricardo Padrón, *The Spacious Word: Cartography, Literature, and Empire in Early Modern Spain* (Chicago: University of Chicago Press, 2004), a challenging examination of the nature of cartographic thought during the age of empire.

9. Tim Cresswell, *The Tramp in America* (London: Reaktion Books, 2001) and *On the Move: Mobility in the Modern Western World* (New York: Routledge, 2006); Don Mitchell, *The Right to the City: Social Justice and the Fight for Public Space* (New York: Guilford Press, 2003).

10. Baker, *Geography and History,* 68.

11. David J. Staley, *Computers, Visualization, and History: How New Technology Will Transform Our Understanding of the Past* (Armonk, N.Y.: M. E. Sharpe, 2003), 4-5.

12. Salem Witch Trials Documentary Archive and Transcription Project, accessed online at etext.virginia.edu/ salem/witchcraft/home.html, and The Valley of the Shadow: Two Communities in the American Civil War, accessed online at valley.vcdh.virginia.edu. Edward L. Ayers and Anne S. Rubin, *Valley of the Shadow: Two Communities in the American Civil War* (New York: W. W. Norton & Co., 2000)—a short book , CD-ROM, and users guide—make the Web-based project's core materials and themes available to students and general readers.

13. Personal communications with Benjamin C. Ray and William G. Thomas III, 2001-2002.

14. Benjamin C. Ray, "Teaching the Salem Witch Trials," in *Past Time, Past Place: GIS for History,* ed. Anne Kelly Knowles (Redlands, Calif.: ESRI Press, 2002), 19-33.

15. William G. Thomas III and Edward L. Ayers, "The Differences Slavery Made: A Close Analysis of Two American Communities," summary printed as "An Overview," *American Historical Review* 108:5 (2003), 1299-1308, full electronic text and media accessed online at www.historycooperative.org/ahr in February 2004. See also Aaron Sheehan-Dean, "Similarity and Difference in the Antebellum North and South," in *Past Time, Past Place,* ed. Anne Kelly Knowles (Redlands, Calif.: ESRI Press, 2002), 35-49.

16. Thomas and Ayers, 1301, 1303.

17. *Journal of Archaeological Science* is a leading publisher of GIS-based archaeological research. On the themes mentioned here, see M. W. Lake, P. E. Woodman, and S. J. Mithen, "Tailoring GIS Software for Archaeological Applications: An Example Concerning Viewshed Analysis," vol. 25 (1998), 27-38; Dennis E. Ogburn, "Assessing the Level of Visibility of Cultural Objects in Past Landscapes," vol. 33 (2006), 405-13; Marcos Llobera, "Building Past Landscape Perception with GIS: Understanding Topographic Prominence," vol. 28 (2001), 1005-14; Timothy S. Hare, "Using Measures of Cost Distance in the Estimation of Polity Boundaries in the Postclassic Yautepec Valley, Mexico," vol. 31 (2004), 799-814; and D. J. Bescoby, "Detecting Roman Land Boundaries in Aerial Photographs Using Radon Transforms," vol. 33 (2006), 735-43. See also Trevor M. Harris, "GIS in Archaeology," in *Past Time, Past Place: GIS for History,* ed. Anne Kelly Knowles (Redlands, Calif.: ESRI Press, 2002), 131-43. Notable textbooks include an anthology of early GIS work in archaeology by K. M. S. Allen, S. W. Green, and E. B. W. Zubrow, *Interpreting Space: GIS and Archaeology* (London: Taylor & Francis, 1990); and Mark Gillings and David Wheatley, *Spatial Technology and Archaeology: The Archaeological Applications of GIS* (London: Taylor & Francis, 2002).

18. The issue is summarized in the forum "GIS: Tool or Science?" *Annals of the Association of American Geographers* 87:2 (1997), 346-73.

19. Bruce M. S. Campbell and Ken Bartley, *England on the Eve of the Black Death: An Atlas of Lay Lordship, Land and Wealth, 1300-49* (Manchester: Manchester University Press, 2006), 2.

20. Ibid.; Bruce M. S. Campbell, *English Seigniorial Agriculture 1250-1450* (Cambridge: Cambridge University Press, 2000); H. Clifford Darby, *Domesday England* (New York: Cambridge University Press, 1977).

21. Brian Donahue, *The Great Meadow: Farmers and the Land in Colonial Concord* (New Haven, Conn.: Yale University Press, 2004); Geoff Cunfer, *On the Great Plains: Agriculture and Environment* (College Station: Texas A&M Press, 2005).

22. David Seaman, "GIS and the Frontier of Digital Access: Applications of GIS Technology in the Research Library," paper presented at Future Foundations: Mapping the Past—Building the Greater Philadelphia GeoHistory Network, held at the Chemical Heritage Foundation, Philadelphia, organized by The Philadelphia Area Consortium of Special Collections Libraries, 3 December 2005.

23. Lynne Heasley, "Shifting Boundaries on a Wisconsin Landscape: Can GIS Help Historians Tell a Complicated Story?" *Human Ecology* 31:2 (2003), quotation on p. 187.

24. Richard G. Healey and Trem R. Stamp, "Historical GIS as a Foundation for the Analysis of Regional Economic Growth: Theoretical, Methodological, and Practical Issues," *Social Science History* 24:3 (2000), 575-612; Healey, *The Pennsylvanian Anthracite Coal Industry, 1860-1902: Economic Cycles, Business Decision-Making, and Regional Dynamics* (Scranton, Pa.: University of Scranton Press, 2007); Anne Kelly Knowles and Richard G. Healey, "Geography, Timing, and Technology: A GIS-Based Analysis of Pennsylvania's Iron Industry, 1825-1875," *Journal of Economic History* 66:3 (2006), 608-34.

25. Michael McCormick, *Origins of the European Economy: Communications and Commerce, A.D. 300-900* (Cambridge: Cambridge University Press, 2001).

26. Bernard Bailyn, comment during discussion of papers at The Geography of Atlantic History, A Workshop of the International Seminar on the History of the Atlantic World, 1500-1825, Harvard University, November 4, 2006.

27. Jim Tice, Erik Steiner, et al., *The Interactive Nolli Website,* http://nolli.uoregon.edu; Keith Lilley, Chris Lloyd, and Steven Trick, *Mapping the Medieval Urban Landscape: Edward I's New Towns of England and Wales,* http://www.qub.ac.uk/urban_mapping; Roy Bradshaw and Robert J. Abrahart, "Widening Participation in Historical GIS: The Case of Digital Derby 1841," RGS-IBG Annual International Conference, London, September 1, 2005.

28. Loren Siebert, "Using GIS to Document, Visualize, and Interpret Tokyo's Spatial History," *Social Science History* 24:3 (2000), 537-74; "Rail Names as Indicators of Enduring Influence of Old Provinces in Modern Japan," *Geographical Review of Japan,* ser. B, 73:1 (2002), 1-26; "Urbanization Transition Types and Zones in Tokyo and Kanagawa Prefectures," *Geographical Review of Japan,* ser. B, 73:2 (2000), 207-24; and "Using GIS to Map Rail Network History," *Journal of Transport History* 25:1 (2004), 84-104.

29. A good example is Jason Gilliland, "Imag(in)ing London's Past into the Future with Historical GIS," paper presented at the Annual Association of Canadian Geographers, June 1, 2006.

30. Diane Favro, "Wagging the Dog in the Digital Age: The Impact of Computer Modeling on Architectural History," paper presented at The Computer Symposium: The Once and Future Medium for the Social Sciences and the Humanities, Brock University, Toronto, May 30, 2006. Urban planners have developed programs such as Space Syntax, developed at University College London, that measured spatial segregation and modeled spatial flows years before standard GIS programs were capable of such modeling.

31. See, for example, Trevor M. Harris, "GIS in Archaeology", 131-143; and Michael Wheeler, "Topography, Politics, and the Erie Canal," paper presented at the Association of American Geographers annual meeting, Chicago, March 9, 2006.

32. David Rumsey and Meredith Williams, "Historical Maps in GIS," in *Past Time, Past Place: GIS for History,* ed. Anne Kelly Knowles (Redlands, Calif.: ESRI Press, 2002), 8–16. See also Rumsey and Edith M. Punt, *Cartographica Extraordinaire: The Historical Map Transformed* (Redlands, Calif.: ESRI Press, 2004).

33. Robert Summerby-Murray, "Analysing Heritage Landscapes with Historical GIS: Contributions from Problem-Based Inquiry and Constructivist Pedagogy," *Journal of Geography in Higher Education* 25:1 (2001), 37–52; and "Historical Geography: Mapping Our Architectural Heritage," in *Understanding Place: GIS and Mapping Across the Curriculum,* ed. Diana Sinton and Jennifer Lund (Redlands, Calif.: ESRI Press, 2007), 237–47.

34. The first book on georeferencing includes discussion of automation: Linda Hill, *Georeferencing: The Geographic Associations of Information* (Cambridge, Mass.: MIT Press, 2006).

35. Anne Kelly Knowles, ed., "Reports on National Historical GIS Projects," *Emerging Trends in Historical GIS, Historical Geography* 33 (2005), 134–58. For an overview of a representative project, see Catherine A. Fitch and Steven Ruggles, "Building the National Historical Geographic Information System," *Historical Methods* 36:1 (Winter 2003), 41–51.

36. Ian N. Gregory's many publications on the GBHGIS and the statistical significance of historically accurate boundaries are summarized in *A Place in History: A Guide to Using GIS in Historical Research* (Oxford: Oxbow Books, 2003). See also John H. Long, "The Case for Historical Cartographic Data Files," unpublished conference paper, American Historical Association, Dallas, Texas, December 1977; and "The Nature of Research into Past County Boundaries and Its Implications for Historical GIS Infrastructure," unpublished conference paper, Social Science History Association, St. Louis, Missouri, October 2002.

37. See also Merrick Lex Berman, "Boundaries or Networks in Historical GIS: Concepts of Measuring Space," *Historical Gegoraphy* 33 (2005), 118–33.

38. Merrick Lex Berman, "Persistence and Scale in Historical Gazetteers," paper presented at Electronic Cultural Atlas Initiative and Pacific Neighborhood Consortium, Honolulu, November 2005, http://www.fas. harvard.edu/~chgis/.

39. Bertrum H. MacDonald and Fiona A. Black, "Using GIS for Spatial and Temporal Analyses in Print Culture Studies: Some Opportunities and Challenges," *Social Science History* 24:3 (2000), 505–36.

40. Lewis R. Lancaster and David J. Bodenhamer, "The Electronic Cultural Atlas Initiative and the North American Religion Atlas," in *Past Time, Past Place: GIS for History,* ed. Anne Kelly Knowles (Redlands, Calif.: ESRI Press, 2002), 164. See http://www.timemap.net and http://ecaimaps.berkeley.edu/clearinghouse.

41. Navin Ramankutty and Jonathan A. Foley, "Characterizing Patterns of Global Land Use: An Analysis of Global Croplands Data," *Global Biogeochemical Cycles* 12 (1998), 667–85; and "Estimating Historical Changes in Global Land Cover: Croplands from 1700 to 1992," *Global Biogeochemical Cycles* 13 (1999), 997–1027. For a review of historical land-use/land-cover datasets, see Kees Klein Goldewijk and Navin Ramankutty, "Land Cover Change over the Last Three Centuries Due to Human Activities: The Availability of New Global Data Sets," *GeoJournal* 61 (2004), 335–44. The gateway to Harvard Forest data is http://harvardforest.fas.harvard.edu/data/archive.html.

42. Lancaster and Bodenhamer, "Electronic Cultural Atlas Initiative," 168–9.

43. University of Pennsylvania, West Virginia University, and Idaho State University.

44. J. B. Owen and Laura Woodworth-Ney, "Envisioning a Master's Degree Program in Geographically Integrated History," *Journal of the Association for History and Computing* 8:2 (2005), n.p.

45. On the history of geography's decline and recent resurgence in U.S. higher education, see Alexander B. Murphy, "Geography's Place in Higher Education in the United States," *Journal of Geography in Higher Education* 31:1 (2007), 121–41.

46. Leading critiques include J. B. Harley, *The New Nature of Maps;* David Woodward, et al., eds., *The History of Cartography,* vol. 1 and vol. 2, books 1, 2, 3 (Chicago: University of Chicago Press, 1987–1998); and Derek Gregory, *Geographical Imaginations* (Cambridge, Mass.: Blackwell, 1994).

47. John Pickles, ed., *Ground Truth: The Social Implications of Geographic Information Systems* (New York: Guilford Press, 1995); Eric Sheppard, "Knowledge Production through Critical GIS: Geneology and Prospects," *Cartographica* 40:4 (2005), 5–21. My thanks to Eric Sheppard for allowing me to read his essay in advance of publication. Apologies to E. M. Forster.

48. Alan M. MacEachren, "Visualization Quality and the Representation of Uncertainty," in *Some Truth with Maps: A Primer on Symbolization & Design* (Washington, D.C.: Association of American Geographers, 1994).

49. Mark Harrower, "Representing Uncertainty: Does It Help People Make Better Decisions?" white paper prepared for the UCGIS Workshop: Geospatial Visualization and Knowledge Discovery Workshop, National Conference Center, Landsdowne, Virginia, November 18–20, 2003; Richard J. A. Talbert, ed., in collaboration with Roger S. Bagnall, et al., map editors Mary E. Downs and M. Joann McDaniel, *Barrington Atlas of the Greek and Roman World* (Princeton, N.J.: Princeton University Press, 2000).

50. Jingxiong Zhang and Michael F. Goodchild, *Uncertainty in Geographical Information* (London, New York: Taylor & Francis, 2002). On error in historical GIS, see Ian N. Gregory and Paul S. Ell, "Error Sensitive Historical GIS: Identifying Areal Interpolation Errors in Time-Series Data," *International Journal of Geographical Information Science* 20 (2006), 135–52.

51. Brandon Plewe, "The Nature of Uncertainty in Historical Geographic Information," *Transactions in GIS* 6:4 (2002), 431–56.

52. For a model of this approach, see the documentation provided for the digital edition of the Atlas of Historical County Boundaries project, available at www.newberry.org/ahcbp.

2

CREATING A GIS FOR THE
HISTORY OF CHINA

Peter K. Bol

Understanding how spatial relationships change over time is fundamental to the study of history. But how do we create a historical GIS useful to many disciplines and appropriate to many historical periods? This is the basic problem of the China Historical GIS project.[1] The China Historical GIS (CHGIS) aims to provide the basic infrastructure for spatially enabled historical research. It is a platform for organizing data with temporal and spatial attributes (population, tax quotas, military garrisons, religious networks, regional economic systems, family history, and so on), representing them graphically and analyzing their relationships.

The data in the CHGIS covers more than 2,000 years—from 222 BC to AD 1911—from the Qin dynasty's establishment of the first centralized empire to the fall of the Qing, the last traditional dynasty. This long period witnessed important changes in administrative structures, economic processes, and culture. The area to be covered changed over time; it cannot be defined by the international borders of the People's Republic of China today and must include multiple regimes simultaneously. The population of the area covered is large, from about 50 million at the start of the database to about 500 million at the end. It had diverse patterns of settlement, social organization, and ethnic identities. Finally, the sources most important to creating a GIS and to spatial analysis changed over time. We have confronted difficult questions about the kinds of data fundamental to other kinds of data, how they relate to existing historical sources, and how our representations of basic spatial information relate to past conceptions of space and place.

The final CHGIS will consist of three elements. The first and most important is a continuous time series of the administrative hierarchy from the capital down to the county, because historical data was collected and reported through the administrative hierarchy. The second element is major nonadministrative settlements, particularly the market towns that proliferated during the last millennium. The third element is historical coastlines, rivers, lakes, and canals.

The China Historical GIS must consider how spatial data was collected and reported, because the GIS is intended to accommodate the kinds of data found in historical sources. We are aided by traditions of geographical record keeping and cartography that originated before the starting point of the CHGIS datasets and became more sophisticated and detailed over time.[2] This essay will explain the nature of Chinese sources and how we designed the CHGIS to suit them. It begins, however, by considering more basic questions raised by this research about how people conceived of the space for which they collected data and how their perceptions of space changed, because these issues affect how a GIS represents spatial relationships. I will argue that in earlier history, administrative space was conceived as a hierarchy of administrative central places (points) rather than as bounded territorial units (polygons). The chapter then discusses the importance of including more than just administrative hierarchy in this GIS by discussing the transformations in Chinese society approximately one thousand years ago that resulted in a dramatic quantitative and qualitative increase in local spatial data.

CONCEPTIONS OF PLACE AND SPACE

The CHGIS intends to establish a common base for the history of an area occupied by successive regimes beginning with the Qin dynasty in 222 BC. For convenience, we refer to these regimes as "Chinese dynasties," but some were empires founded by people, such as the Mongols and Manchus, who conquered Chinese territory. For the history of conceptions of space and place, we can draw on a cumulative tradition of texts and maps written in Chinese that located the origins of civilization in the remote past and typically sought to relate the geography of the present to the geography of the past. Table 2.1 (pages 30–31) gives the chronology of dynastic periods, notes the existence of different kinds of geographical sources, and offers an overview of the size of the territorial administration during the period covered by the CHGIS database.

Check marks signify the existence of "Treatises on Geography" in the official dynastic histories, other national administrative geographies, physical geographies, local gazetteers, and national and local maps. The number of province, commandery or prefecture, and county level units are given for selected years. Blank entries indicate that no data is available for a given dynasty and category.

The physical versus the political

The earliest comprehensive geographic text is the "Tribute of Yu," a chapter in the *Book of Documents* from the late Zhou period. It tells how the (legendary) sage king Shun of a millennium and a half earlier, seeking a worthy successor, tested Yu by assigning him the task of controlling the great floods that had inundated the land. Yu succeeded and became king in turn. The "Tribute of Yu" is both a foundational geography and a grand assertion of the human ability to bring order to the landscape and its inhabitants: Yu changes river courses, levels the plains, drains the marshes, registers the local products, assesses the quality of the fields, determines the appropriate crops, and describes the inhabitants.[3]

Table 2.1 Chronology of dynasties and geographic texts

Dynasty (Legendary Rulers)	Beginning	Ending	Treatise on Geography	Other national administrative geographies	Local gazetteers
Xia (uncorroborated)	−21st c.?	−16th c.?			
Shang	ca.−1600	−1045			
Zhou	−1045	−256			
Warring States	−475	−221			
Qin	−221	−206			
Han	−202	220	✔		
Three Kingdoms	220	280	✔		
Jin	265	420	✔		
Sixteen Kingdoms	304	439			
Northern and Southern Dynasties	420	581	✔		
Sui	581	618	✔		
Tang	618	907	✔	✔	
Five Dynasties and Ten Kingdoms	907	979			
Liao	916	1125	✔		
Jin	1115	1234	✔		
Song	960	1279	✔	✔	✔
Yuan	1206	1367	✔	✔	✔
Ming	1368	1644	✔	✔	✔
Qing	1616	1911	✔	✔	✔

Table 2.1 **Chronology of dynasties and geographic texts** *(continued)*

Extant maps	Year for count of administrative units	Number of provinces	Number of commanderies or prefectures (jun, zhou, fu)	Number of counties (xian)
✔	−210		49	319
✔	7		99	1,341
	140		103	1,088
	262		168	1,073
	281		193	1,098
	612		193	1,241
	740		328	1,473
✔	1111		300	1,193
	1208a		254	738
✔	1330	13	400	1,127
✔	1582	19	390	1,144
✔	1820	18 core	276	1,215

Sources: Chronology from Endymion Wilkinson, Chinese History: A Manual *(Cambridge, Mass.: Asia Center, Harvard University Press, 2000), modified; count of local administrative units from Charles O. Hucker,* Dictionary of Official Titles in Imperial China *(Stanford: Stanford University Press, 1985) and Zhang Minggeng and Zhang Mingju* 張明庚 張明聚 *eds.,* Zhongguo lidai xingzheng quhua: gongyuan qian 211–gongyuan 1911 nian 中國歷代行政區劃: 公元前 211–公元 1991年, *(Beijing: Zhongguo Huaqiao chuban she, 1996). In 1208, Song dynasty territory did not include the North China plain.*

The "Tribute of Yu" contains two contradictory perspectives on the land. The dominant one is essentially physical geography. It sees regions in terms of mountains, rivers, climate, and soil, and includes the local people as part of the natural landscape. From this vantage, government is imposed upon a preexisting natural geography and must organize itself around it. The other perspective, very briefly mentioned in the "Tribute" and possibly a later addition, is political geography. It supposes that a political center organizes the world into a series of concentric zones at set distances from the capital (figure 2.1), simply ignoring the natural landscape.

The physical and political perspectives reappear in the "Treatises on Geography," the section of the official dynastic histories devoted to accounts of the administrative system of the empire. The introduction to the "Treatise" in the Jin dynasty (265–420) history, for example, begins with the creation of the world, the initial existence of human beings as part of the natural landscape, and the gradual development of civilized life. In this text, the physical universe is the primary context: landscape features mark the empire's extent, and governing requires propitiating the spiritual powers in the landscape.[4]

> In the past the primordial embryo had no image, the plain element flowed into form, and by responding to what was in heaven some became leaders. Of this [time] the *[Book of] Rites* says: "In the winter they lived in mounds and caves, in the summer they lived on twig platforms and nests. They drank blood and ate [the meat of things with] feathers and fur; they had yet neither hemp nor silk."[5] Then Fireman invented fire-making. Baoxi began the project [of government], he transformed his clan and continued the legacy. Yan continued the glorious project and marked out territory [for farming] in the unknown. They all were part of a single plan. The Yellow Emperor then went east to the sea and south to the great river; he climbed into emptiness and ascended Mount Tai. Reaching the Kun range [in the west] he pulled on the reins, at the Kong mountains he asked about the Way. He preserved it all on bamboo slips so that nothing would be mistaken. King Gaoyang relied on the spirits particular to the place. King Diku accorded with heaven and performed the ceremonies. East past Crooked Tree [Mountain], west across the Flowing Sands, north to the Dark Mounds, and south to Jiaozhi,[6] in all that the sun and moon passed through, everywhere that cart and boat could reach, none were not subjects of the King and they did not depart from this realm.[7]

The Jin dynasty failed in its attempt to reestablish a unitary centralized empire, but it saw a burgeoning of interest in religious experience and the natural world. Against this, the introduction to the "Treatise on Geography" in the history of the Sui dynasty (581–618) begins with the supremacy of political power, which dominates the natural world and organizes territory as it sees fit.

> Since antiquity all the sage kings who received the mandate to govern have marked out the capital and measured the lands so as to set the axis for humanity. Above they were in correspondence with the orbits of the planets; below they divided the mountains and rivers. They created borders and they drew boundaries; they established a capital and they bestowed fiefs.[8]

After almost four centuries of division, the Sui had reestablished a single centralized empire, uniting northern and southern dynasties. The introduction bears witness to its own effort to reorganize the empire administratively.

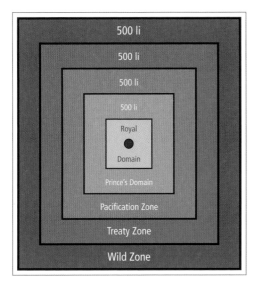

FIGURE 2.1

The "Five Dependencies" scheme for the organization of territory in the "Tribute of Yu." Concentric squares in bands of 500 *li* (1 *li* =1/3 mile) radiate from the Royal Domain. However, the bulk of the text is devoted to a description of the natural geography, which does not fit this scheme.

A spatial understanding of the empire involved the administrative and the physical because administrative centers were located in the midst of mountains and rivers. Yet in practice, geographers could give primacy to one perspective. We can see this in two maps of approximately the same date, both presenting themselves as cartographic representations of the "Tribute of Yu." The first (figure 2.2) is from Shui Anli's *Ready Charts of Geography through the Ages,* the earliest extant printed historical atlas in human history, finished at the end of the eleventh century.[9] Shui Anli's goal in his atlas is to establish correspondences between past and contemporary and administrative places.[10] The atlas includes a rough representation of coasts and rivers, but the focus is on the identification of administrative places rather than physiographic space. Contrast this with another "Map of the Traces of Yu" from the same period (figure 2.3), which gives priority to the representation of physical geographic space.

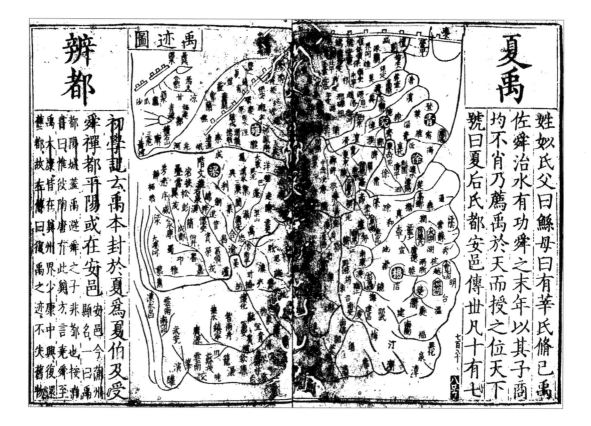

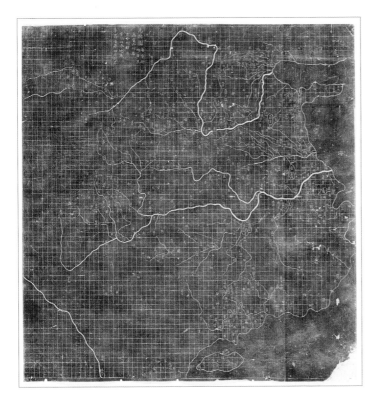

FIGURE 2.3

"Map of the Traces of Yu" 禹跡圖. This rubbing of an engraving was made in 1136 but shows the Yellow River course as of 1080. The legend states that it is scaled at 100 li (approximately 30 miles) to the square. It names rivers and mountains found in the "Tributes of Yu" chapter in the Classics, as well as past and present names of administrative units to the prefectural level. For a redrawing, see Cao Wanru, *Zhongguo gudai ditu ji,* vol. 1, plate 56.

Courtesy of The Photograph Collections, Fine Arts Library, Harvard College Library.

◀ **FIGURE 2.2**

"Map of the Traces of Yu" 禹跡圖. The Nine Regions in the "Tribute of Yu" are labeled in white on black. The prefectural designations are of the eleventh century. The accompanying text explains who Yu was and notes the diverse view of the location of his capital.

Shui Anli, Ready Charts of Geography through the Ages, *printed in the twelfth century.*

One implication of this difference will be pursued below: the physical geography perspective gave priority to the depiction of extensive physical space marked by mountains and rivers, whereas the administrative perspective was more concerned with the places that served as seats of government in the administrative hierarchy. Again, these were not exclusive perspectives. Administrative geographies typically noted the outstanding mountains and the major river in a jurisdiction. Nevertheless, some scholars such as Zheng Qiao 鄭樵 (1104–62) argued that physical geography provided a more consistent way of understanding space through time than did the ever-changing hierarchy of administrative places.[11]

Place and space in representing the administrative hierarchy

Maps today depict administrative entities as territorial units with clearly marked boundaries. In the United States, administrative units are likely to have names different from the town in which the administrative seat of government is located. But this has not been the typical assumption in China's history. From early times, the administrative seat defined the administrative unit, rather than a clearly bounded territorial unit. To illustrate, if the state of Massachusetts were in China, its administrative seat would be called Massachusetts rather than Boston. In earlier historical sources, the state would be depicted on a map by the point location of its administrative seat. In China, the national capital was the seat of the court (chao 朝), the center of power and wealth, and for much of history, a planned city. It was the "pivot of the four quarters," standing against the uncultivated wilds (ye 野), just as the light of the "son of heaven" in a central plain was in the midst of the forces and deities in the darkness of the surrounding mountains.[12] The depiction of administrative units, which obviously had jurisdiction over surrounding villages, is evident in the two maps in figures 2.2 and 2.3 (pages 34 and 35), where the prefectures are named points rather than territories.[13] This was not because a national map of limited size impeded the depiction of boundaries. Surviving county and prefectural maps from the thirteenth century represent prefectures and counties as central places. An example from 1261 (figure 2.4) depicts physical features (mountains, rivers, and lakes) graphically and the prefectural and county seats planimetrically, as square, enclosed cities. Even the subcounty administrative units that were territorial units without fixed seats (the "township" or "canton" xiang) are merely labeled.

The difference between this square map and one that depicts an administrative unit as bounded territory is evident in two maps of the same place from 1892.

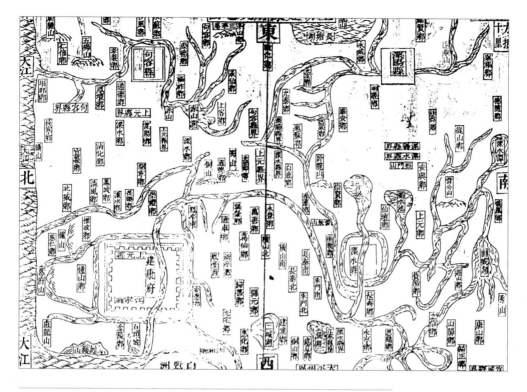

FIGURE 2.4

General map of Jiankang Prefecture (modern Nanjing) in 1261. East is at the
top. The large, walled square (lower left) is the prefectural seat. County seats are
smaller squares. Cantons and other features are only labeled. This is a later tracing of the original map; it preserves a note in the upper right specifying the scale
of the grid but does not show the grid.

From Jingding Jiankangzhi *(1809 ed.).*

Figure 2.5A is a traditional page-filling square of a county: it shows the seat and physical features and labels of subcounty cantons. It characteristically magnifies the county seat and locates the county relative to the surrounding counties by cartouches along the perimeter at the eight compass points (N, NE, E, etc.) reading "north to Yiwu county," and so on. Figure 2.5B, which comes from the same source, shows roads connecting villages to the county seat. For the first time in the case of this county, the map also represents the administrative unit as bounded space.[14]

Although there were precedents, the popularity of depicting the county as isolated bounded territory became popular in the nineteenth century and is probably due to the influence of European cartography.[15]

In her review of studies of the "Treatises on Geography" *(di li zhi)* in the dynastic histories, Vera Dorofeeva-Lichtmann offers the following proposition:

> The term *di li* (which I propose to translate as "terrestrial organization") is a conception of an orderly administrative territorial division established by the ruler and aimed at symbolizing world order. The geographical matters are then presented in the context of the so-called "world-making" activities of the ruler with the aim of establishing an orderly hierarchical organization of the terrestrial space."[16]

Leaving aside for the moment the question of organizing terrestrial *space,* the important insight here is the idea of administrative hierarchy. This sense of a hierarchy of administrative central places continued in China. Even today, a villager likely sees the village as subordinate to the county (by which the county seat is meant) rather than as being "in" the county.[17] The administrative hierarchy to which a given settlement belonged mattered because the government saw itself as governing through a hierarchy of administrative centers.

Into the eleventh century, national geographic treatises were written from the perspective of the central government; they focused on the resources local government could command. Li Jifu's *Maps and Treatises on Commanderies and Counties in the Yuanhe Reign Period* from 806–814 is still extant, although its

---

FIGURES 2.5A and B ▶

Yongkang County, Jinhua Prefecture, Zhejiang Province. Figure 2.5A shows military installations (with flags) but not villages and makes no attempt to suggest the actual dimensions of the county, as depicted in figure 2.5B.

From Yong Kang xianzhi *(1892 ed.).*

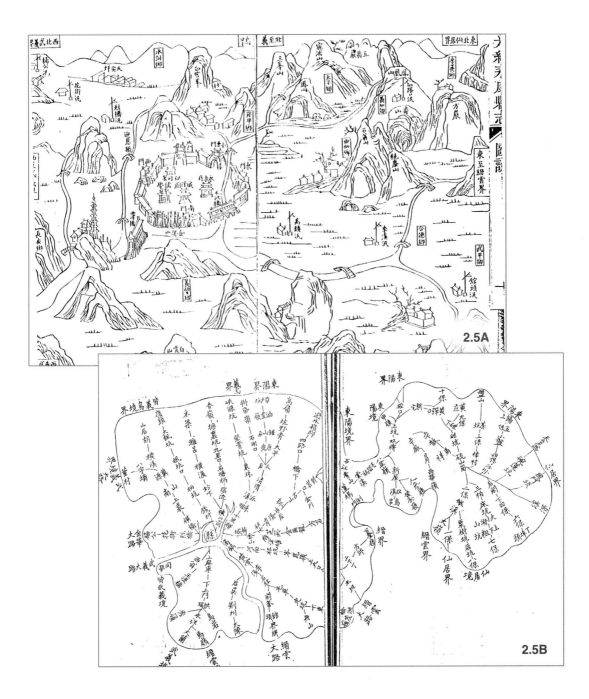

2.5A

2.5B

accompanying maps have been lost. For each prefecture, it gives the name, rank, population, total number of cantons (defined at the time as units of five hundred registered households) in the prefecture, its administrative history, the goods it supplied to the court, and the distance by road and river to the surrounding prefectural capitals. For each county, it gives its rank, the origin of its name, the major river and source of the flow, and significant mountains. Recognizing that the prefecture extends through space, Li Jifu's work gives the extent of the prefecture measured east to west and north to south but does not try to define boundaries. It locates points in space (as do later works) by giving the direction and distance from the prefectural seat to surrounding prefectural seats and from the county seat to the prefectural seat.[18] Figure 2.6 illustrates this for one prefecture.

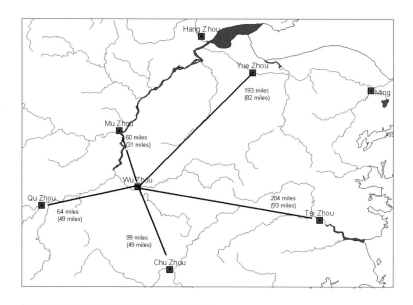

FIGURE 2.6

Distances between Wu zhou 婺州 (previously Dongyang jun, later Jinhua fu) and surrounding prefectures *(zhou)* circa AD 1000, according to the *Taiping huanyu ji* (1793 ed.), 97.5b–10b. In this map, all distances have been converted to miles. The distances given in the text are travel distances (actual distances based on straight lines between points on a modern map are given in parentheses). The original text gives both directions by the eight compass headings and the distances in *li* 里 (e.g., "Southeast to Tai zhou 612 *li*").

China Historical GIS.

This does not mean that Chinese historians and administrators could not conceive of boundaries or space as bounded territory. Beginning in the eleventh century, for reasons that will be discussed later, greater attention came to be paid to the territorial extent of prefectures in both geographies and maps.[19] Although surveying techniques for measuring direct distance were known at this time, extant maps and geographies did not yet attempt to depict the boundaries of administrative units.[20]

The focus on central places, the limited resources of government, and above all the nature of the tax system, which registered land and population separately, help explain the lack of interest in delineating administrative boundaries. The population was registered according to decimal-based systems of ten to a thousand households. The register, not the village, was the unit of registration. Land parcels were measured and their productivity assessed in order to assign the tax burden of each parcel. In the north China plain into the eighth century, registers were used for the equitable distribution of lands to taxpayers.[21] Once land was redistributed through the private market, this was done to grade households by wealth and collect land tax from the owner of each parcel. However, correlating the land registers with the population registers depended on recording all land transactions or regular cadastral surveys, neither of which happened. Land registers could have provided a basis for defining administrative units as bounded territory, but only if all land was farmed in some fashion. The idea of creating new maps to serve as an integrated guide to land and population did occur to some. For example, Yuan Xie 袁燮 (1144–1224) proposed that each unit of ten households should draw a map with paddy and dry fields, mountains and rivers, and roads. The inhabitants of the area depicted would write their names and livelihood on the map and presumably identify the fields they owned. The maps would be collected and merged at the next level of the administrative system until finally a map of the entire county was created. For Yuan, a complete county map could serve as an information management system: "In taxation, legal disputes, and arresting bandits, things could be decided simply by turning to the map."[22] Yuan's proposal supposes a hierarchical population registry system within the county; it does not suppose a clearly defined hierarchy of territorial units below the county. Given the private market in land, over time the land held by households in a given registration group would change so that to depict their registration unit as bounded space would make it even more difficult to collect taxes. This suggests that unless there were natural barriers such as rivers or mountain ranges that created clear lines of jurisdiction, people at the time thought of the territorial boundaries that divided administrative units as flexible zones. From an administrator's perspective the real question was who he had to collect taxes from. He had to know which settlements fell under his jurisdiction and what property was held by the inhabitants of those settlements; he did not need absolute boundaries.

This preference for zones of jurisdiction was sometimes true at the national level as well. Militarized borders had lines of control at a given moment, but these lines also shifted as troops moved back and forth. In the late eleventh century, faced with multiple hostile states to the north, the court debated defining the northern border as a zone or a line. The proponents of a zone carried the day with the argument that ambiguity reduced conflict.[23] Two twelfth-century national maps of the relations between the Song and the surrounding states identify prefectural seats but do not draw national boundaries.[24] Neither does the great map of the Eurasian landmass, the *Amalgamated Map of Great Ming* from 1389, which extends from the Pacific to the Atlantic Ocean.[25]

For much of the last millennium, demarcating boundaries was the exception rather than the rule. Some sixteenth-century national maps imply national borders by drawing provincial borders.[26] The *Enlarged Terrestrial Atlas* of circa 1553 includes a series of provincial maps that show provinces as isolates and mark prefectures as bounded territory rather than as prefectural seats alone.[27] The national geography of 1820 outlines the borders of prefectures, although not of the counties.[28]

Most prefectural and county gazetteers, which began to appear in large numbers in the twelfth century, remained oriented toward the administrative seat, noting the direction and distance to mountains, bridges, reservoirs, markets, and religious sites as measured from this one central point. But some depicted the county as bounded territory. Such works typically identified subordinate administrative units within the county as spatial units within the county and located features within these spaces. Figure 2.7 is from a gazetteer that depicts counties as bounded space in semi-isolation.

This map adopts the perspective of physical geography rather than administrative geography. It depicts mountains, rivers, and the natural villages along the major road, but it gives only the county seat (the square in the lower middle) and ignores administrative divisions within the county. Although some argued that the county should be treated as a "natural" spatial unit rather than a series of points networked to the administrative seat, this did not become the dominant view until the nineteenth century under the influence of European surveying techniques and cartography.[29] The author of a similar county map from 1823 states that it was

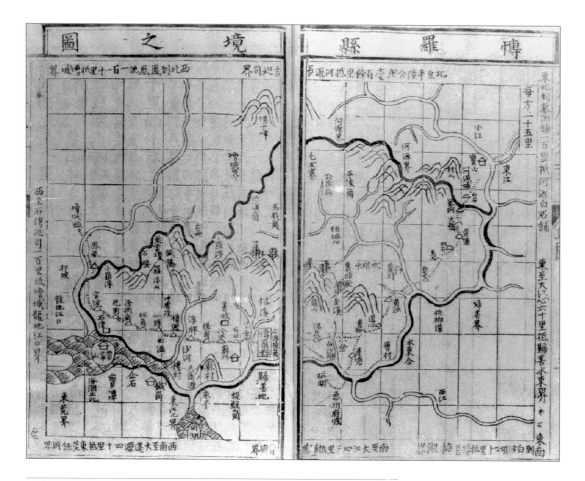

FIGURE 2.7

"Boundary Map of Boluo County" 博羅縣境之圖, Guangdong.

From Huizhou Fuzhi 惠州府志 (1595 ed.).

influenced by the Qing empire maps of 1718 created by the Jesuits with European surveying techniques (figure 2.8).[30]

The gazetteer used this map as a template for other maps, such as one showing administrative districts within the county drawn as bounded spatial units, although without geographical exactness. Even today, the government frequently alters the administrative hierarchy and reorganizes administrative units within the county. Although contemporary cartography follows the Western style of depicting units as bounded space, the government is only now systematically using modern surveying techniques to define county boundaries exactly.

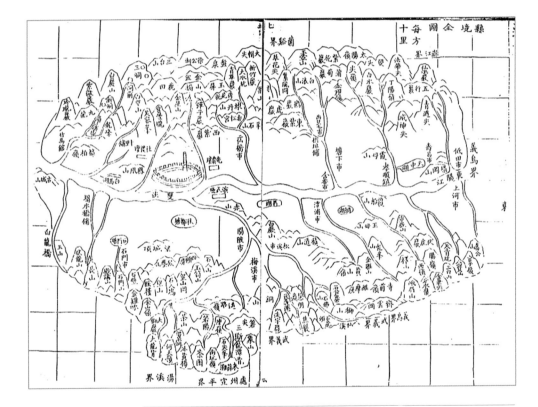

FIGURE 2.8

Overview of Jinhua County, from the *Jinhua xianzhi* 金華縣誌 (1823 ed.), said to be influenced by the Jesuit maps of the Qing empire of 1718.

From Jinhua xianzhi 金華縣誌 (1823 ed.).

From historical conceptions to a historical GIS—points and polygons

Tracing changes in the administrative hierarchy is fundamental to creating a GIS for Chinese history because the government collected data according to its administrative structure. The central government ruled territory through a system of prefectures and subordinate counties. Centrally appointed officials governed this system, supervising locally hired personnel according to legal and administrative codes. (By the thirteenth century, a provincial administration had also emerged.) Local governments maintained the road and postal station network and systems for land and household registration, justice, and security. By the thirteenth century, it had become common in the south of China to create "local gazetteers" for counties and prefectures to preserve extensive local data. China has the longest continuous historical record in human history. The combination of central and local records has provided a massive amount of data with spatial attributes. A bilingual historical GIS will make much of this data available for scholarship without first requiring sinological training.

The importance of the administrative system to the organization of historical information has led to three fundamental design decisions: (1) to build the GIS around the administrative structure, (2) to keep track of this structure by tracing all known changes (in name, location, and place in the administrative hierarchy) in administrative units in a continuous time series rather than documenting selected slices-in-time, and (3) to make extensive use of points in representing administrative units visually. CHGIS is thus a base GIS because it provides the fundamental database: the record of changes in the administrative units and the changes in the points, lines, and polygons that represent them. We must first correctly identify and locate the administrative units that reported data; without that we lack a reliable means of spatially analyzing data such as population records.[31] A common-base GIS makes diverse datasets compatible and shareable, making it possible to combine, for example, demographic data with county tax receipts and a dataset of temples and monasteries.

CHGIS thus depends ultimately on time-consuming historical geographical research, even with the aid of important slice-in-time printed historical atlases and studies of changes in administrative units.[32] It is succeeding thanks to the senior historical geographers at the Center for Historical Geography at Fudan University, many of whom took part in the compilation of the *Historical Atlas of China* under the late director Tan Qixiang. Their work contains extensive notes, included in the CHGIS database, which quote from primary sources, cite secondary sources, and justify all their choices.

How should CHGIS represent administrative units? The Chinese historical record suggests that we should conceive of them for much of history as a hierarchy of points extending from the capital down to the counties. Further, we should understand that the data collected by a prefecture or county refers not necessarily to a bounded space but to data collected from settlements within the reach of the local government. Conceiving of the county as bounded territory became less problematic once population increased and marginal lands were brought into cultivation so that settlements filled the area, a process that took place in the south from the eighth century on. A historical GIS for China can better represent administrative units as points rather than following the Western convention of representing them as polygons, a tradition that takes advantage of (but is perhaps also limited by) two centuries of mathematical cartography. CHGIS can extend backward in time because the "points" at which administrative seats were located can be determined with a fair amount of accuracy, as can the start and end dates for administrative units.[33]

At the same time, cartographers and GIS researchers in China and abroad expect that a GIS will represent administrative units as bounded territory. Area also figures importantly in density analysis. CHGIS can address this in two ways. For recent history, we can take recourse to the mathematical cartography that Chinese geographers began to use widely in the late nineteenth and early twentieth centuries to create county boundaries for circa 1911, the end of the database coverage. Working backward in time, approximate county boundaries for some areas can be drawn, although these boundaries will not be highly exact at a 1:1,000,000 scale. County boundaries and physical features have proved particularly useful in approximating prefectural boundaries, which CHGIS seeks to provide for all periods. Although the introduction of mathematical cartography helped establish the idea of using clearly delineated boundaries, researchers should consider treating all CHGIS administrative boundaries as approximations and use point data whenever possible.

The second method for approximating county areas is to maximize the point coverage by including as many settlements within the county as possible, thus allowing the use of Thiessen polygons to give approximate areas. Increasing the point coverage within an administrative unit produces correspondingly better approximations of the area of the administrative unit.

The value of increasing the point coverage goes beyond improving the representation of administrative space. Maximizing the number of points is the best means of taking into account the extraordinary increase in locally preserved data in local gazetteers from the twelfth century on.

LOCAL DATA AND THE FUTURE COURSE FOR THE CHINA HISTORICAL GIS

For the first millennium of CHGIS coverage, most of the available historical data comes from sources compiled by the central government and relates to the county and prefecture as administrative units. For the second millennium, particularly for southern China, it is often possible to identify the administrative units and villages within the county.[34] The most important attributes of the tens of thousands of named places outside the administrative seat were economic, familial, cultural, and religious rather than administrative. Geographies and maps best represented the administrative system,[35] but collected data also recorded various nonadministrative networks. It is precisely information about nonadministrative places that has made possible G. William Skinner's "Hierarchical Regional System" model for the analysis of contemporary Chinese society and earlier periods.[36]

The background to the appearance of local data lies in the transition from the Tang (617–907) to the Song (960–1279). Into the ninth century, the North China plain dominated what we consider China. The plain contained most of the population, produced the largest share of tax revenues, and provided most government officials. Its contested northern border was the focus of foreign relations and a major site of military expenditure. Regional systems analysis becomes important when other regions began to rival North China demographically, economically, and politically. This happened in the ninth and tenth centuries, when the south gained population and divided into regional kingdoms as the Tang dynasty (617–907) disintegrated.[37]

Beginning in the twelfth century, one important consequence of these changes was the appearance of local histories, known as local gazetteers (地方志). The Tang dynasty had been led by a state-sponsored aristocracy of great clans that, having become divorced from their earlier local power bases, made government service the family occupation. The Tang ideal was a unified hierarchy of power, wealth, social status, and culture centered on the court. At least in the north China plain, the government controlled the land, redistributing it to farmers in return for an assessment per adult of a set amount of tax in kind and labor. Trade was strictly controlled and long-distance trade was largely limited to luxury goods. Three things happened as this centralized system deteriorated. First, as a private land market emerged, the state lost control of the land and changed its tax system to tax households according to their land and wealth.[38] Second, the state stopped restraining commerce and learned to tax it. As a market economy took shape, the state increased the money supply.

In 740, the annual mint had been about 275,000 "strings" (nominally 1,000 coins) of bronze cash. By the 1080s, the annual mint was about 4.5 million strings.[39] Third, the identity of the national elite changed from a group of families of aristocratic pedigree to a national elite of "literati," men educated in local state schools and private academies and chosen for office through competitive examinations. Although only a few were chosen, there was a dramatic expansion of the educated elite: in the mid-thirteenth century, as many as 450,000 people participated in local examinations in the triennial examination cycle, out of whom only about 600 went on to obtain the highest examination degree.

State institutions did not expand, either to employ the larger elite or to maintain services to the larger population, to reflect population growth.[40] The later imperial government's role in society, economy, and culture was limited. At the local level, the growing number of well-to-do educated local families filled the gap. Officials and their immediate kin, the most privileged elements in society, thus belonged to a national elite constituted by local literati elites, groups of families that kept up literati education and social practices but, because members rarely served in government, remained locally resident. They supported the state but also defended local interests in the face of state demands.[41]

The local gazetteers, the most important source for detailed information about local physical, administrative, social, religious, cultural, and economic geography and history, incorporated the earlier form of local data compilation and added a new layer. Prior to this, local administrative units compiled local records for their own purposes (of which only a few remnants remain). In contrast, local literati were generally the compilers of local gazetteers. Their communities wanted histories of the places in which they resided and the social, economic, and cultural world in which they lived, in addition to the records of local government. Thus, for example, local gazetteers began to have extensive sections devoted to local biography, educational institutions, literary selections, and examination registers. Gazetteers represented a confluence of interests between local officials and local elite families, those with the ability to educate their children, organize local defense militias, establish water conservancy pacts, and contribute to schools, bridges, walls, and religious institutions.[42]

The writing of local gazetteers was part of the growing interest in using locality to catalogue the nation's cultural history. The first privately compiled national geographies drew on national records and local gazetteers and culled literati writings to give accounts of famous local sights, customs, stele inscriptions, and biographies. Two of the earliest are still extant: Wang Xiangzhi's (王象之) two-hundred-chapter *Record of the Best Sights of the Realm* (輿地紀勝) and Zhu Mu's (祝穆) seventy-chapter

Finest Sights of the Realm (方 輿 勝 覽). Collections of local biographies and literary writings also became popular.[43] Beginning in the fourteenth century, state-compiled national geographies reflected this change and new "unified gazetteers" summarized the contents of cultural geographies and local gazetteers.

Although only thirty gazetteers remain from the Song and Yuan (1279–1368) periods, most southern prefectures and many counties had their own gazetteers by the late thirteenth century. By the end of the sixteenth century, much of the north was producing local gazetteers. They were cumulative, with later editions incorporating much of the material from earlier editions. Today, more than 8,000 editions of gazetteers are extant, totaling 125,000 chapters.[44] In short, we have data-rich sources, covering the area inhabited by about 90 percent of the population, for between four and eight centuries. Beginning in the 1980s, all counties once again began to publish local gazetteers.[45]

What are our priorities as we look ahead to the work of adding nonadministrative point data to CHGIS? As historical gazetteers become published as searchable databases, we face the prospect of integrating large amounts of local historical data into spatial analysis. Market towns, lineages and lineage villages, and religious networks are three of the most promising areas of interest.

Market towns

From early times, settlements were connected vertically to local government through administrative systems to register land and population. By the eleventh century, they were coming to be linked vertically and horizontally through market networks. The growth of the private market economy created regional hierarchical economic networks that no longer corresponded to administrative hierarchy.[46]

Sources vary for historical market towns. For some periods, merchant route books provide a geographical source grounded in the commercial economy rather than the state apparatus.[47] Local gazetteers record market towns too, and research has shown that in many places, market towns continued from the Song period through later history, outlasting every dynasty.[48]

Lineages and lineage villages

In the eleventh and twelfth centuries, a new vision of kinship appeared, in which descendents of a common founding or migrant ancestor were encouraged to maintain kinship ties. The result was extended networks of kin organized into lineages or descent groups that maintained their own membership records. In some places and for some periods, a single lineage dominated villages, as is true today. Because successful lineages segmented and branches grew in new areas, lineage networks spread not only within a county or canton but also across administrative boundaries.

By the fourteenth century, the compilation and updating of lineage "genealogies" had become commonplace. These works have survived in large numbers and are being recompiled once again today.[49] By the sixteenth century, the ancestral halls of powerful lineages had become centers of village life. Lineage genealogies offer a major (but often highly unreliable) nonadministrative resource for studying local society and maps of lineage villages, land parcels, and graves. Some local gazetteers also provide evidence. Figure 2.9 is a map of a canton from a county gazetteer in which villages are identified not by village name but by the surname of the dominant lineage.

Gazetteers rarely provide such a graphic account of dominant lineages, but the current revival of interest in compiling genealogies and in family history suggest that

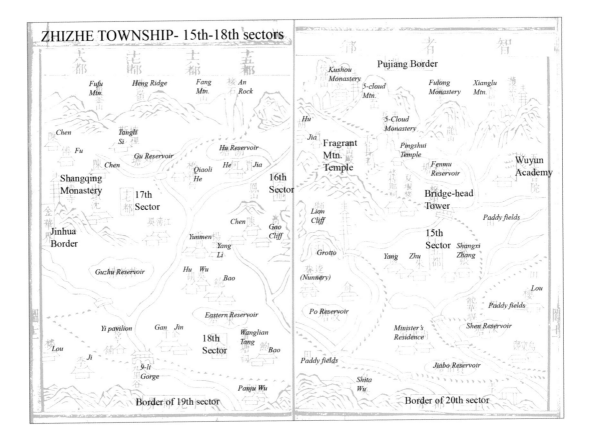

if CHGIS can add point data for historical settlements, it will become possible to study the spatial distribution of lineage networks.

Religious networks

Records of religious sites are a third abundant source of spatiotemporal point data that reveal nonadministrative networks. Despite the state's occasional attempts to suppress them, monastic institutions and local shrines continued to proliferate. Monastic institutions depended on patronage, either state gifts of revenue from land or private patronage. Periods of private economic growth were also periods of temple building, for example during 1100–1400 and 1550–1700 (and once again today).[50] Buddhist institutions were important to local cultural life and the local economy.[51] In some instances, a Buddhist monastery became the site of a settlement and market town. Like Buddhism, Daoism was also a national religion, although it was institutionally much smaller. Buddhist and Daoist institutions formed various kinds of networks as a result of the sources of patronage or traditions of doctrine and practice.

The growth of market and lineage networks was accompanied by the emergence of regional deities. Temples devoted to a local god might spread throughout a region. Networks of shrines devoted to figures such as Five Manifestations (五顯), King Zhang (張王), Zitong (梓童), and the Heavenly Consort (天后) appeared, and local supporters successfully sought official recognition from the court.[52] During the last millennium, hierarchies of local gods and temples appeared and cults often became the vehicle for local leadership. Cults often provided an alternative form of social organization and in some places have been able to impose taxes in support of religious activities on the local community.[53]

◄ **FIGURE 2.9**

Zhizhe Township (or Canton) in Yiwu County, Jinhua Prefecture, depicting named mountains, rivers, bridges, roads, religious sites, academies, and lineage villages. Lineage villages are marked by houses with names, either a single surname (e.g., Hu, Wu, Bao) or a choronym (i.e., a place name plus surname, such as Shantou Shen, or the Shen lineage of Shantou). Although these villages are known by different names today, many of them are still inhabited by descendants of the families noted here. The gazetteer has a map for each of its townships.

From Yiwu xianzhi 義烏縣誌 (1596 ed. Rpt. 1640); translated.

Many gazetteer maps include leading religious institutions, and some include comprehensive lists of religious sites. From these, it is clear that religious institutions dominated the landscape to a far greater extent than did local government, providing the bulk of public space. Gazetteer maps give uneven coverage but contain more extensive lists than a map of customary size could represent. The 1480 Jinhua prefectural gazetteer, for example, lists 824 religious establishments in its eight subordinate counties, each identified by name, travel distance, and direction from the county seat, and often the date of founding.[54] These can be plotted in a GIS. However inexact, such maps tell us something about the spatial distribution of religious sites: those deemed worth recording are overwhelmingly Buddhist, they are for the most part located at the periphery of the county rather than the capital, and (something that would only be apparent with a GIS) they are located in the hills rather than in the populated plains. A historical GIS lets us study the spatial pattern of religious sites in a natural geographic and demographic context and in an administrative context.

SOME THOUGHTS ABOUT HISTORICAL GIS

This case study has made a series of related arguments.

Any historical GIS would seem to need a spatial thread running through history, recognizing that such continuity can be achieved only by accommodating change. The Chinese case achieves that continuity by tracing changes in the administrative hierarchy. It is a justified approach, because administrative hierarchy effectively collected and reported data with spatial attributes.

But how should we represent the administrative hierarchy spatially in a GIS? Our intuition, one supported by work on historical GIS for Europe and the United States, is that administrative units are polygons. Summarizing conclusions derived from a recent collection of studies on historical GIS, Anne Kelly Knowles writes that "accurate spatial boundaries are key to all calculations derived from geographically located data. Without using historically correct and accurate unit area boundaries, one cannot tell whether statistical changes reflect changes in population, changes in boundary lines, or both."[55] But what do we do when we have a lot of data but lack accurate unit area boundaries, as is the case for most of Chinese history?

Practical and conceptual answers seem to make sense. In practical terms, expedient methods generate approximate, provisional boundaries for modes of analysis based on measurement of area. These approximations will improve over time as the amount of point data increases. To do this, we must maximize point data available for many regions for the last millennium. Moreover, the same sources that allow us to increase point coverage and better identify the territory under a particular jurisdiction also allow us to develop information about economic, social, and religious networks that were not a function of the administrative hierarchy.

The expanded acquisition of point data will help us ensure that CHGIS, which is meant to be *the* common base of history for two thousand years, can serve many fields and their methodologies, not all of which depend on measuring area. However, exploring economic, social, and cultural networks requires identifying point locations and considering the attribute data associated with those points. For earlier periods, we cannot assemble the breadth of attribute data used in Skinner's hierarchical regional system model for contemporary China. We have only begun to explore the possibilities for spatial datasets in Chinese history.

In conceptual terms, greater reliance on point data is justified. This case study has introduced evidence that the administrative hierarchy was conceived as hierarchies of central places rather than as bounded territory, which governed through its ability to register populated settlements and landholdings of the inhabitants. In other words, administrative units were not purely conceived of as bounded territory. Administrative geographies and early cartography support this view. Administrative places were located in space relative to other administrative places, and the notable physical features of the landscape within the jurisdiction were recorded. However, a strong sense of precisely bounded territory was lacking except when it was crucial to define, as was the case along roads, where one jurisdiction ended and another began.

A belief in sovereign territory has been part of the conception of the modern nation state and makes the idea of bounded territory seem natural. This fits with modern cartography, making it possible to draw absolute boundaries irrespective of the realities of geography. This does not fit much of the history of China. We may also ask how appropriate it is to the history of Mediterranean civilization before the fifteenth century. If bounded territories are misleading or otherwise inadequate, then the development of historical GIS for the premodern West will also have to deal in points rather than polygons.

This does not mean that the top-down, point-based administrative perspective was the only possibility in China before the adoption of Western cartography. From the start, the natural geographical discourse in China supposed a world influenced but not determined by the administrative perspective. Moreover, the rise of local gazetteers, a consequence of social, economic, cultural, and institutional changes during the Tang–Song transition from the eighth through the twelfth century, brought something akin to a bottom-up perspective: an intensive examination of the elements of local society. Gazetteers recognize the administrative perspective. But at the local level, they see it in the context of a locality with its own historical landscape. A GIS for Chinese history must take into account such historical shifts in sources and spatial conceptions. Ultimately, inhabitants adopted administrative units imposed on the landscape then tried to make them their own and give them a history they would define. As this happened, ideas about bounded space became more prevalent, even if boundary-making was not seen as fundamental to administration.

A guiding principle in our creation of a historical GIS for China has been the need to take into account characteristics of the Chinese historical record. Ultimately, CHGIS should become part of a historical GIS for the Eurasian landmass. The idea of a national historical GIS works for an era of nation states. But for earlier periods, when populations moved, tribal confederations and sedentary states rose and fell, and power was contracting and expanding, our spatial understanding of history would surely benefit from the many perspectives of a world historical GIS. When that day comes, the China Historical GIS project will provide one vital piece of a more complex whole.

NOTES

1. For a short description of the project see Peter K. Bol and Jianxiong Ge, "China Historical GIS," *Historical Geography* 33 (2005): 150–2. Datasets can be downloaded at http://www.fas.harvard.edu/~chgis.

2. The first detailed English-language introduction to geography, cartography, and surveying in China was Joseph Needham, *Science and Civilisation in China,* vol. 3 (Cambridge, Cambridge University Press, 1959), 497–590. This has been superseded by Cordell D. K. Yee, "Cartography in China," in *The History of Cartography: Cartography in Traditional East and Southeast Asian Societies,* vol. 2, book 2, ed. J. B. Harley and David Woodward, (Chicago: University of Chicago Press, 1994), 35–202, 228–31. The earliest known geographical treatise is the "Tribute of Yu" chapter of the *Book of Documents,* one of the Confucian Classics. Although purportedly relating events of 2200 BC, it is a work of the first millennium BC. The earliest extant maps include topographic, administrative, and land-use attributes and date from the third century BC; discussed in Cordell D. K. Yee, "Cartography in China," 37–40; and Mei-ling Hsu, "The Qin Maps: A Clue to Later Chinese Cartographic Development," *Imago Mundi* 45 (1993): 90–100.

3. For a translation of this text see Bernard Karlgren, "The Book of Documents: Yu gong (Tribute of Yu)," *Bulletin of the Museum of Far Eastern Antiquities* 22 (1950): 12–18.

4. The "Five Dependencies" scheme is discussed in Yee, "Cartography in China," pp. 75–6.

5. Citing the "Li yun" chapter of the *Book of Rites.*

6. Citing the "Virtue of the five emperors" chapter of the *Book of Rites.*

7. Fang Xuanling 房玄, *Jin shu* 晉書 (*Scripta Sinica* ed. Beijing: Zhorghua shuju, 1974), 14.405

8. Wei Zheng 魏徵, and Linghu Defen 令狐德棻, *Sui shu* 隋書 (*Scripta Sinica* ed. Beijing: Zhonghua shuju, 1973), 29.806.

9. Shui Anli 稅安禮, *Lidai dili zhizhang tu* 歷代地理抵掌圖 (rpt. of 12th c. ed. Shanghai: Shanghai guji chuban she, 1989). The original is held by the Toyo Bunko in Tokyo. Discussed in Tan Qixiang's preface. Also see Cao Wanru 曹婉如 and et al., eds., *Zhongguo gudai ditu ji* 中國古代地圖集, vol. 1 (Beijing: Wenwu chuban she, 1990), notes for maps 94–101.

10. In this Shui does in graphic form what Ouyang Min does in narrative form in his *Extended Record of the Realm* from the 1120s; see Ouyang Min 歐陽忞, *Yudi guangji* 輿地廣記, (Chengdu: Sichuan da xue chu ban she, 2003).

11. Zheng Qiao 鄭樵, *Tong zhi* 通志 (Beijing: Zhonghua shuju, 1987), 40.541A. However, this led Zheng to ignore what he certainly knew: that rivers, particularly the Yellow River, had changed course over time.

12. My thinking about this owes much to Sarah Jo-Shao Wang, "Out of Control: The Place of Shanshui (Mountains and Rivers) in the Geographical Discourse of Early Imperial China" (PhD thesis, Ann Arbor, University of Michigan, 1999); and Paul Wheatley, *The Pivot of the Four Quarters: A Preliminary Enquiry into the Origins and Character of the Ancient Chinese City* (Chicago: Aldine, 1971).

13. This is true for all of the maps in Shui Anli's historical atlas.

14. The representation of county units as bounded space appears for the first time in late eighteenth century county gazetteers for Jinhua Prefecture (formerly Wuzhou, formerly Dongyang Jun), to which Yongkang belongs. See Huang Jinsheng, ed., *Jinhua xianzhi* (1823 ed.); Tang Rensen, ed., *Lanxi xianzhi* (1888 ed.); and Xue Dingming, ed., *Pujiang xianzhi* (1779 ed.).

15. For the adoption of European methods see Iwo Amelung, "New Maps for the Modernizing State: Western Cartographical Knowledge in Late 19th Century China," in *Graphics and Text in the Production of Technical Knowledge in China: The Warp and the Weft,* ed. Francesca Bray, Vera Dorofeeva-Lichtman, and Georges Métailié (Leiden: Brill, forthcoming). As Zou Zhenhuan points out in his authoritative study of Western geography in China, Western knowledge introduced in the late Ming did not have a transformative impact; see Zou Zhenhuan 鄒振環, *Wan Qing xifang dili xue zai Zhongguo: yi 1815 zhi 1911 nian xifang dilixue yizhu de zhuanbo yu yingxiang wei zhongxi* 晚清西方地理學在中國：1815至1911年西方地理譯著的轉播與影響為中心 (Shanghai: Shanghai guji chuban she, 2000).

16. Vera Dorofeeva-Lichtman, "Geographical Treatises in Chinese Dynastic Histories: "No Man's Land" Between Sinology and History of Science," Proceedings of the XXIst International Congress of History of Science (Mexico City, 2001), 11.

17. For example, Henrietta Harrison, "Village Identity in Rural North China: A Sense of Place in the Diary of Liu Dapeng," in *Town and Country in China: Identity and Perception,* ed. David Faure and Tao Tao Liu (Houndsmills: Palgrave, 2002), 85–106.

18. Taking the section on Wu zhou as an example, see Li Jifu 李吉甫, *Yuanhe jun xian tu zhi* 元和郡縣圖志 (*Wuying dian ju zhen ban* ed.), 27.4b–7a. Later examples include Yue Shi's *The Taiping Reign Period Record of the World* from 976–983 and Wang Cun's extremely summary *Treatise on the Nine Regions in the Yuanfeng Reign Period* from 1078–85. See Yue Shi 樂史, *Taiping huanyu ji* 太平環宇記 (1793 ed.), 97.5b–10b. Wang Cun 王存, *Yuanfeng jiuyu zhi* 元豐九域志 (1784 ed.), 5.16a–b.

19. Wang Cun, *Yuanfeng jiuyu zhi* (Beijing: Zhonghua shuju, 1984), 5.212–19, a national administrative geography from 1078–85, for the first time gives distances from the prefectural seat to the border of the adjoining prefecture. The overview maps of Jiankang Prefecture from 1261 depict the prefecture and county seats graphically and labels boundary points between counties; see Zhou Yinghe 周應合, *Jingding Jiankangzhi* 景定建康志 (1809 ed.). In both cases, I assume that the distances and points are given with reference to roads between administrative seats.

20. The great polymath Shen Gua 沈括 (1031–1095) argued that by using surveying techniques and twenty-four rather than eight compass headings it was possible to measure the "as the bird flies" distance between points. The value of this, he claimed, was that with a table of directions and distances a scaled map could be drawn when necessary. See Needham, *Science and Civilisation,* vol. 3, 576; and Yee, "Cartography in China," 113–17.

21. Frank Leeming, "Official Landscapes in Traditional China," *Journal of the Economic and Social History of the Orient 23,* parts 1–2 (1980): 153–204, uses 1:50,000 and 1:100,000 maps to argue that road systems reveal the system of land allotments in the North China plain according to the Tang "equitable fields" land redistribution system and an underlying older well-field system.

22. *Song shi* 宋史 (*Scripta Sinica* ed.), 400.12146. Noted in Needham, vol. 3, 518. A similar argument is found in a late twelfth century handbook for local officials; see *Zhou xian tigang* 州縣提綱 (Congshu jicheng ed.), 2.22.

23. Christian Lamouroux, "Geography and Politics: The Song-Liao Border Dispute of 1074/75" *China and Her Neighbours: Borders, Visions of the Other, Foreign Policy, 10th to 19th Century,* ed. Sabine Dabribghaus and Roderich Ptak (Weisbaden: Harrassowitz Verlag, 1997), 1–28.

24. Huang Shang's map from 1190 covers the territory of the Song dynasty and two northern states, the Jin dynasty of the Jurchens and the Xia dynasty of the Tanguts. It names 368 prefectures, 623 military bases, 73 rivers, 27 lakes, 180 mountains, and 24 passes, but it does not draw state boundaries; reproduced from Cao Wanru, *Zhongguo gudai ditu ji,* vol. 1, plate 72. The same holds for an earlier map covering international relations, the "Map of the Chinese and the Tribal Peoples" 華夷圖, engraved in 1136 but describing the situation as of 1117; reproduced and discussed in Cao Wanru, *Zhongguo gudai ditu ji,* vol. 1, plates 54-6.

25. *Da Ming hunyi tu* 大明混一圖, Cao Wanru, *Zhongguo gudai ditu ji,* vol. 2, plates 1-5.

26. Examples include the "Map of the Realm with Notes by Yang Ziqi" (楊子器跋輿地圖) from 1512-13 and "Map of the Eternal Unification of the Ming" (大明萬世一統圖) from 1638; reproduced and discussed in Cao Wanru, *Zhongguo gudai ditu ji,* vol. 2, plates 1-5, 96.

27. Guang Yu tu 廣輿圖 of circa 1553; reproduced and discussed in Cao Wanru, *Zhongguo gudai ditu ji,* vol. 2, plates 147-56.

28. For examples, see the maps included in the *Jiaqing Chongxiu Da Qing yitong zhi* 嘉慶重修大清一統志.

29. For one such example, see Timothy Brook's study of the cartography of Ye Chunji, contemporary with the author of the Boluo County map in figure 2.7. Brook notes that this model was not followed until the nineteenth century. See "Mapping Knowledge in the Sixteenth Century: The Gazetteer Cartography of Ye Chunji," *The [Princeton University, Gest] East Asian Library Journal* 7:2 (1994): 5-32. Note that in the 1763 edition the Boluo County gazetteer reverts to a traditional administrative seat-centered perspective on the county in its maps and dispenses with borders. Cf. fig 10, a late 16th century map that also adopts a bottom-up perspective.

30. This is the "Map of the Complete Vista of the Imperial Realm" (Huangyu quanlan tu 皇輿全覽圖), cited as the source for overview map of Jinhua County. See Huang Jinsheng, *Jinhua xianzhi* 金華縣誌 (1823 ed.); *juanshou* 9b.

31. Various printed maps exist that claim to show the spatial distribution of population at various points in Chinese history without, however, providing the level of spatial detail that would allow one to check the figures for accuracy. As an example, see Hans Bielenstein, "Chinese Historical Demography, A.D. 2-1982," *Bulletin of the Museum of Far Eastern Antiquities* 59 (1987): 1-288.

32. The authoritative historical atlas is Tan Qixiang 譚其驤 ed., *Zhongguo lishi ditu ji* 中國歷史地圖集, 8 volumes (Shanghai: Ditu chubanshe, 1982-1987). The most important single source for changes in administrative units is Zhang Minggeng and Zhang Mingju 張明庚 張明聚 eds., *Zhongguo lidai xingzheng quhua: gongyuan qian 211-gongyuan 1911 nian* 中國歷代行政區劃: 公元前 211 - 公元1991年 (Beijing: Zhongguo Huaqiao chuban she, 1996).

33. CHGIS has rules for dating that reflect the degree of precision found in the historical record.

34. One of the unique aspects of the CHGIS database is the "Part-of Table," which makes it possible to see what administrative unit a given place belonged to in the administrative hierarchy. Probably the most important decision that must be made in extending this downward concerns the levels of hierarchy that should be included as the institutional system changes. For example, because in the middle period the "canton" (*xiang* 鄉) played a significant role in village administration, it makes sense to list known villages as "part of" both a particular canton and a particular county. The CHGIS database has been constructed so that a village can be listed both as "part of" a canton and "part of" a county without creating any conflict.

35. This point is made in Hu Bangbo, "Maps and Political Power: A Cultural Interpretation of the Maps in *The Gazetteer of Jiankang Prefecture*," *Journal of the North American Cartographic Information Society* 34 (1999): 9-22, and "Cartography in a Chinese Gazetteer of 1268, The Gazetteer of Linan Prefecture," *Middle States Geographer* 32 (1999): 61-70.

36. G. William Skinner, Mark Henderson, and Jianhua Yuan, "China's Fertility Transition through Regional Space: Using GIS and Census Data for a Spatial Analysis of Historical Demography," *Social Science History* 24:3 (2000): 613-48; G. William Skinner, "Marketing and Social Structure in Rural China," *Journal of Asian Studies* 24:1-3 (1964-1965); "Cities and the Hierarchy of Local Systems," in *The City in Late Imperial China*, ed. G. William Skinner (Stanford: Stanford University Press, 1977), 275-354; and, for a major statement of his view that regional analysis is fundamental to the study of Chinese history, "The Structure of Chinese History," *Journal of Asian Studies* 44:2 (1985): 271-92. For a theoretical discussion of the value of regional scale explanation, see Richard G. Healy and Trem R. Stamp, "Historical GIS as a Foundation for the Analysis of Regional Growth: Theoretical, Methodological, and Practical Issues," *Social Science History* 24:3 (2000): 575-612.

37. For a discussion of this transition, the development of regional systems and cycles, and its consequences for the makeup of the elite, see Robert M. Hartwell, "Demographic, Political, and Social Transformations of China, 750-1550," *Harvard Journal of Asiatic Studies* 42:2 (1982): 365-442.

38. For the Tang elite, see David Johnson, *The Medieval Chinese Oligarchy* (Boulder: The Westview Press, 1977). On the diminution of central authority, see Charles A. Peterson, "Court and Province in Mid- and Late T'ang," in *The Cambridge History of China*, vol. 3, *Sui and T'ang China, 589-906*, ed. Denis Twitchett (Cambridge: Cambridge University Press, 1979), 464-550. On the changes in the financial system, see Denis C. Twitchett, *Financial Administration under the T'ang Dynasty* (Cambridge: Cambridge University Press, 1963).

39. Gao Congming 高聰明, *Songdai huobi yu huobi liutong yanjiu* 宋代貨幣與貨幣流通研究. (Baoding: Hebei daxue chuban she, 1999), 103.

40. G. William Skinner points out that the centrally appointed bureaucracy and the total number of counties and prefectures did not grow with the population, which increased from 100 million at the end of the eleventh century to 450 million by the end of the nineteenth. See his "Introduction: Urban Development in Imperial China," in *The City in Late Imperial China*, ed. G. William Skinner (Stanford: Stanford University Press, 1977), 3-32.

41. On the role of the examination system, see John W. Chaffee, *The Thorny Gates Learning in Sung China: A Social History of Examinations* (Cambridge: Cambridge University Press, 1985). The nature of the social transition was defined most clearly by Robert Hartwell, "Demographic, Political, and Social Transformation of China, 750-1550," *Harvard Journal of Asiatic Studies* 42:2 (1982): 365-442; and Robert P. Hymes, *Statesmen and Gentlemen: The Elite of Fu-Chou, Chiang-hsi, in Northern and Southern Sung.* (Cambridge: Cambridge University Press, 1986). For a survey of the relevant literature, see Peter K. Bol, *"This Culture of Ours"—Intellectual Transitions in T'ang and Sung China* (Stanford: Stanford University Press, 1992), chap. 2.

42. On local gazetteers as scholarly and elite endeavors, see James M. Hargett, "Song Dynasty Local Gazetteers and Their Place in the History of *Difangzhi* Writing," *Harvard Journal of Asiatic Studies* 56:2 (1996): 405-42; and Joseph Dennis, "Between Lineage and State: Extended Family and Gazetteer Compilation in Xinchang County," *Ming Studies* 45-46 (2001): 69-113.

43. Peter K. Bol, "The Rise of Local History: History, Geography, and Culture in Southern Song and Yuan Wuzhou," *Harvard Journal of Asiatic Studies* 61:1 (2001): 37–76.

44. E. P. Wilkinson, *Chinese History: A Manual* (Cambridge, Mass.: Harvard University Asia Center for the Harvard-Yenching Institute, distributed by Harvard University Press, 2000), 154.

45. On the new style of gazetteer, see Stig Thogersen and Soren Clausen, "New Reflections on the Mirror: Local Chinese Gazetteers (*difangzhi*) in the 1980s," *Australian Journal of Chinese Affairs* 27 (1992): 1–24.

46. Guo Zhengzhong 郭正中, *Liang Song chengxiang shangpin huobi jingji kaolue* 兩宋城鄉商品貨幣經濟考略 (Beijing, Jingli guangli chuban she, 1997) 229–301. Cf. Shiba Yoshinobu 斯波義信, "*Sōdai* no toshika wo kangaeru" 宋代の都市化を考える. *Tōhōgaku* 東方學 102 (2001): 1–19.

47. These route books and the vision of the nation implied by them is the subject of Du Yongtao, "Translocality, Place Making, and Cultural Formation: Huizhou Merchants in Late Imperial China, 1500–1800" (PhD diss., University of Illinois, Urbana-Champagne, 2005).

48. Shiba Yoshinobu, "Ningpo and Its Hinterland," in *The City in Late Imperial China,* ed. G. William Skinner, (Stanford: Stanford University Press, 1977), 391–440.

49. The Shanghai Library holds over 2,000 editions of genealogies for Jinhua Prefecture alone.

50. Following Wolfram Eberhard, "Temple Building Activities in Medieval and Modern China: An Experimental Study," *Monumenta Serica* 23 (1964): 264–318. These conclusions were based on case studies of religious sites recorded in local gazetteers. Jinhua was one of the cases.

51. Huang Minzhi 黃敏枝, *Songdai fojiao shehui jingjishi lunji* 宋代佛教社會經濟史論集 (Taibei: Xuesheng shuju, 1989).

52. Valerie Hansen, *Changing Gods in Medieval China* 1127–1276 (Princeton: Princeton University Press, 1990), 128–59.

53. For a discussion of the ways in which cults functioned in local society, see Barend Ter Haar, "Local Society and the Organization of Cults in Early Modern China: A Preliminary Study," *Studies in Central and East Asian Religions* 8 (1995): 1–43; David Faure, "What Weber Did Not Know: Towns and Economic Development in Ming and Qing China," in *Town and Country in China: Identity and Perception,* ed. D. Faure and T. T. Liu (Houndsmills, Palgrave, 2002), 58–84; and Richard von Glahn, "Towns and Temples: Urban Growth and Decline in the Yangzi Delta, 1100–1400," in *The Song-Yuan-Ming Transition in Chinese History,* ed. Paul Smith and Richard von Glahn (Cambridge: Harvard University Asia Center, 2003): 176–211.

54. Zhou Zongzhi, ed., *Jinhua fuzhi* (1480 ed.), 13.1a–54b.

55. Anne Kelly Knowles, "Introduction," *Social Science History* 24:3 (2000), 451–67 (452).

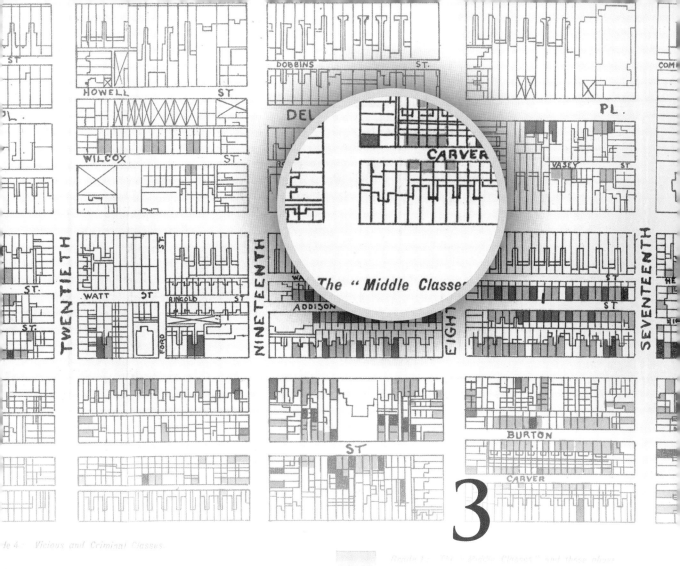

3

TEACHING WITH GIS

Robert Churchill and Amy Hillier

PART I: THE VALUE OF GIS FOR LIBERAL ARTS EDUCATION

By Robert Churchill

Early advocates of GIS[1] argued that the technology was somewhat analogous to Galileo's telescope in that they both allowed us to see old problems in different and innovative ways and accommodated exciting discoveries. Early critics worried that GIS was the latest effort of positivists to reassert themselves and expressed deeper fears that the technology readily facilitated sociospatial engineering: one more strike against the proletariat.[2] Many students chose a practical, rather than philosophical or moral, stand in the belief that GIS was an acronym for guaranteed income security. Proponents and critics alike, however, now acknowledge that GIS is more than a passing fad or fetish that can be wished away.[3] GIS is embedded in the academy, with numerous journals and conferences and well-established curricula and infrastructure in many colleges and universities. The technology may be more assimilated in mainstream society, with examples ranging from simple Web applications like MapQuest to dashboard navigation systems. Long used in environmental planning and resource management, GIS is now employed across a variety of industries such as real estate, banking and investment, insurance, and marketing, to name a few of the more prominent examples. In the near future, some form of GIS software will likely become nearly as common on the desktop as word processors and spreadsheets. The rapid diffusion and the ubiquity of GIS in academia and society have occasioned what Pip Forer and David Unwin refer to as a changing "dialectic with human processes."[4]

Moreover, GIS alters the ways in which we envision space and spatial relationships, as conveyed by a very simple example.[5] With formal schooling as a geomorphologist, I once studied watersheds, which were measured and represented by a number of indices taken at particular locations within the drainage basin. In other words, a continuous area feature was reduced to a series of point measurements. With GIS, however, the watershed can be envisioned and processed as a continuous feature (figure 3.1). And properties of the watershed such as ground slope, once expressed as a maximum or a mean, also can be determined as a continuous surface.[6]

The ubiquity and analytic power of geographic information systems in the public and private sectors warrant ongoing consideration of the place of GIS in higher education. While a lot has been written about GIS and education, much of this work begins with the assumption that students are destined toward a career in related fields or at the very least will make intensive use of GIS as an essential research tool. For students who fall outside of these categories, the limited consensus is that GIS, like the liberal arts in general, is good for them. But just how does GIS add value to their education? Part I of this chapter proposes that GIS offers at least four distinct benefits beyond training professionals, scientists, and technicians. First, GIS can teach valuable analytical and problem-solving strategies that transcend disciplinary boundaries. Second, GIS emphasizes visualization and underscores the indispensable value of the visual by using maps to communicate results.[7] Third, GIS engages a variety of important and timely social, economic, and political issues. Finally, GIS can provide a pedagogy that at once serves and cuts across traditional disciplines.

FIGURE 3.1

Watershed as a continuous surface. Raster GIS representations like this of the Rancocas Watershed Management Area in New Jersey can be made from publicly accessible data using desktop GIS software.

New Jersey Department of Environmental Protection (NJDEP), Office of Information Resources Management (OIRM), Bureau of Geographic Information and Systems (BGIS), 10-Meter Digital Elevation Grid of the Rancocas Watershed Management Area (WMA 19).

ANALYTICAL THINKING AND PROBLEM SOLVING

At the very least, GIS provides a forum to teach a number of rudimentary concepts—ideas that should be familiar to college and university students but which often seem to be foreign. This became particularly apparent to me after spending an inordinate amount of time attempting to convince an otherwise bright student that longitude was not a measure of north–south position on the earth. In addition to longitude and latitude, the concepts include datums and basic geodesy, planar geometry and coordinate systems, and fundamental map-reading skills. Working knowledge of these concepts alone might justify GIS education, but GIS also teaches analytical thinking and the ability to solve problems. Even more basically, the informed use of GIS to address any problem first requires the ability to understand and articulate that problem.

GIS tools are powerful in part because they can be applied to a wide variety of problems. For example, there is no button that evaluates the socioeconomic impact of redrawing school district boundaries, only the capacity to conduct map overlays and queries that can evaluate their impact. Students must deconstruct the problem to determine how GIS can be applied. But for any given problem, the particular steps in the deconstruction process are dictated to some degree by the GIS toolbox. This point may be illustrated most effectively with reference to a particular problem.

Used early on to segregate Chinese immigrants in San Francisco, zoning has its origins in discrimination and remains subject to discriminatory practice.[8] Unfortunately, determining whether zoning is discriminatory is confounded because pertinent socio-economic data is rarely collected by zoning class (figure 3.2) and instead is mostly aggregated by census enumeration units. Before demographic data representing race, income, and age structure can be mapped by zoning districts, these variables must first be reaggregated, a process commonly approached using either area-weighted or population-weighted averaging (see chapter 5 in this volume). While GIS software can do this, students must understand the procedure and learn to organize it into a series of distinct steps that can be performed using GIS tools at hand. Teaching GIS in the context of a particular problem helps students appreciate and understand the substantive problem and the appropriate analytical techniques. Deconstructing the problem is essential in the research process. However, the lesson has value beyond knowing the operation of overlays, buffers, and dissolves.

FIGURE 3.2 ▶

Land-use map of Middlebury, Vermont. To analyze demographic data by zoning areas, students need to learn how to reaggregate data from census units, such as block group or census tract, to zoning classes.

Shapefiles courtesy of Addison County Regional Planning Commission.

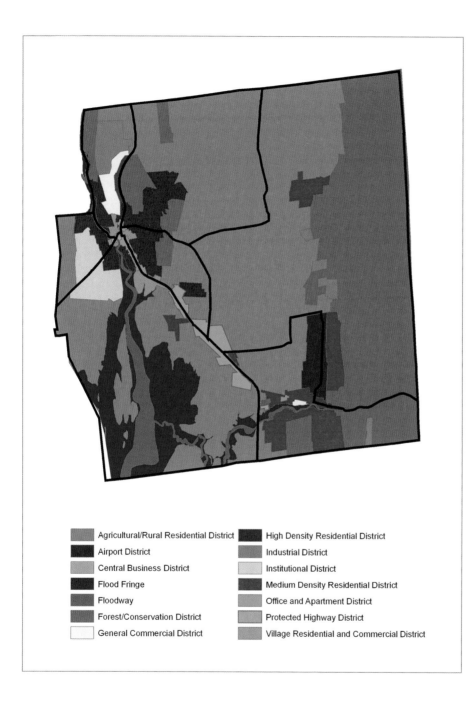

	Agricultural/Rural Residential District		High Density Residential District
	Airport District		Industrial District
	Central Business District		Institutional District
	Flood Fringe		Medium Density Residential District
	Floodway		Office and Apartment District
	Forest/Conservation District		Protected Highway District
	General Commercial District		Village Residential and Commercial District

VISUALIZATION

Spatial patterns and relationships that may have significant explanatory power often are revealed only when the information is presented visually in the form of a map. In his popular book, *Mapping the Next Millennium,* Stephen Hall argues that data has become so voluminous and complex that mapping data is the only way to make sense of it and investigate it visually.[9] After reviewing the history of mapping, Hall explores how visualization made its way into a variety of fields beyond geography. In the years since Hall conducted this examination, scientific visualization has become a familiar term in the lexicon, an important research tool pervasive across many fields and itself the subject of substantial research.[10] In geography, visualization is gaining favor as a term that subsumes traditional cartography, GIS, and related technologies such as animation and multimedia.[11]

When people look at a map on paper or screen, however, their first instinct is to locate their home or a familiar frame of reference. Maps draw people in. Some years ago, our lab took on a project for a local town. In revising and updating its plan, all but one member of the town select board wanted to build a digital database. The lone holdout was dubious of computers, all related technology, and GIS in particular. On visits to our lab, he maintained considerable distance from the workstations, as if he might contract some horribly contagious malady. When the database was completed and displayed, however, this skeptic inched his way toward the monitor and excitedly began to point out his farm, buildings, and fence lines. Even the simplest maps are engaging; they break down language barriers and facilitate dialogue. With capabilities that extend well beyond conventional maps, GIS accommodates an impressive and effective set of visualization tools.

As a young teacher, I struggled to have students see a three-dimensional (3D) surface from what appeared as a disorganized mass of brown squiggles. I hoped the class would make sense of photographs of selected areas juxtaposed with their contour representations. This approach was questionable at best and almost certainly not worth the time and effort required. Now, the touch of a button produces a shaded relief representation that talented Swiss cartographers once would have spent countless hours constructing with an airbrush. Software quickly renders 3D representations of landscape, which people can virtually fly over or drive through. Today, we have the ability to represent visually, and in a variety of ways, subjects that are too vast or too abstract to envision otherwise. This may be one of the most simple and obvious—and one of the greatest—strengths of GIS technology.

Referring to Walter Benjamin's comparison of photography and painting, John Pickles contends that "GIS directs our attention to the multiple fragments, multiple views, and layers that are assembled under the new laws of ordering and reordering . . . ."[12] Pickles argues that GIS enables students to explore the character and characteristics of images that give meaning to space and place. As a leading voice for the critical GIS movement, Pickles also challenges the notion that GIS is value-neutral and that maps are objective. But perhaps even more fundamentally, the ability to create one's own symbology, to add and remove text and toponyms, to literally shape the picture of place, helps to expose the social and cultural subjectivity of maps.

During the Enlightenment, the development of visual argument brought about a view of the map as scientific and objective. This view was reinforced through much of the twentieth century and no doubt still prevails outside the academy.[13] While students learn from an early age to question what they read, the maps they study tend to remain unassailable. But as GIS students design maps to frame their analyses and support their arguments, they begin to realize that maps are visual arguments, that every map is a proposition with a distinct point of view. Corollary to this point, we may more readily see how the design and construction of maps influence and are influenced by our sense of place. In his intriguing work *Landscape and Memory*, postmodernist historian Simon Schama argues that landscape is a construct of cognition and perception.[14] As a primary force in geographical cognition, the map may contribute nearly as much to landscape as memory does, while in recursive fashion, this sense of landscape informs the map. A recent paradigm shift recognizes maps not only as subjective social constructs but also emphasizes their textual nature.[15] The irony might be that while the image is generally held as subordinate to text, the visual has always been privileged in geography.[16]

ENGAGING STUDENTS IN SOCIAL AND POLITICAL ISSUES

GIS is used in a variety of applications that raise important and timely ethical questions. In an early indictment of geographic information systems, social theorist and geographer Neil Smith labeled the 1991 Gulf War as the first GIS war and, in the same paper, used as a section title the provocative phrase *GIS über alles*.[17] Is GIS a tool for good or harm? Is the technology morally neutral, or does it somehow facilitate unbalanced exercise of power? From a social standpoint, one could argue that answering these questions is more important than the science or technology itself. Issues related to access to GIS and how it is used provide students with opportunities to reflect critically on all the tools and skills they acquire during their education. The social and political dimensions of geographic information systems thus have considerable relevance in a liberal arts education, as made clear by a brief look at several indicative examples.

Predicated on the argument that "More indigenous territory can be defended by maps than by guns," geographer Bernard Nietschmann founded the Mayan Mapping Project to involve indigenous peoples in southern Belize in mapping and documenting their homelands.[18] Among other threats, the Belizean government advocated multinational logging operations on traditional Mayan lands. While it can be argued that appropriation of territory has often and necessarily involved maps *and* guns, Nietschmann believed that mapping would go some way toward government recognition and legalization of Mayan claims to their lands. Using basic technology, local people mapped their homelands, with Nietschmann and his colleagues serving in an advisory capacity. The results of this work are presented in the *Maya Atlas,* which includes some of the first published maps by indigenous people using geospatial technologies to document traditional land use.[19]

GIS also plays a role in current controversies relating to personal privacy. These controversies go well beyond the role of information technologies alone, explaining why they have garnered appreciable popular attention.[20] GIS is relevant to these debates because location is the key to many of the databases that raise concerns about privacy.[21] Commercial geodemographic data provides detailed information down to the level of the nine-digit ZIP Code, typically a few households, while fidelity cards and similar devices accumulate data at the individual level.[22] Geographer Michael Curry, another outspoken voice in the critical GIS literature, worries that the practices of geodemographic firms are invasive, replacing real people with digital syntheses to the point that people and place become shallow digital caricatures.[23]

These examples of the intersection among GIS and social and political systems are far from exhaustive. As financial institutions adapt the technology, the issue of redlining reemerges, but the misuse of GIS may allow far more selective and indiscernible discrimination in lending than something as obvious as areas circled in red on paper maps. Industrial and government applications raise questions about equitable access to data and technology. Is GIS, for example, limited to the privileged who have requisite financial resources, education, and skills? What can be done to make it more widely available and to help close the digital divide?[24] Are there situations in which public data is best kept private? These are questions for students who are studying GIS in a liberal arts environment to consider.

GIS AS PEDAGOGY

Elbridge Gerry (figure 3.3) was a signatory of the *Declaration of Independence,* a cofounder of the Library of Congress, and a vice president of the United States. But it was in his capacity as governor of the Commonwealth of Massachusetts that, in name at least, he achieved lasting if dubious distinction.

In 1812, Gerry's political party reapportioned state senatorial districts. In the process, he packed a number of townships into a single, shoestring district. Noting a resemblance to the shape of a salamander, the editor of the *Boston Gazette* dubbed this district a gerrymander, which inspired Elkanah Tisdale's famous cartoon (figure 3.4, page 70) and gave rise to the term gerrymander as a pejorative for the act of creating districts that give distinct advantage to some particular faction and to such districts themselves.[25]

The reapportionment process has received extensive scrutiny since Gerry's time, most recently after 1992, when the Justice Department under President George H. W. Bush adapted a literal interpretation of the 1985 Amendments to the Voting Rights Act to create so-called minority–majority congressional districts. Across the country, black and Hispanic voters were packed into districts in which they comprised an overwhelming majority and arguably weakened the Democratic vote.[26] Understandably, reapportionment is of considerable interest to political scientists

and legal scholars alike. Yet at the most fundamental level, the process is geographic and cartographic. The U.S. Supreme Court underscored this point when it ruled that the shape of districts is a significant factor in assessing gerrymandering.[27] Gerrymandering predates GIS technology, but GIS makes it much faster to experiment with different redistricting plans. As GIS is now the

FIGURE 3.3

Gerrymandering, the process of reshaping political districts for partisan advantage, was named after Massachusetts Governor Elbridge Gerry, who reapportioned state senatorial districts in 1812.

National Portrait Gallery, Smithsonian Institution.

FIGURE 3.4

Elkanah Tisdale's political cartoon of Massachusetts gerrymandering. Tisdale emphasized the similarity between the reapportioned Massachusetts state senatorial districts and a salamander in this 1812 *Boston Gazette* political cartoon.

Boston Gazette, *1812.*

tool of choice in political redistricting, critics worry about the potential of people using the technology to create spatially compact districts without tortured shapes that gave gerrymandering its name.[28] The better that students understand the technology, the more potential abuses can be prevented.

GIS provides a pedagogic context in which to explore and understand the redistricting process, if for no other reason than its rapidly growing and extensive use. Students can use relatively simple redistricting routines in some software packages to explore basic concepts of reapportionment in a single class session. At the other extreme, sophisticated third-party extensions for proprietary software provide the basis for extensive study over an entire term.

Mark Rush, a political scientist and scholar of reapportionment, used this approach in teaching a course that used GIS to explore principles and issues of geographically based representation through the reapportionment of Virginia's congressional districts. His classroom experience showed that redistricting offers excellent examples of how GIS technologies are shaping our world. It provides a platform for integrating learning about constitutional law, judicial process, partisan politics, and demographic trends with the simplest of GIS techniques such as displaying data, dissolving boundaries, and computing summary statistics.[29] Students are forced to consider the geographic basis for political representation and inevitably weigh in with opinions about what is fair and reasonable.

Turning from the political process, literature often both evokes and imparts a strong sense of place. In this context, a colleague has proposed using GIS to facilitate appreciation of Terry Tempest Williams's *Refuge*. In this biographical reflection, Williams explores, as reciprocal metaphors, her mother's confrontation with cancer and profound changes in the Great Salt Lake Basin where she studied as a biologist.[30] GIS allows students to learn about place and about themselves by facilitating the exploration of different geographical elements, cartographic representations, and imagery at different points in time.[31] GIS accommodates modeling and analysis of change in lake levels, change in salinity, and change in habitats. Visualizing the lake's changes strengthens its metaphorical connection to Williams's mother as she copes with the changes wrought by her illness. GIS is being used to map literary landscapes, trace the journeys of fictional protagonists, and compare literary texts to virtual images of the actual places where they are set.

These examples illustrate the instructive use of GIS as pedagogy. One can easily imagine other compelling examples. Patterns and processes of off-shore industrial location encompass interwoven temporal and spatial elements that students might more effectively study and understand with GIS. Health care presents many issues with important spatial dimensions, from the diffusion and geographical patterns of disease to the distribution of human and material resources at different scales to the geographical variation in practitioner cultures. In showcasing a variety of historical studies in *Past Time, Past Place,* Anne Kelly Knowles suggests additional subjects for which GIS might prove a productive pedagogy, as do Diana Stuart Sinton and Jennifer J. Lund in *Understanding Place.*[32] Once faculty members embrace GIS, they see many ways to use it proactively and productively in the classroom.

GIS AND LIBERAL ARTS EDUCATION

GIS goes beyond mechanics and even conceptual frameworks to provide a number of universal and lasting benefits that are of value to students whether or not they pursue GIS-related careers. Part 1 of this chapter has focused on four such benefits: problem solving, visualization, social and political issues, and GIS as a pedagogical framework. And while arguments have been presented for each in turn, they are rarely so clearly segregated in practice.

Attempting to evaluate both the purported economic benefits and the social costs of carving a new school district from the existing structure provides a context in which GIS is more clearly understood but also requires operational definition of the problem and formulation of specific research questions. These are particularly valuable exercises, because students face a great challenge in defining and deconstructing a problem in a meaningful way that they can assess. Beyond articulating questions, the problem requires the skills to determine the questions that can be answered and the ones that cannot. Students may realize that questions depend on how the problem is cast. A different perspective might cause the questions to be framed differently, suggest a different choice of data, and require alternative analytical techniques. In addition, redrawing boundaries of any sort and attendant reaggregation of information within those boundaries are inherently geographical problems that require spatial reasoning and the ability to map and make sense of information at different scales of analysis. Finally, redrawing boundaries nearly always raises ethical questions that go beyond tools and techniques. Put more generally, is GIS an empowering technology that enables people to visualize choice, or is it another form of hegemony controlled by those who have requisite skills and access to the information and the resources?

Answering these questions, which means comprehending the reach, strength, and limitations of GIS, requires more than a superficial understanding and demands appreciation of applications, mechanics, and methods. Education can provide this familiarity, while encouraging responsible practice and promoting dialogue about the evolving role of GIS in science and society. These tasks are also education's imperative, because whether envisioned simply as a powerful tool or a recasting of geographical space, GIS is a big business that will become even more embedded in our society with time.

PART II: A GUIDE TO TEACHING HISTORICAL GIS
By Amy Hillier

Skeptics among us may continue to ask, is it necessary to teach GIS in history classes, or can the same teaching goals be met in other ways? These goals include teaching problem-solving and visualization and engaging students in important social and political issues, as described in part I of this chapter. In the context of history classes, goals might also include teaching students to find and assess historical sources and to incorporate spatial thinking into historical research.

Even if some teachers believe they can teach the same principles and skills in more traditional ways, GIS offers a unique tool for a technology-savvy generation to make discoveries about history. Students attending colleges and universities these days grew up looking for driving directions and music on the Internet, using e-mail and instant messaging to communicate with friends, and designing profiles and Web sites for dating and social networking. By applying these computer skills to mapping history, they can see the past in ways that most historians have not. The new computer skills they learn with GIS, such as naming and organizing files, building databases, writing queries, and learning to use graphics to communicate an argument, are transferable to other areas. Making maps is no substitute for writing, but students can learn how to complement good writing with visual representations.

One may accept the value of GIS in liberal arts education and teaching history, but from a practical point of view, how can history teachers begin to integrate GIS into their classes? Part II of this chapter provides examples from an introductory GIS course in urban history at the University of Pennsylvania. Twentieth-century urban history is full of examples of how place matters and how GIS has the potential to transform the approach to teaching and scholarship in this field. But beyond their value for urban history, these examples highlight transferable ideas about finding spatial data, framing research questions, and engaging students in work that is analytical and not just technical. As the examples in other parts of this book demonstrate, scholars are using historical GIS to make new contributions in ancient, rural, environmental, religious, political, and Civil War history. These fields are also ripe for courses that introduce GIS.

FINDING HISTORICAL SPATIAL DATA

Finding spatial data is one of the main obstacles to teaching historical GIS, but this sometimes frustrating process offers many opportunities for teaching students to recognize what is spatial in historical data, assess spatial data as a historical source, and convert historical data into map layers. Map layers ready to use with GIS software are increasingly available on the Internet. State GIS repositories, the U.S. Census Bureau, and the U.S. Geological Survey are among the most common sources of GIS data in the United States, providing access to basic map layers such as elevation, waterways, street networks, municipal boundaries, and census administrative units. These readily available sources rarely provide historical data. Many online and professional GIS training programs use generic GIS data with the expectation that users will translate examples to applications in their own industry. But using GIS examples with historical data is necessary for most undergraduate history students to understand the possibilities and make the connections to their work. Historical spatial data comes in many familiar formats, including paper maps, tables of aggregate data, and lists of addresses. With a little work, students can convert these formats to digital map layers for use in GIS. A major goal of the urban history course is to teach students to recognize and take advantage of this abundance of historical spatial data.

Old paper maps constitute the bedrock of historical GIS. (See Anne Kelly Knowles's presentation in the digital supplement for examples.) They often feature elegant cartography, intriguing distortions, dramatic color choices, and fraying edges. Among the jewels within urban history are Charles Booth's maps of poverty in London,

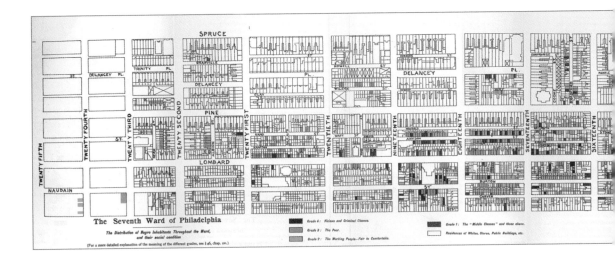

the maps Hull House residents created of their Chicago neighborhood, W. E. B. Du Bois's map of social class in *The Philadelphia Negro* (figure 3.5), and the color-coded residential security maps created for U.S. cities by the Home Owners' Loan Corporation (HOLC).[33]

These maps convey the values and prejudices of the people and institutions that created them. Booth drew attention to London's widespread poverty in the 1880s

FIGURE 3.5

W. E. B. Du Bois's map of social class from *The Philadelphia Negro,* shown here in its entirety and with an enlarged detail. W. E. B. Du Bois chose to represent the findings from his 1896 door-to-door survey of Philadelphia's Old Seventh Ward with this map color-coded by social condition.

Courtesy of University of Pennsylvania Archives.

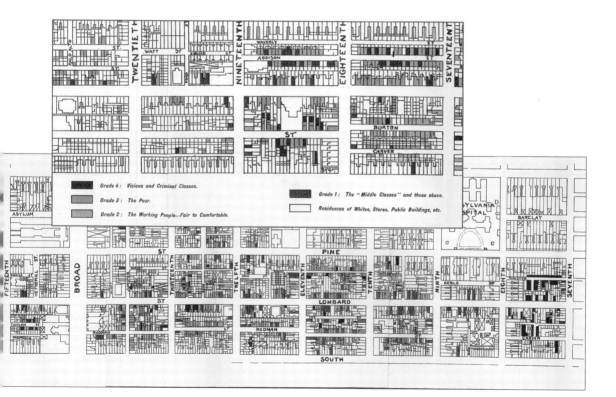

with his extensive survey while using a classification system that perpetuated ideas about deserving and undeserving poor. Like Booth, Du Bois referred to "vicious and criminal classes" in his efforts to distinguish them from decent working poor and middle-class blacks living in Philadelphia in the 1890s. The HOLC maps used the color red to indicate which neighborhoods it considered "hazardous" in the 1930s, invariably including areas with blacks and certain groups of new immigrants in supposed danger zones. These maps and others like them capture the racial and class prejudice of their makers, exposing students to an unfiltered representation of predominant attitudes and practices of a different era. Teaching historical GIS means taking the time to assess the meaning of these sources for historical communities and for us today.

Through georectifying, scanned paper maps can be converted to GIS layers and mapped with other data sources, including contemporary data. This process is done visually by lining up features on the scanned historical map with current GIS layers. A block-level map displaying data about race, ethnicity, housing values, and commercial activity in Philadelphia by appraiser J. M. Brewer in 1934 provides one example. A high-resolution scanned image allows students and researchers a chance to pour over its detail and interpret its story. Georectifying the digital image using a current street centerline file, available for free from the U.S. Census, makes it possible to compare past and present residential patterns. Figure 3.6 shows how 2000 U.S. Census data can be mapped on top to show how the black population in Du Bois's Old Seventh Ward along the southern edge of Center City has shifted farther south and west over the last hundred years as a result of gentrification in neighborhoods known as Rittenhouse Square, Washington Square, and Society Hill.

Scanned historical maps are increasingly available on the Internet through sites such as the map collections of the Library of Congress and David Rumsey.[34] Local libraries, historical societies, and planning commissions may also make digital images available on their Web sites. The GeoHistory Network of the Philadelphia Area Consortium of Special Collection Libraries (PACSCL) has made a number of fire insurance and land-use maps from the Free Library of Philadelphia available on the Internet.[35] The University of Pennsylvania's Fine Arts Library scanned its collection of neighborhood planning reports, sources with many maps, and made them available through its Philadelphia Neighborhoods Web site.[36] The University of Pennsylvania's Van Pelt Library has scanned many other historical maps, including those of historical township, ward, and census tracts.[37] All of these are available to students via the

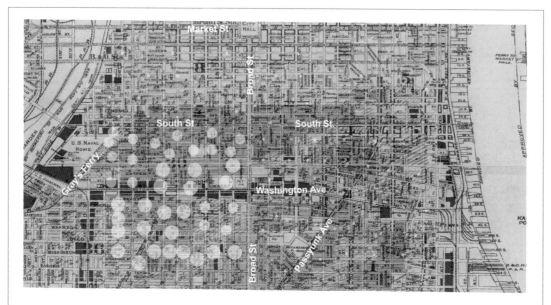

JM Brewer's 1935 Racial Concentrations

Jewish   Italian   Colored

Complete or Substantially
Complete Concentration

Predomination

Minority

Source: JM Brewer's 1935

African American 2000 Population

—— Block group

0% - 24%

25% - 49%

50% - 74%

75% - 100%

Source: US Bureau of the Census

FIGURE 3.6

Historical neighborhood conditions with 2000 U.S. Census data. The 1934 map
created by real estate appraiser J. M. Brewer was scanned and georectified as a
lab exercise in an introductory course on historical GIS. Students can compare
historical demographic and housing patterns with current patterns by layering
2000 census data on top. Here, block group-level data showing where blacks live
illustrates how the concentration of blacks in 1934 had shifted south and west by
2000 as the result of gentrification.

Map Collection, Free Library of Philadelphia.

Internet. Historical maps that have not been scanned are much more common and can be found within atlases, historical books, archives, and government agencies, among other places. Desktop scanners are generally capable of producing digital images of small maps that are adequate for classroom exercises and student projects. Large-format scanners may be needed for larger maps.

Historical data, aggregated by political and administrative units, such as towns, counties, and census tracts, provides another valuable source of GIS data. The National Historical Geographic Information System (NHGIS) project aims to make all of the aggregate census data from 1790 to 2000 available for free downloads.[38] Aggregate data like this can be mapped and analyzed alone or with scanned historical maps. During one class exercise, students layered 1950 census data with a scanned historical map of the expressways planned for Philadelphia. As in New York, where Robert Moses pushed through the Brooklyn–Queens Expressway, Cross–Bronx Expressway, the Belt Parkway, and other projects, city planners in Philadelphia designed an ambitious network of expressways. Some of these, like the Vine Street Expressway (I-676), were built while others, like the Cobbs Creek Parkway and Cross-town Expressway, were not. Urban historians have argued that expressway development in American cities, including Philadelphia, disproportionately affected poor, working class, and black neighborhoods.[39] Using a map scanned from a 1966 planning report with tract-level data from the 1950 census, students can analyze the relationship between the planned expressways and the income and racial composition of nearby areas (figure 3.7).

Because administrative boundaries change over time, the process of finding and analyzing aggregate historical data becomes more challenging. But this potential nightmare for researchers may provide important teaching opportunities for students. How have boundaries changed over time? Why have they changed? How can students analyze changes in the data when boundaries change? These questions are at the heart of the Great Britain Historical GIS project, which has carefully documented changes in parish boundaries during a 200-year period.[40] The challenge of reaggregating demographic data to zoning districts described earlier in this chapter is recreated endlessly in efforts to match historical data to changing boundaries.[41]

When digital boundary files are not available, they must be created. This involves digitizing, a tedious process of using GIS tools to trace boundary lines based on existing GIS layers. Digitizing produces files that can be used repeatedly. It also provides an opportunity for students to understand how GIS works, how existing GIS layers store spatial data, and how to generate and document spatial errors.

Lists of addresses provide a third major source of historical spatial data. Police arrest records, health department birth and death records, city directories, church directories, real estate directories, mortgage records, and manuscript decennial

FIGURE 3.7

Planned expressways in Philadelphia and highways actually constructed. This map is part of a report created by the Philadelphia Planning Commission in 1966. The network of planned expressways is shown in a semi-transparent layer. The yellow layer on top is the current centerline file for highways. It shows how few of the planned highways were actually built. The green shaded areas are 1960 census tracts showing different concentrations of black residents at the time the expressway network was planned.

University of Pennsylvania Libraries.

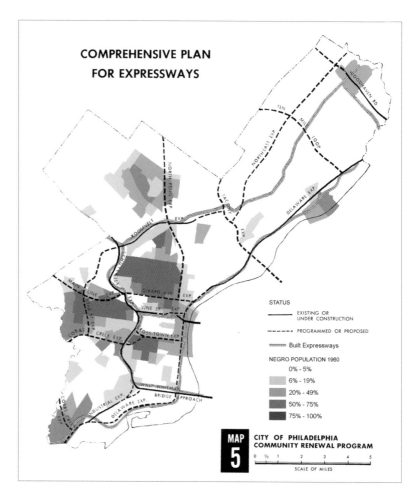

census records from 1930 or earlier are among the many different sources of information about individuals and households that include street address. Mapping current street addresses, whether using GIS desktop software or online systems that provide driving directions, involves a process of identifying the approximate location of an individual property along a street segment. Each street segment has a known range of house numbers and odd and even sides, so, theoretically, any house number can be located. Changing streets, street names, or house numbering systems can greatly complicate this process. Undergraduate Brandon Gollotti encountered this problem while trying to map addresses of tuberculosis patients in Philadelphia from 1896. To determine how streets and street names had changed, he consulted historical maps, aerial photographs, and an online historic street index.[42] Among other findings, his research revealed that Philadelphia General Hospital, which provided treatment to a number of the tuberculosis patients who lived at addresses he was trying to map, was located at 34th and Pine Street, an address that no longer exists because of the creation of a civic center and several new hospitals.

Framing research questions

My urban history class culminates in a final research project in which students collect and map their own data in order to answer a specific research question. Much of the urban history literature is based on broad narratives, some of which have not been well supported by empirical research.[43] Even when previous research has been well supported, it has rarely used GIS to look at the spatial dimension. Therefore, students may look to familiar books and articles to find questions that have not been asked through a spatial lens. Student Benjamin Berman found his research question in a journal article about the elimination of Philadelphia's Skid Row as part of urban renewal efforts in the 1960s.[44] His project (figure 3.8) asked, how did construction of the expressway affect Skid Row? Do maps showing how institutions and demographics changed over time challenge or support the existing

FIGURE 3.8 ▶

Philadelphia's Skid Row in 1952 with Vine Street Expressway. Student Benjamin Berman scanned and georectified a map of Skid Row from a 1952 Health and Welfare Council report. He added a layer of businesses geocoded from lists of addresses in *Yellow Pages* directories. Finally, he mapped the Vine Street Expressway, constructed between 1957 and 1959, using a current street centerline file.

Temple University Libraries, Urban Archives, Philadelphia, Pennsylvania.

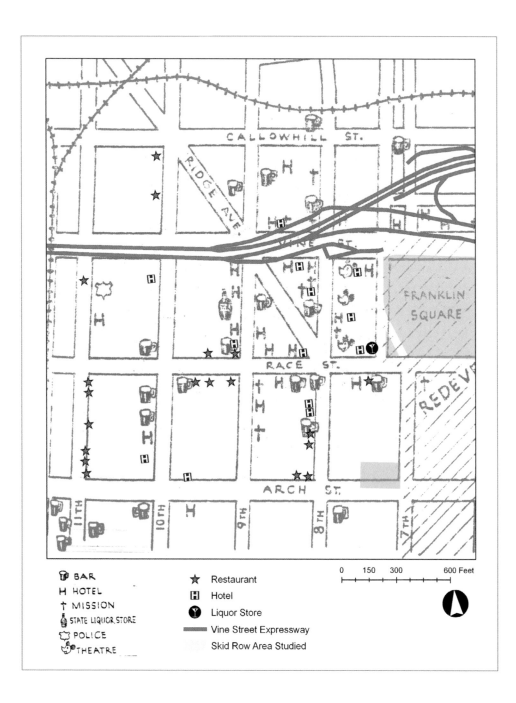

BAR	★ Restaurant
H HOTEL	H Hotel
✝ MISSION	Y Liquor Store
STATE LIQUOR STORE	Vine Street Expressway
POLICE	Skid Row Area Studied
THEATRE	

0   150   300   600 Feet

narrative that changing economic conditions and political support for urban renewal led to displacement of hundreds of poor, itinerant single men? Berman collected information about rooming houses and restaurants from business directories and block-level housing and population data from the U.S. Census. He mapped these together with a scanned paper map of Skid Row from a 1952 report about the area and a current street file showing where the Vine Street Expressway was eventually built. The resulting map in figure 3.8 (page 81) shows how the expressway wiped out the area that had been home to missions, liquor stores, hotels, theaters, and a population of 3,000 mostly older white men.

Student Dickon Waterfield found his research question in two classic texts of urban history, Clifford Shaw and Henry McCay's *Juvenile Delinquents and Urban Areas* (1942) and Ernest Burgess's essay on the growth of cities in the 1928 classic, *The City*.[45] Burgess presented his theory that cities develop along a series of concentric zones, with a commercial core, zone of transition, the working classes, and higher-class residential and commuter zones in the outlying areas. Shaw and McCay's book includes a 1940 map of Philadelphia showing where juvenile delinquents lived. Waterfield asked whether this pattern of juvenile delinquency followed Burgess's theory about the growth of cities and social disorganization. If social disorganization decreased with distance from the central city, as Burgess theorized, juvenile delinquency rates should decrease in the outlying areas. Waterfield scanned the map from the Shaw and McCay book and, using the buffer function in GIS, superimposed concentric rings around City Hall at the center of Philadelphia's downtown (figure 3.9). He concluded that Burgess's model largely fit 1940 Philadelphia, with some exceptions that are explained by Philadelphia's north–south growth along the Delaware River and the development of industry.

FIGURE 3.9 ▶

Visualizing Robert Park's and Burgess's concentric zones in Philadelphia. Student Dickon Waterfield created this map as part of his final project in a historical GIS course. The bottom layer is a scanned map of juvenile delinquency in Philadelphia in 1940 from Shaw and McCay's classic book, *Juvenile Deliquents and Urban Areas*. He created the top layer, a series of buffered zones around Center City shaded according to the rates of male juvenile delinquency.

Shaw and McCay, Juvenile Delinquency and Urban Areas, *1969 reprint edition, map 27, page 199; final GIS map created by Dickon Waterfield for URBS430 class at University of Pennsylvania. Shapefiles used by permission of the City of Philadelphia.*

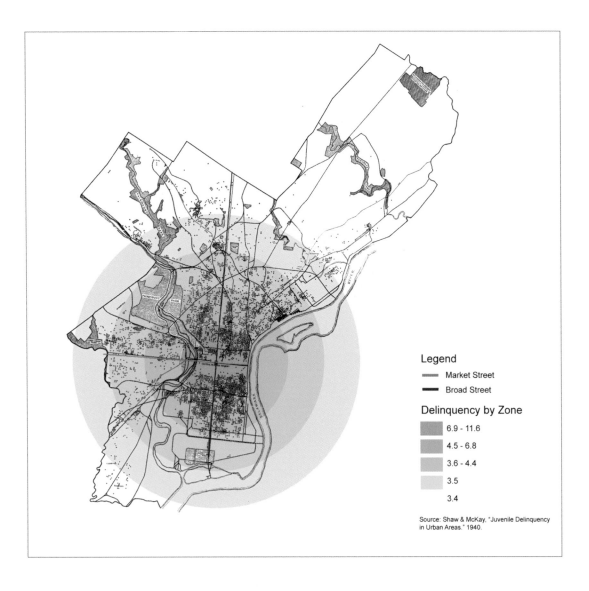

Legend

— Market Street

— Broad Street

Delinquency by Zone

6.9 - 11.6

4.5 - 6.8

3.6 - 4.4

3.5

3.4

Source: Shaw & McKay, "Juvenile Delinquency
in Urban Areas." 1940.

For her final class project, student Amelie Davidson recreated a section of South
Street in Philadelphia (figure 3.10) to test the much discussed but little documented
hypothesis that the planned Cross-town Expressway negatively affected businesses,
even though it was never built. Using building ownership data from 1940 to 1970
for a five-block area on the eastern end of South Street, Davidson showed a change
in the type of businesses along South Street before and after the Cross-town contro-
versy. She determined that most of the Jewish-owned neighborhood businesses, such
as Levy's Hardware Store, were eventually replaced by destination businesses, such
as clubs, theaters, and galleries (figure 3.10). While this did not reflect a direct process of displacement, the negative effect expressway plans had on property values
and residential stability did create the opportunity for a new class of merchants who
focused on leisure rather than the needs of local residents.

FIGURE 3.10

Business along Philadelphia's
South Street, 1960. Student
Amelie Davidson collected
information on businesses
along three blocks of South
Street from the *Bell Telephone
Directories* for 1940, 1950,
1960, and 1969. She matched
information about the name
and type of business to a
current parcel map, amending
boundaries as needed, since
property lines changed during
this period.

Map created by Amelie Davidson.

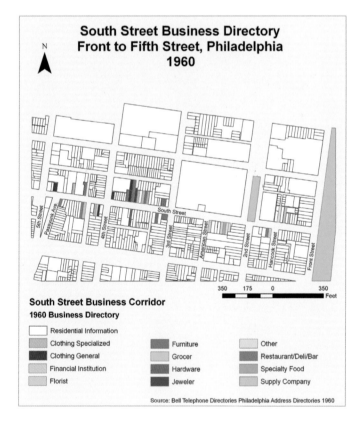

Undergraduate Sarah Bertozzi engaged directly in a historiographical debate in her final project and senior urban studies thesis on "vicious geography" and the spatial distribution of prostitution in Philadelphia during the twentieth century. To test prevailing theories that prostitution was spatially concentrated in the nineteenth century and dispersed in the twentieth century, she collected and mapped prostitution arrest data for Philadelphia from 1913 to 1961. Her results indicate a more complicated picture than that described in the literature, with prostitution centralized at some points and decentralized at others in response to policing, downtown investment, and residents' political capital (figure 3.11). Her findings challenged notions that prostitution in cities became more dispersed over time as street-walking replaced brothels and other place-based forms of prostitution.

FIGURE 3.11

Prostitution arrests in 1930 Philadelphia. Student Sarah Bertozzi mapped archival data from the Vice Squad Register of Arrests with hotel and restaurant listings in the *Classified Yellow Pages* of 1930 to assess the relationship between prostitution arrests and other sources of nightlife in Philadelphia.

Map created by Sarah Bertozzi. Shapefiles used by permission of the City of Philadelphia.

Urban history is full of topics like these that have had little or no empirical research or spatial methods applied. Simple descriptive research questions offer a good starting place for students who are studying new topics. Where did new immigrant groups settle in relation to each other and in relation to different types of industry? When and where did patterns of racial segregation emerge? Where were public housing projects located? Where was public transportation developed? Questions about the effect of these developments take research a step further. How did new immigrant groups affect housing construction and residential patterns? What was the impact of public housing projects on racial composition and housing values? How did new highways affect existing neighborhoods and suburban development? Students will gain a more thorough understanding of GIS and the scientific research process if they make their own maps using data related to their own interests. In doing so, they will learn to review a literature that interests them, identify a spatial question that needs answering, identify or create a dataset, and analyze the data using GIS techniques.

ENGAGING IN ANALYTICAL THINKING

Anyone who teaches a GIS class faces the challenge of devoting enough time to help students learn and use the software while focusing on GIS as an analytical tool. Technical success does not automatically translate into analytical accomplishment. New GIS users risk becoming enamored with the first color maps they make, even if the maps themselves say nothing. The following kinds of questions can help new users focus on the larger picture.

What is spatial about this research? Why does space matter? While much of the research in urban history relates to geography, students need to explicitly consider the causal mechanism behind a spatial relationship. Why did rivers affect the development of manufacturing? How did street cars and trains affect a suburban housing development? Why did disease cluster in a certain neighborhood? Was it because the disease was transmitted by human contact, caused by exposure to a toxic facility, or because people who are poor are more likely to contract it? Proving causality is nearly impossible in urban history, but students should be challenged to understand the temporal ordering of events and to develop a plausible explanation for why geography matters. GIS may be the best tool for a spatial research question, but students must first understand what makes it spatial.

What relationships does the map reveal? A simple map showing the distribution of a single variable, such as population density, across space has little analytical value. A map showing population density with natural geographic features, such as rivers and parks, and transportation, housing, and employment opportunities suggests why population density varies across space. Layering maps so that two different variables can be understood together, creating a series of maps so that each shows a different variable, and using queries are all ways to understand relationships. These simple visual correlations may not hold up in the peer-review research process, but they can help students generate hypotheses and look for initial evidence of relationships. Another way to explain this to students is that good maps tell a story. Map titles, labels, and other text can make a story clearer, but the relationships shown on the map should be at the heart of the story.

How else could the same data be modeled? Students need to understand that GIS maps are one representation of a complex world. Qualitative representations such as diaries, photographs, oral histories, and written stories offer alternative ways of understanding history. Students in my class read the historical novel, *Tumbling,* about the impact of the planned Cross-town Expressway.[46] A map is a complement, not a substitute, for such a book. Other quantitative representations include line charts and graphs, time series analysis, and regression models. When GIS is an appropriate method, students should be encouraged to consider the implications of their choice of data source and GIS technique. How different might a map look if address-level administrative data were used rather than aggregate census data? What might a raster GIS map—converting data to tiny pixels to create a continuous surface— reveal that vector points, lines, and polygons do not? (See Peter K. Bol's presentation in the digital supplement for more about raster and vector data.) What would the same data look like at a different scale? Training students to constantly ask these questions helps protect against the attitude that GIS is inherently superior to other methods or that there is only one way to make a map.

An in-class exercise on historical mortgage redlining introduces students to basic technical skills while paying attention to these broader analytical questions. Redlining is a form of housing discrimination characterized by restricted access to mortgages (or property insurance) based on the racial composition of a neighborhood. It takes its name from the actual and figurative process of lenders drawing red lines on maps around areas where they refused to lend. With map layers showing individual mortgages and aggregate housing values, housing tenure, the location of blacks, immigrants, and native whites from the 1950s, students can begin to understand the relationship between lending and neighborhood characteristics. Figures 3.12A and B show a random sample of loans made in Philadelphia by two different lenders, Metropolitan Life Insurance Company and Berean Savings and Loan Association.

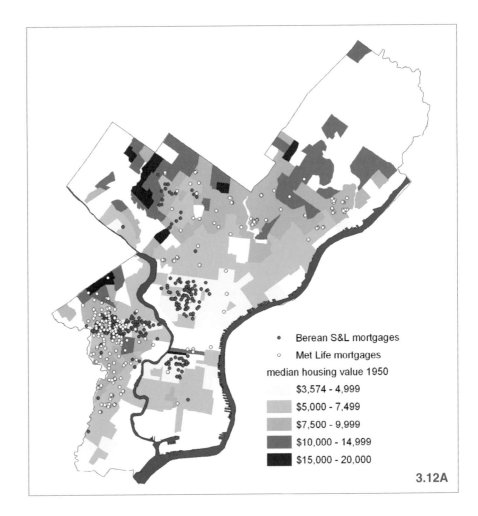

- Berean S&L mortgages
- Met Life mortgages

median housing value 1950

- $3,574 - 4,999
- $5,000 - 7,499
- $7,500 - 9,999
- $10,000 - 14,999
- $15,000 - 20,000

3.12A

FIGURES 3.12A and B

Sample of mortgages with housing values and percent black, 1950. A random sample of loans made by two different lenders between 1940 and 1960 was collected from the mortgagee index at the City of Philadelphia Archives and geocoded using a current street centerline file. By layering the point data with census data from that time, students can explore the relationship between the type of lender and housing values and the concentration of blacks.

Shapefiles used by permission of the City of Philadelphia and the University of Pennsylvania Libraries.

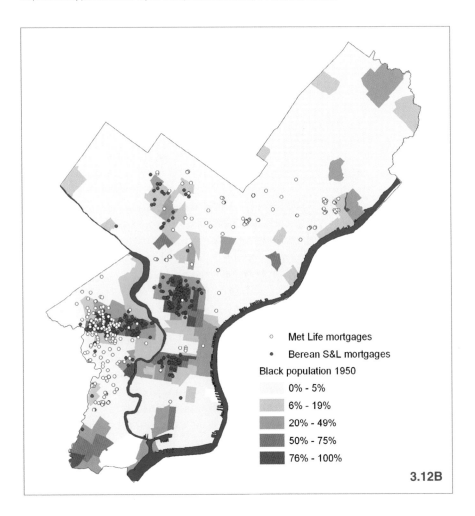

Met Life mortgages

Berean S&L mortgages

Black population 1950

0% - 5%

6% - 19%

20% - 49%

50% - 75%

76% - 100%

3.12B

The map indicates that the two lenders chose only slightly overlapping areas to service. Met Life tended to lend to wealthier areas and largely avoided areas where blacks lived, while Berean provided loans to areas with a high proportion of blacks almost exclusively. It comes as little surprise when students learn that Berean was the leading black-owned lender of that day, started by Berean Presbyterian Church in Philadelphia, while Met Life was a major national insurance company (for more on this research on historical redlining, see Amy Hillier's presentation in the digital supplement). Mapping address-level mortgage data makes it possible to see the amount of clustering within individual lender portfolios. The relationship between these patterns and neighborhood characteristics becomes visible when layered with housing and demographic data, allowing students to imagine the process lenders used in deciding where to make loans. Completing this exercise requires a certain amount of technical skill to map and symbolize the layers, but once mapped, students can focus on the story the data tells.

For some students, the ability to answer an important historical question may provide the incentive for working through technical challenges. For others, the technical challenges may provide the incentive to uncover an important historical relationship. To be successful, history classes that teach GIS need to blend technical and analytical lessons. Introductory lessons in layering and symbolizing maps should use real data that can tell a story. Discussions of theoretical readings about how cities have developed should include consideration of how students can map concepts such as suburbanization, gentrification, and sprawl. Striking this balance will help ensure that students learn to appreciate GIS as an analytical tool and not just another new technology to master.

CONCLUSION

GIS can be an effective teaching tool for liberal arts education generally and history classes specifically. We can use it to teach students about problem solving and visualization even if their research interests and career goals have nothing to do with GIS. Furthermore, basic GIS skills enable students to explore important social and political issues like redistricting and redlining. GIS lessons inevitably cut across academic disciplines, providing opportunities to teach students basic lessons in physical geography and political representation. In the context of a history class, GIS requires students to assess the quality and spatial dimension of historical data as they create and analyze their own map layers. Students can learn about the research process as they build their own GIS to answer specific research questions. Because

GIS applications in historical research are still relatively rare, students can use their new spatial skills to ask an endless number of questions. Ensuring that GIS deepens analytical thinking rather than just technical skills requires careful thought and planning. GIS is not necessarily a tool to make teaching easier; it is a tool for making teaching more engaging and meaningful.

Those of us interested in taking the steps to integrate GIS into our teaching must be prepared to deal with our colleagues' doubts and our own anxieties. Questions raised in part I of this chapter about how GIS can and should shape our world will continue to emerge as GIS technologies are applied in more settings. We need not resolve every question about the appropriate place of GIS in scholarship, teaching, science, and society before we integrate it with our teaching. We should wrestle with such issues alongside our students. Those of us who are doing the teaching may be the ones who learn the most.

ACKNOWLEDGMENTS

Special thanks to Julie Donofrio for her assistance with figures 3.6–3.12.

NOTES

1. I recognize that in recent years, GIS has taken on several meanings: geographic information systems, geographic information science, and geographic information studies. See, for example, Paul Longley, Michael F. Goodchild, David J. Maguire, and David W. Rhind, eds., *Geographic Information Systems and Science* (New York: John Wiley & Sons, Inc., 2001). While I appreciate the distinction, I use GIS to mean geographic information systems, somewhat as a matter of convention but also because the discussion here cuts across geographic information systems, science, and studies.

2. Peter J. Taylor and Ronald J. Johnston, "GIS and Geography," in *Ground Truth: The Social Implications of Geographic Information Systems,* ed. John Pickles (New York: Guilford Press, 1995), 51–67.

3. John Pickles, "Representations in an Electronic Age: Geography, GIS, and Democracy," in *Ground Truth: The Social Implications of Geographic Information Systems,* ed. John Pickles (New York: Guilford Press, 1995), 1–50.

4. P. Forer and D. Unwin, "Enabling Progress in GIS and Education," in *Geographical Information Systems,* ed. Paul A. Longley, Michael F. Goodchild, David J. Maguire, and David W. Rhind (New York: John Wiley & Sons, Inc., 1999), 748.

5. Daniel Z. Sui, "GIS, Cartography, and the 'Third Culture': Geographic Imaginations in the Computer Age," *Professional Geographer* 56 (2004): 62–72.

6. Douglas Fischer, Stephen V. Smith, and Robert R. Churchill, "Simulation of a Century of Runoff across the Tomales Watershed, Marin County, California," *Journal of Hydrology* 186 (1996): 253–73.

7. Nicholas Chrisman, *Exploring Geographic Information Systems,* 2d ed. (New York: John Wiley & Sons, Inc., 2002).

8. Rebecca Solnit, *Hollow City: The Siege of San Francisco and the Crisis of American Urbanism* (New York: Verso, 2000); J. Maantay, "Zoning, Equity, and Public Health," *American Journal of Public Health* 91:7 (2001): 1033–41.

9. Stephen Hall, *Mapping the Next Millennium* (New York: Random House, 1992).

10. See, for example, Patrizia Palamidese, *Scientific Visualization: Advanced Software Techniques* (New York: Ellis Horwood, 1993); Clifford A. Pickover and Stuart K. Tewsbury, eds., *Frontiers of Scientific Visualization* (New York: John Wiley & Sons, Inc., 1994).

11. Anne Kelly Knowles, "A Case for Teaching Geographic Visualization without GIS," *Cartographic Perspectives* 36 (2000): 24–37; Alan M. MacEachren and Fraser Taylor, *Visualization in Modern Cartography* (London: Elsevier, 1994).

12. Pickles, "Representations," 9.

13. Matthew H. Edney, "Reconsidering Enlightenment Geography and Map Making: Reconnaissance, Mapping, Archive," in *Geography and Enlightenment,* ed. David N. Livingstone and Charles W. J. Withers (Chicago: University of Chicago Press, 1999), 165–98; Arthur H. Robinson, *The Look of Maps* (Madison, Wis.: University of Wisconsin Press, 1952); Arthur H. Robinson and Barbara Bartz Petchenik, *The Nature of Maps: Essays toward Understanding Maps and Mapping* (Chicago: University of Chicago Press, 1976).

14. Simon Schama, *Landscape and Memory* (New York: Random House, 1996).

15. J. B. Harley, "Maps, Knowledge, and Power," in *The Iconography of Landscape,* ed. Denis Cosgrove and Stephen Daniels (Cambridge: Cambridge University Press, 1988), 277–312; J. B. Harley, "Deconstructing the Map," *Cartographica* 26 (1989): 1–20; Denis Wood, *The Power of Maps* (New York: Guilford Press, 1992).

16. Barbara Maria Stafford, *Good Looking: Essays on the Virtue of Images* (Cambridge, Mass.: MIT Press, 1996).

17. N. Smith, "Real Wars, Theory Wars," *Progress in Human Geography* 16 (1992): 257–71. Smith's phrase was doubly provocative as an echo of the Nazi slogan *Deutschland über alles* and as an encapsulation of the view he and other critics held that GIS was taking over geography.

18. Michael Stone, "Map or Be Mapped," *Whole Earth* (Fall 1998): 54; Tim Norris, "Maya Atlas: The Struggle to Preserve Maya Land in Southern Belize," *Natural History* (April 1998): 10.

19. Maya Mapping Project, *Maya Atlas: The Struggle to Preserve Maya Land in Southern Belize* (Berkeley: North Atlantic Books, 1997).

20. David Brin, *The Transparent Society* (Reading, Mass.: Addison-Wesley, 1998); Amitai Etzioni, *The Limits of Privacy* (New York: Basic Books, 1999); Ellen Alderman and Caroline Kennedy, *The Right to Privacy* (New York: Knopf, 1995).

21. Michael Curry, "Rethinking Privacy in a Geocoded World," in *Geographical Information Systems: Principles and Applications,* 2nd ed., ed. Paul Longley, David J. Maguire, Michael F. Goodchild, and David W. Rhind, eds. (New York: John Wiley & Sons, Inc., 1998), 757–66.

22. Mark Monmonier, *Spying with Maps* (Chicago: University of Chicago Press, 2002).

23. Michael Curry, "The Digital Individual in the Private Realm," *Annals of the Association of American Geographers* 87 (1997): 681–99; Michael Curry, *Digital Places: Living with Geographic Information Systems* (London: Routledge, 1998).

24. Jeremy Crampton, *The Political Mapping of Cyberspace* (Chicago: University of Chicago Press, 2003).

25. Mark Monmonier, *Drawing the Line* (New York: Henry Holt, 1995).

26. Gary W. Cox and Jonathan N. Katz, *Elbridge Gerry's Salamander: The Electoral Consequences of the Reapportionment Revolution* (Cambridge: Cambridge University Press, 2002).

27. While the minority-majority districts may have benefited Republicans in the subsequent congressional elections, litigation that emerged as a consequence of the 1992 reapportionment drew the U.S. Supreme Court into a more proactive role in redistricting than has been the case historically. See Mark Monmonier, *Bushmanders and Bullwinkle: How Politicians Manipulate Electronic Maps and Census Data to Win Elections* (Chicago: Univeristy of Chicago Press, 2001).

28. Peter J. Taylor and Ronald J. Johnston, "GIS and Geography"; Monmonier, *Bushmanders and Bullwinkles.*

29. Mark E. Rush, "Teaching Reapportionment Using GIS." Paper presented at the Associated College of the South GIS symposium. Georgetown, Tex., February 2003. See also, Mark Rush and John Blackburn, "Political Science: Redistricting for Justice and Power," in *Understanding Place: GIS and Mapping across the Curriculum,* ed. Diana Stuart Sinton and Jennifer J. Lund (Redlands, Calif.: ESRI Press, 2007), 128-39.

30. Terry Tempest Williams, *Refuge: An Unnatural History of Family and Place* (New York: Vintage, 1992).

31. P. C. Meuhrcke, "The Logic of Map Design," in *Cartographic Design: Theoretical and Practical Perspectives,* ed. C. H. Wood and C. P. Keller (New York: John Wiley & Sons, Inc., 1996), 271-8.

32. Anne Kelly Knowles, *Past Time, Past Place: GIS for History* (Redlands, Calif.: ESRI Press, 2002); Diana Stuart Sinton and Jennifer J. Lund, *Understanding Place: GIS and Mapping across the Curriculum* (Redlands, Calif.: ESRI Press, 2007).

33. See http://booth.lse.ac.uk/ and http://cml.upenn.edu/redlining.

34. http://www.loc.gov/ammem/gmdhtml/ and http://www.davidrumsey.com.

35. http://philageohistory.org/geohistory/index.cfm.

36. http://www.sceti.library.upenn.edu/PhilaNeighborhoods/index.cfm.

37. http://www.library.upenn.edu/datasets/philamaps.html.

38. http://www.nhgis.org/.

39. See Raymond Mohl, "Planned Destruction: The Interstates and Central City Housing," in *From Tenements to the Taylor Homes,* ed. J. F. Bauman, R. Biles, and K. M. Szylvian (University Park, Penn.: Pennsylvania State University Press, 1985), 226-45; Kenneth Jackson, *Crabgrass Frontier: The Suburbanization of the United States* (New York : Oxford University Press, 1985).

40. Ian N. Gregory, C. Bennett, V. L. Gilbam, H. R. Southall, "The Great Britain Historical GIS Project: From Maps to Changing Human Geography," *Cartographic Journal,* 39:1 (2002): 37-49; Ian N. Gregory, "Time-variant GIS Databases of Changing Historical Administrative Boundaries: A European Comparison," *Transactions in GIS* 6:2 (2002): 161. See also, http://www.port.ac.uk/research/gbhgis/.

41. Geolytics, a for-profit data vendor, sells the Neighborhood Change Database (NCDB), which reaggregates historical census tract data for the U.S. from 1970, 1980, and 1990 to 2000 census tract boundaries to allow for change-over-time analyses.

42. The Historic Street Index was developed by Philadelphia's Department of Records and Avencia, Inc. See http://www.phillyhistory.org/HistoricStreets/.

43. See, for example, Robert A. Beauregard, "Federal Policy and Postwar Urban Decline: A Case of Government Complicity," *Housing Policy Debate* 12: 1 (2001): 129-51.

44. Stephen Metraux, "Waiting for the Wrecking Ball: Skid Row in Postindustrial Philadelphia," *Journal of Urban History,* 25:5 (1999): 691-716.

45. Clifford R. Shaw and Henry D. McKay, *Juvenile Delinquents and Urban Areas* (Chicago: University of Chicago Press, 1942); Robert E. Park and Ernest W. Burgess, *The City* (Chicago: University of Chicago Press, 1925).

46. Diane McKinney–Whetstone, *Tumbling* (New York: Morrow, 1996).

4

SCALING THE DUST BOWL

By Geoff Cunfer

THE DUST BOWL IN AMERICAN CULTURE

The story of the Dust Bowl is strong in American culture. New Deal reformers created the narrative in the 1930s, building into it a justification for their radical efforts to reorganize American agriculture. The tale, in brief, runs like this: In the late nineteenth century, American pioneers moved into the Great Plains to make farms. They plowed prairie sod in Kansas, Oklahoma, Texas, and northward through the Dakotas and Montana. Farmers sometimes did well for a few years, but they had unwittingly entered a landscape that, because of limited rainfall, was unreliable for crop agriculture. The World War I era and the 1920s saw a second assault on the grassland when industrial farmers using tractors plowed even more sod for commercial cash crop enterprises. When a long and deep drought arrived in the 1930s, the southern plains were all plowed up and the grass sod that had held soils in place was gone. Flatland winds picked up the topsoil and blew it into enormous dust storms that eroded farms and devastated the region (figures 4.1 and 4.2). Hundreds of thousands of destitute "Dust Bowl refugees" collected their meager belongings and moved to California looking for work. The Dust Bowl was caused by misuse of a fragile ecosystem. Recent research

questions the spatial assumption of the traditional story: that dust storms happened where the most land was plowed.[1] This chapter questions the temporal assumption of the New Deal story: that dust storms happened only after the massive plow-up of the 1920s.

The traditional Dust Bowl story persists in our collective memory, in part because of the great art that surrounds it. Woody Guthrie's Dust Bowl ballads and John Steinbeck's *Grapes of Wrath* evoke the story. Poignant photographs by Dorothea Lange, Russell Lee, and Arthur Rothstein illustrate it (figures 4.3, 4.4, and 4.5).[2] Donald Worster's powerful

FIGURE 4.2

Dust storm, Prowers County, Colorado. April 1935.

Library of Congress, Prints and Photographs Division, FSA-OWI Collection, LC-USF343-001617-ZE.

◄ **FIGURE 4.1**

Dust storm approaching Stratford, Texas. April 18, 1935.

Photograph by George E. Marsh. National Oceanic and Atmospheric Administration (NOAA). Coast and Geodetic Survey Historic Image Collection, National Oceanic and Atmospheric Administration Central Library.

and beautifully written monograph, *Dust Bowl: The Southern Plains in the 1930s*, has become required reading, not just in environmental history classes, but also in many U.S. history survey courses over the past two decades.[3] As recently as 2006, Bruce Springsteen's album *We Shall Overcome: The Seeger Sessions,* included a track called "My Oklahoma Home" that reprises the story. Various authors emphasize different aspects of the story: the role of technology as farmers converted from horses to tractors, the social injustice of tenant farming, the ecological damage caused by commercial

FIGURE 4.3

Heavy black clouds of dust rising over the Texas Panhandle. March 1936.

Photograph by Arthur Rothstein. Library of Congress, Prints and Photographs Division, FSA-OWI Collection, LC-USZ62-125986.

FIGURE 4.4

Dust Bowl farm. Coldwater District, north of Dalhart, Texas. This house is occupied; most of the houses in this district have been abandoned. June 1938.

Photograph by Dorothea Lange. Library of Congress, Prints and Photographs Division, FSA-OWI Collection, LC-DIG-fsa-8b32396.

agriculture. Some blame farmers, some pity them, some intend to help them do better, but the underlying theme asserts that farmers caused the Dust Bowl by misuse of the land, whether because of innocent ignorance or because of thoughtless greed.

This chapter turns a critical eye on the standard Dust Bowl story, contending in particular with the historical narrative presented by Worster.[4] His *Dust Bowl* develops a powerful argument that the cause of the dust storms was capitalism, which led farmers to misuse their land. The increasingly commercial character of American agriculture prompted farmers to plow land unfit for cropping, to treat their fields as factories that could yield short-term profits, and to pay little attention to the limits and fragility of the plains ecosystem. The result of this misguided rush for cash was one of the world's three worst ecological disasters. Worster writes,

> During the laissez-faire, expansionist 1920s the plains were extensively plowed and put to wheat—turned into highly mechanized factory farms that produced unprecedented harvests. Plains operators, however, ignored all environmental limits in this enterprise. . . . In a more stable natural region, this sort of farming could have gone on exploiting the land much longer with impunity. But on the plains the elements of risk were higher than they were anywhere else in the country, and the destructive effects of capitalism far more sudden and dramatic. There was nothing in the plains society to check the progress of commercial farming, nothing to prevent it from taking the risks it was willing to take for profit. That is how and why the Dust Bowl came about.[5]

In Worster's narrative, responsibility for the Dust Bowl rests firmly with farmers. They took a pristine wilderness that had been nurtured by Native Americans for ten thousand years and turned it into a wasteland in a matter of decades.[6]

Dust Bowl is built around two case-study locations: Cimarron County, Oklahoma, and Haskell County, Kansas (figure 4.5). Six chapters of the book address the particular experience and history of these two sites in the heart of the Dust Bowl. It is in part this case-study approach that gives the book its power. Reading it, we meet real people with names and faces and dramatic personal stories of suffering, loss, and perseverance. We find heroes and villains. We leave the story feeling that we know the place well and understand the role of local farmers who created and then lived through the Dust Bowl. Using case studies in this way is a powerful storytelling device, and a firmly established method for researching and writing history.

Worster develops the stories of these two counties, then asserts that their experience represents the southern plains generally. When Worster researched his study in the 1970s, historians did not have ready access to computer-supported methods of geographic analysis. GIS was in its infancy. Only a handful of technicians using mainframe computers could have contemplated a systematic analysis of regional geographic trends. The idea of researching and analyzing more than two hundred

FIGURE 4.5

Farmer and sons walking in the face of a dust storm. Cimarron County, Oklahoma. April 1936.

Photograph by Arthur Rothstein. Library of Congress, Prints and Photographs Division, FSA-OWI Collection, LC-USZ62-11491.

counties on the southern plains was simply unrealistic thirty years ago. The case study approach was an obvious choice.

The easy availability of GIS technology today means that one can now evaluate the causes of the Dust Bowl using an entirely different method.[7] Incorporating data about all of the counties on the southern plains into a GIS allows the researcher to view the question at a different geographical scale. This chapter argues that varying scale can dramatically alter our understanding of the past. What seems clear when viewed up close in one or two communities can look quite different when zoomed out to the whole region. Worster's case studies appear to bear out his thesis: in Cimarron and Haskell counties, farmers plowed a lot of land, and the dust storms followed soon after. But looking at the plains region of New Mexico, Texas, Colorado, Oklahoma, and Kansas—208 counties in all, instead of just 2—raises some contradictions.[8] For example, a dozen counties on the southern plains had little plowed cropland, less than 10 percent of their entire area, yet still suffered from serious dust storms. The shift in scale throws into doubt the primary causative force of the plow in creating the Dust Bowl. This regional method sacrifices the detailed description possible with case studies for systematic and comprehensive coverage of a broader region.

A similar critique applies to temporal scale. *Dust Bowl* focuses primarily on two decades: the 1920s, when the wheat boom led to additional sod plow-ups; and the 1930s, when the dust storms rolled in. In this brief context, the story of plow-up followed closely by dust storms suggests a direct causal relationship. Zooming out to a broader temporal scale clouds the picture. There is unequivocal evidence of routine dust storms on the southern plains throughout the second half of the nineteenth century, when native grasses had yet to succumb to the plow to any great extent. These dust storms were just as intense as those of the 1930s (figure 4.6). The primary difference, it appears, is that they simply were not as well documented. In 1880, one of the dustiest years in Kansas history, there was no systematic national weather system, no activist federal government to hire world-class photographers and journalists as publicists to cover and promote the story, no recording and radio industry to popularize folk ballads. The story of the nineteenth century Dust Bowls are virtually unknown today because they went largely unreported and unpublicized. One might view the persistence of the Dust Bowl story as a result, in part, of twentieth-century mass marketing.

FROM CASE STUDY TO REGIONAL ANALYSIS

A few years ago, at this time of the year we were cursed with disagreeable, suffocating and provoking sand storms. Sometimes they would last for several days in succession. We firmly believe we shall have none of consequence this spring. The climate is surely improving.
–Salina, Kansas, *Journal,* March 1, 1877

Assembling available data into a GIS allows analysis not only of individual localities but of entire regions.[9] The county makes an excellent unit of analysis for topics that are regional in scale. It is general enough to be manageable yet precise enough to reveal detailed variations across large areas. The county is the basic reporting unit for key land-use data from agricultural censuses conducted by the federal government every ten years until 1920 and about every five years since then.[10] The state of Kansas conducted annual agricultural censuses, published at the county level, from

FIGURE 4.6

A dust storm passes over Midland, Texas, on February 20, 1894, when more than 96 percent of the Texas Panhandle remained in unplowed, native grass.

Photograph by H. G. Symonds. National Archives and Records Administration, Still Picture Branch, U.S. Weather Bureau, RG27, Series S, Item 2.

1874 through the present.[11] On the other hand, weather data, systematically collected by the National Weather Service since 1895, is available for weather station point locations and must be interpolated up to the county unit.[12]

Several kinds of county-level data help us understand where and when dust storms occurred and what caused them. When the land is wet, there is very little wind erosion. Only dry soils erode readily, so a central concern in understanding the occurrence of dust storms is the rainfall record.[13] Animation 1 (see the digital supplement) shows annual precipitation for counties on the southern plains between 1895 and 1942 (excerpt in figure 4.7). The legend breaks at 500 mm of annual precipitation, which is the rough minimum necessary to grow wheat, the most common plains cash crop. On these maps, counties in white had insufficient moisture to sustain wheat in the given year; counties in light blue had enough rain to do so, while the middle blue got enough moisture to support wheat or an even thirstier corn crop. On rare occasions, counties appear in dark blue, indicating extraordinarily wet years. The main thing to watch is the wild fluctuation between successful wheat crops and unsuccessful ones.

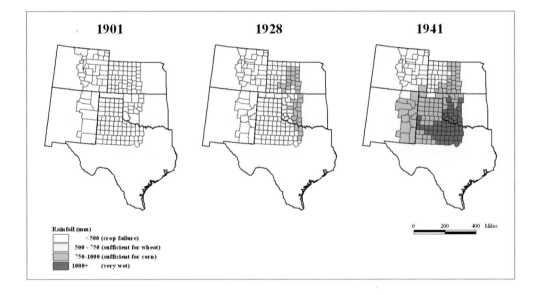

FIGURE 4.7

Excerpt from Animation 1 (see the digital supplement). Examples of dry, moderate, and wet years in southern plains counties.

Data courtesy of ArcUSA, U.S. Census and ESRI, 2006 Data & Maps, CD-ROMs, states.shp.; Carville Earle and Changyong Cao, The Historical U.S. County Boundary Files, 1850-1970, Geoscience Publications (Baton Rouge: Department of Geography and Anthropology, 1991).

Animation 1 shows how variable plains climate is. Dry years were common, but very wet ones could come at any time. Some counties had enough rainfall for a good wheat crop over several consecutive years, only to succumb to drought later. Farmers new to the grassland must have had difficulty anticipating the coming season. Yet they also realized quickly that in much of the plains, crops would fail in two, three, or four years out of ten, even if they could not predict which ones.

Animation 2 depicts the progress of the plow-up in the southern plains over 65 years, from 1880, just after the beginning of agricultural settlement, through 1945 (excerpt in figure 4.8). The counties mapped in white had 90 percent or more of

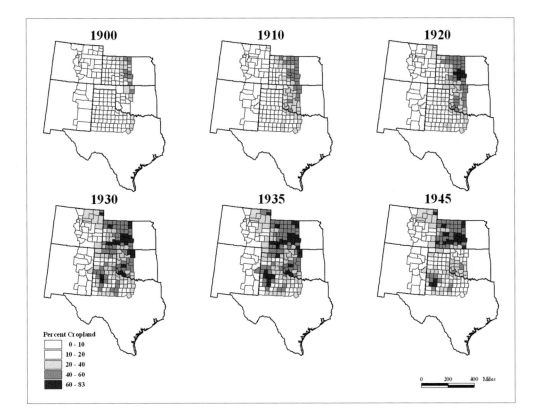

FIGURE 4.8

Excerpt from Animation 2. Percent of total county area devoted to cropland.

Data courtesy of ArcUSA, U.S. Census and ESRI, 2006 Data & Maps, CD-ROMs, states.shp.; Carville Earle and Changyong Cao, The Historical U.S. County Boundary Files, 1850-1970, Geoscience Publications (Baton Rouge: Department of Geography and Anthropology, 1991).

their entire area in unplowed native grassland. Counties in pale yellow retained at least 80 percent of their land in grass, while those in tan and brown had 40 to 80 percent of their original land cover intact. Only about 15 percent of the counties ever dropped below 40 percent grassland and thus into the darkest brown category. Animation 2 shows that pioneer farmers made little progress at plowing up the plains in the nineteenth century. As late as 1900, farmers in less than three dozen counties along the eastern edge of the plains had plowed more than 20 percent of their land. The big plow-up came in the early decades of the twentieth century. A lot of new land went into crops just fifteen or twenty years before the onset of the Dust Bowl in 1934.

Figure 4.9 overlays the 1935–1936 dust storm region on the county maps of plowed area.[14] As late as 1925, relatively little land within the Dust Bowl boundaries had been plowed. In that year, more than half of the native grass sod was intact in 58 of the 60 Dust Bowl counties; in 40 counties on the western side of the region more than 80 percent of the original grass remained. Cropping expanded considerably in the decade before 1935, especially in the Texas and Oklahoma panhandles and in southwestern Kansas. By then, 14 Dust Bowl counties had less than 40 percent of their original grass sod, exposing considerable amounts of plowed cropland to the winds. Haskell County, Kansas, for example, consisted of 71 percent cropland and 29 percent grassland in 1935. In the Texas Panhandle, a dozen recently plowed counties tracked closely the outline of the Dust Bowl's southern lobe. In these locations, the fresh plow-up was likely a contributor to wind erosion. But the Dust Bowl was a big region, including 42 counties with more than half of their native grass intact and 15 where 80 percent or more of the grassland had never been plowed.

The least plowed counties on the western fringe of the southern plains were as dusty as the hardest hit core of the Dust Bowl. Only 9 percent of the native sod was plowed for crops in Harding County, New Mexico, for example, but severe dust storms visited the area repeatedly in the mid-1930s. Employees of the federal government's Agricultural Adjustment Administration (AAA) in the town of Mills reported that "the physical discomfort and menace to health occasioned by the almost continuous blinding dust storms which have swept the area during the past three months, have rendered it distinctly unsuitable for human occupancy." Significantly, even unplowed grassland was subject to wind erosion: "the soil has been completely cut away from the roots of native grasses by blowing sand and gravel."[15] These dusty, little-plowed western counties were upwind of the more cultivated eastern parts of the plains. Prevailing winds throughout the area are from the northwest. While dust storms can be regional phenomena, traveling hundreds of miles, they do not move upwind. If anything, the dry, little-plowed western portion of the Dust Bowl was the contributor to, not the recipient of, dust storms from afar. Figure 4.9 suggests that the big plow-up of land in the 1920s did contribute to the Dust Bowl. It also suggests that there is more to the story.

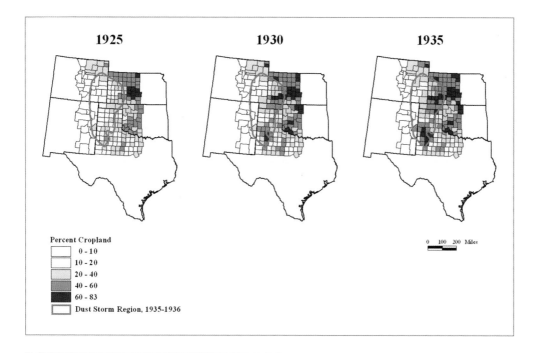

FIGURE 4.9

Percent of total county area plowed compared to 1935–1936 dust storm region.

Data courtesy of ArcUSA, U.S. Census and ESRI, 2006 Data & Maps, CD-ROMs, states.shp.; Carville Earle and Changyong Cao, The Historical U.S. County Boundary Files, 1850-1970, Geoscience Publications (Baton Rouge: Department of Geography and Anthropology, 1991); and Dust Storm Region digitized by author from "Great Plains Area" map, Soil Conservation Service, March, 1954, held in National Archives and Records Administration, College Park, MD, RG 114, Entry 5, 330/c/17/1-2.

Drought explains the location of dust storms in the 1930s better than land use. Figure 4.10 maps rainfall shortages in the southern plains. It presents a sequence of maps in which the drought and the dust storms moved roughly in tandem from year to year. Each item in the figure shows a dust region overlaid on a map of county rain shortage for the five years prior to that dust season.[16] The figure maps rainfall deficits relative to average rainfall for each county. The first conclusion to be drawn from figure 4.10 is that the drought was deep and extensive during the 1930s. Only a handful of counties had more rain than average between 1932 and 1940, and very few fell into the -10 to 0 percent category. The majority of counties had rain shortfalls of greater than 10 percent, and more than 80 counties, mapped in maroon, were at least 20 percent drier than average. Across the region

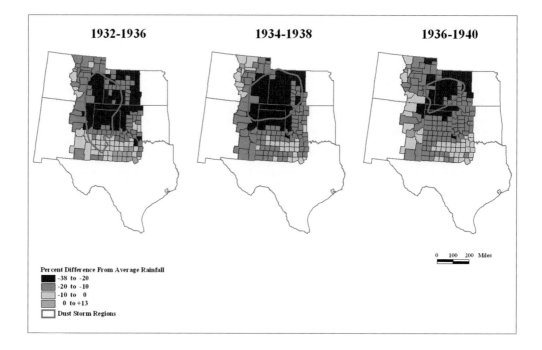

FIGURE 4.10

Percent differences from average rainfall for five-year periods preceding dust seasons, 1932–1940.

Data courtesy of ArcUSA, U.S. Census and ESRI, 2006 Data & Maps, CD-ROMs, states.shp.; Carville Earle and Changyong Cao, The Historical U.S. County Boundary Files, 1850-1970, Geoscience Publications (Baton Rouge: Department of Geography and Anthropology, 1991); and Dust Storm Regions digitized by author from "Great Plains Area" map, Soil Conservation Service, March, 1954, held in National Archives and Records Administration, College Park, MD, RG 114, Entry 5, 330/c/17/1-2 and from "The Dust Bowl: Agricultural Problems and Solutions, U.S. Department of Agriculture Editorial Reference Series No. 7, July 15, 1940, NOAA Central Library.

the drought was deep, extensive, and persisted for nearly a decade. The 1930s was the driest time Euro-American farmers have faced in the 110 years since systematic weather monitoring began on the plains. A second conclusion from figure 4.10 is the marked coincidence between rain shortfalls and dust storm locations. The Dust Bowl followed the movement of drought during the decade. As dry weather moved northeastward and contracted, dust storms did likewise.

Viewing the Dust Bowl from a regional scale broadens our understanding of the sequence of events leading up to the storms and their spatial progression over nine years. It also suggests that the cause of the Dust Bowl may combine human activity and natural phenomena in complex ways. In figure 4.10, the Dust Bowl followed the drought quite closely. The exception was in the Texas Panhandle in 1935–1936, where it was not as relatively dry as in other parts of the southern plains. The Texas Panhandle, however, is just where much new sod had been broken only five to ten years earlier. These maps suggest that while drought has the power, regardless of human activity, to cause considerable wind erosion and dust storms on the Great Plains, human land use can tip the balance in some cases, enhancing the likelihood of blowing soil.

DUST STORMS BEFORE THE BIG PLOW-UP, 1854-1896

When the March winds commenced raising dust Monday, the average citizen calmly smiled and whispered "so natural!"
–Salina, Kansas, *Journal,* March 12, 1885

The howling winds of Monday lifted the surface of the earth into the air. . . . The earth did not go up in minute particles of dust, but bodily.
–Salina, Kansas, *Journal,* February 7, 1889

One of the seven wonders of the world. We haven't had a dust storm for a week.
–Salina, Kansas, *Herald,* June 21, 1895

In addition to shifting the spatial scale, it is useful to expand the temporal scale to understand dust storms on the southern plains. Implicit in the traditional Dust Bowl story is an assumption that the 1930s dust storms were extraordinary and unprecedented. If they were a new occurrence, then it makes sense to ask what changed just before their advent. The most obvious answer is the big plow-up that happened between 1910 and 1935, but broadening the temporal scale casts a different light on the story. The occurrence of dust storms in the 1930s is thoroughly documented, in newspapers, in photographs, in oral histories, and in the documents of federal government employees dispatched to the region to try to solve the crisis. But dust storms were not really new in the 1930s. Consider this report from central Kansas in 1880:

> Another windy, dusty, trying, headache-producing, vexatious, disgusting, terrific, upsetting, tearing, rearing, careering, bumping, sign-lifting, chimney absorbing, lung slaying, garment destroying, eye blinding, and rip-roaring storm, last Monday. The gale which prevailed here last Saturday seems to have been an installment which came up from the south over a large area of country, and which occasioned much damage in certain parts of the state. It was furious, and in this locality summoned all the dust between here and Kingdom come to the august presence of the Salinaites. The buildings seemed on the point of being lifted from their foundations and the day was uncommonly dark from the clouds of dust.[17]

Local newspapers from throughout the region contain unequivocal evidence that dust storms happened on the southern plains throughout the late nineteenth century, before a significant amount of the grassland had been plowed.

In the 1940s, historian James Malin meticulously sifted through enormous numbers of newspapers archived at the Kansas State Historical Society. Weekly newspapers from the first forty years of Kansas's Euro-American history, 1854–1896, revealed that dust storms were quite common throughout the settlement era. In an extraordinary 71-page article published over three consecutive issues of *Kansas Historical Quarterly,* Malin laid out evidence of intense, routine, and anticipated dust storm activity at dozens of locations throughout the state, all before 1900.[18] The article is unwieldy—it reads more like Malin's research notes, chronicling hundreds of dust storms, one after another, than like a carefully honed scholarly argument. But it brings home the fact that these were not freak events; they were the norm. Dust storms did not come every year, but they were routine, and often occurred in conjunction with extended droughts. When dust storms arrived, usually in spring, sometimes in early fall, they seldom happened in isolation. All of the drama revealed by the photographers, journalists, documentary filmmakers, and songwriters of the 1930s Dust Bowl are present in these obscure and forgotten newspaper clippings from one-horse Kansas villages.

The documentary record of dust storm activity culled by Malin from local newspapers and government weather summaries illustrates the widespread and routine character of blowing dust on the southern plains. He identified hundreds of reports of dust storms in Kansas, such as this item from Atchison in April 1860: "During nearly three months we have had dry weather, with hardly even a sprinkle of moisture. And now that the soil is perfectly dry, the wind is doing its best to blind every inhabitant of this section of country with dust. And such clouds of it! It penetrates everywhere; and has grown to be a most intolerable nuisance."[19] Other items come from across the southern plains. Central Kansas and eastern Colorado, 1882: "Monday was a regular, old-fashioned dusty day. . . . On Monday when the dust was flying here [Salina, Kansas] to all points of the compass, there was a terrific sand storm on the Colorado desert. . ."[20] Midland, Texas, in January 1886: "a heavy sandstorm occurred at 10 AM, of the 26th, during which it was impossible to see objects one hundred yards distant."[21] Residents of El Reno, Oklahoma, reported in April 1895 that "About 4 o'clock yesterday afternoon a cloud of sand came up from the southwest and totally obscured the sun. Buildings could not be seen fifty yards and the sand was scattered along as though sown broadcast from a great hand. The falling of the sand continued for more than an hour, and those out in it had a hard time to breathe."[22]

Malin's extensive excerpts demonstrate that while dust storms did not happen every year, they happened often enough to be received without surprise. "Kansas is herself again. The wind blows and the dust and sand flies, but no rain descends."[23] Newcomers reacted with shock and dismay, more experienced people with resignation. "The month of March thus far has not been the 'regulation March' of Kansas. We have had few dust storms and very fine weather most of the month. Last Sunday was a Kansas March day in every respect. The clouds of dust were stupendously suffocating all day."[24] Malin's article documents hundreds of dust storms at dozens of locations around the state, including many years when dust storms were daily or nearly daily occurrences for a month or more, and some years—1855, 1879, 1880, 1881, 1894, 1895—when they persisted for several months.

The descriptions of these dust storms match those reported in the Dirty Thirties. As in the 1930s, nineteenth-century dust storms penetrated the interiors of buildings, coating homes and furnishings with dirt: "the dust and dirt in some houses was nearly an inch deep" (1880).[25] Dust storms darkened the sky at midday: the wind "filled the air with such clouds of dust that darkness of the 'consistency of twilight' prevailed. Buildings across the street could not be distinguished" (1879).[26] Storms drifted soil from farm to farm: "the past few weeks a large amount of real estate, in the shape of dust, has changed ownership" (1882).[27] In extreme cases dunes formed: "drifts of sand six feet deep are piled up along the railroad tracks at the west line of the state [Kansas] (1895).[28] Some storms carried dust across the continent, depositing it many hundreds of miles eastward: "This process of raising great clouds of dust, carrying them south and east and depositing the dust. . . must have begun in Montana on the 10th to be concluded in Ohio, Kentucky, Louisiana, and Texas on the 12th and 13th. . ." (1895).[29] Figure 4.6 shows a black blizzard in 1894 that appears as ferocious as any of the photographs from 1934. And all of this happened when farmers had plowed only a tiny fraction of the immense Great Plains.

Most of the dust storms described in newspapers must have come from unplowed native grassland. The occurrence of dust storms in conjunction with dry years is a regular component of southern plains ecology. Deep wind-blown loess soil deposits around the region are the geological accumulation of thousands of years of dust storms and wind erosion. Farmers suffered from the dust storms considerably, and they exacerbated the phenomena in some cases. But they did not single-handedly cause the Dust Bowl. The southern plains have weathered Dust Bowls for a very long time.

Using GIS methods, it is possible to map the dust storm observations that Malin unearthed. Animation 3 uses a simplified legend to apply rough categories to a dataset that represents a messy shoebox full of newspaper clippings (excerpt in figure 4.11). These are qualitative sources, not quantitative, and therefore are challenging to incorporate into a GIS. The present approach is to evaluate the newspaper descriptions and assign them to one of four categories for each year between 1854 and 1896. Some accounts describe a single dust storm for a given location in a given year; these are coded as category 1. Others describe several dusty events in one place, and are coded as category 2. It is not unusual for the newspaper record to reveal an entire month of dusty conditions and in some places a whole season of several months of blowing dust in a particular year; they are coded as categories 3 and 4. These groupings are admittedly vague. It is not always clear where to draw the line between categories 2 and 3—when do "several" dust storms merge into a whole "month" of dusty weather? I have tried to be conservative. When in doubt, I rounded down.

There is a danger that the implied authority of a statistical and cartographic rendering of this dust storm activity might suggest more comprehensive knowledge than is possible with qualitative sources. There is no way to evaluate nineteenth-century dust storms systematically. Large sections of Kansas—including the driest, western parts of the state where dust storms were most severe in the 1930s—had few observers who might write down or publish accounts. There were undoubtedly many dust storms that went unobserved or unreported. Such events are absent from these maps. In the 1850s the only Euro-American settlements, and thus the only newspapers, were in the eastern part of the state. By the 1870s, newspapers were emerging in central Kansas. Much of western Kansas was only settled in the 1890s, just as the map series in animation 3 ends. Given the known geography of 1930s dust storms, it is likely that in very dusty years like 1879–1881, western Kansas had a lot of wind erosion. We just do not have any accounts from there.

Historians are used to this type of incomplete information. Traditional narrative history is built upon the scraps of information left behind—what happened to get

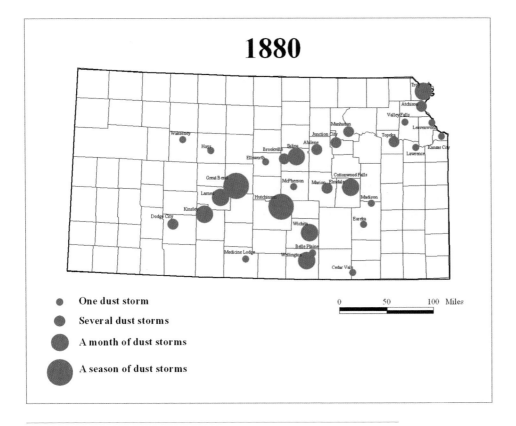

FIGURE 4.11

Excerpt from Animation 3 (with place-names added). Kansas dust storms, 1880.
Proportional circles appear at each newspaper's city of publication.

Data courtesy of ArcUSA, U.S. Census and ESRI, 2006 Data & Maps, CD-ROMs, states.shp.; Carville Earle and Changyong Cao, The Historical U.S. County Boundary Files, 1850-1970, Geoscience Publications (Baton Rouge: Department of Geography and Anthropology, 1991); James Malin, "Dust Storms," Kansas Historical Quarterly 14 (1946).

written down, what happened to be preserved, what the researcher happened to find. Historians acknowledge a level of incompleteness in their sources and are comfortable with it. The maps in animation 3 do not indicate where or when dust storm activity was greatest in Kansas, but rather where and when it is known to have occurred. These maps do, however, offer powerful evidence that wind erosion was not an anomaly in the 1930s. Dust storms were, in fact, quite common throughout Kansas history, not just at a handful of places or on rare occasions, but year after year, often for months at a time, and at dozens of sites.

SOD-BREAKING AND PLOWED CROPLAND IN KANSAS, 1874–1936

While newspaper descriptions of dust storms are neither systematic nor quantitative, censuses are. Kansas conducted the most thorough and long-running census of agriculture of any state in the United States. Beginning in 1874, and continuing annually through the end of the twentieth century, Kansas surveyed all farmers about their agricultural practices—acreage devoted to various crops, number of horses, cattle, and hogs, and, later, number of tractors. County totals appeared in the *Biennial Reports* of the Kansas State Board of Agriculture. The totals are available in paper form for 1874 through the present. They are available in electronic form for 1874 through 1936, and it is the latter dataset that supports the maps of cropland in animation 4 (excerpt in figure 4.12).[30]

Euro-American settlement began in Kansas around 1853, but was spatially limited and confined to the eastern third of the state until the 1870s. Between 1870 and 1890 settlers occupied most of the rest of the state, homesteading farms, creating rural villages, fencing pasture for grazing, and plowing land for crops. The process of occupation and sod-breaking moved generally from east to west across the state.

Animation 4 shows the sequence of cropland expansion (and occasional contraction) from 1874 to 1936. The series begins when agricultural settlement was already underway in eastern and central Kansas, but most of the state was still unplowed; only 27 eastern counties had more than 10 percent of their land plowed for crops, and only 11 of them exceeded 20 percent. During the 1870s, settlers poured into Kansas to take free homesteads or to buy farms from railroad land agents. The eastern half of the state saw rapid sod-breaking that decade as many counties moved into the 20–40 percent plowed category. But the westward expansion was not straightforward. It flowed around the Flint Hills in east central Kansas. These hills, with their shallow, rocky soils, were unsuited to crop agriculture, although they provided exceptional grazing. The dozen counties of the Flint Hills remained as an island of mostly native grassland in a sea of expanding cropland.

By 1888, every county had at least 1 percent cropland. The western third, however, was still more than 90 percent native pasture. The maps reveal a temporary contraction of cropped land in 1890 that coincided with a severe drought and significant out-migration. But by 1891, cropland levels matched those of the 1880s, and a slow cropland expansion resumed through the rest of the 1890s. During that decade, many central Kansas counties moved up by one map category to more than 40 percent cropland, and the far northwest of the state now plowed more than 10 percent of its land for the first time. Still, two dozen counties in southwest Kansas remained practically unplowed as late as 1900.

The high crop prices and patriotic incentives surrounding World War I led farmers to increase cropland. Between 1915 and 1930, farmers expanded cropland in the western third of the state. By the peak in 1931, every county had more than 10 percent cropland. Although many western counties still had less than 40 percent

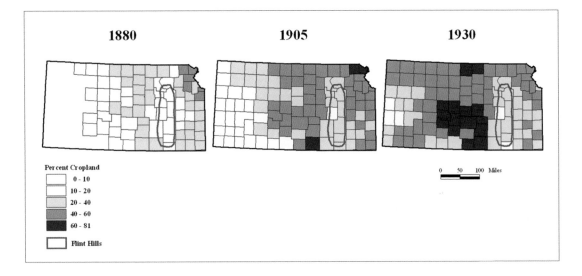

FIGURE 4.12

Excerpt from Animation 4. Percent of total county area devoted to cropland, Kansas.

Data courtesy of ArcUSA, U.S. Census and ESRI, 2006 Data & Maps, CD-ROMs, states.shp.; Carville Earle and Changyong Cao, The Historical U.S. County Boundary Files, 1850-1970, Geoscience Publications (Baton Rouge: Department of Geography and Anthropology, 1991); Flint hills layer drawn by author.

cropland, most of the state was over 20 percent; 19 counties across central Kansas plowed more than 60 percent of their land. Cropland declined again as the century-drought of the 1930s set in, though only in small measure. Animation 4 shows a 60-year chronology of the human impact on vegetative cover during the half century leading up to the Dust Bowl.

Although they only overlap for a couple of decades, it is interesting to compare the series of dust storms reported in Kansas newspapers (1854-1896) with the cropland series (1874-1936). Animation 5 shows the newspaper accounts of dust storms overlaid on the map of cropland for the period 1874 to 1896, when both are available (excerpt in figure 4.13). This series is difficult to interpret. Most of the dust storms occurred in counties with 80 percent or more of their land in unplowed native grass. Some happened in counties with 90 percent or more grassland. On the other hand, the circles representing dust storms often appear over the darker, more plowed counties on the map. This could indicate that dust storms were more common where

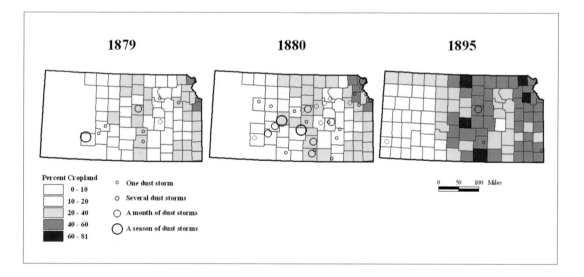

FIGURE 4.13

Excerpt from Animation 5. Percent of total county area devoted to cropland, Kansas, with dust storm overlays. Sample maps from near the beginning and the end of the time series show wide spatial distribution across the state.

Data courtesy of ArcUSA, U.S. Census and ESRI, 2006 Data & Maps, CD-ROMs, states.shp.; Carville Earle and Changyong Cao, The Historical U.S. County Boundary Files, 1850-1970, Geoscience Publications (Baton Rouge: Department of Geography and Anthropology, 1991); James Malin, "Dust Storms," Kansas Historical Quarterly 14 (1946).

more land was plowed. It could also be because counties with higher crop acreages generally had more people, more towns, and thus more eyes to observe and more newspapers to report.

The question of observational power, of the need for a critical mass of people to be present for an event to enter the historical record, is crucial. It helps us understand not only the plains dust storm record but also the American consciousness of Dust Bowl history. The Dust Bowl of 1879–1881 is virtually unknown to the public because there were not many people living in the plains then. Those few who experienced the dust storms were disinclined to tell anybody about them. Newspaper editors were always the biggest boosters in newly settled towns, all of which hoped to attract more settlers, to become the next Chicago, the next Denver. Great Plains newspapers were routinely tight-lipped about drought, crop failure, and out-migration. It is remarkable that we have any newspaper record of dust storms at all. M. M. Murdock, editor of the Wichita, Kansas, *Eagle* acknowledged the tension, writing,

> the probability is that the individuals in this valley are scarce who would have the temerity to assert that the *Eagle* has ever proven remiss in blowing Kansas. But we come now to acknowledge that the blowing she has done for herself the past week has nipped our blowing pretensions in the bud. It may as well be asserted here and now that Kansas as a paradise has her failings, not the least of which is her everlasting spring winds. If there is man, woman or child in Sedgwick county whose eyes are not filled with dust and their minds with disgust, he, she, or it must be an idiot or awfully pious.[31]

Few in the plains were advertising dust storms in the nineteenth century or promoting them to a national audience.

That changed in the 1930s. Plains residents were still reticent about their troubles, to be sure, but now there was a federal bureaucracy and a cadre of modern journalists prepared to spread the Dust Bowl news to the nation. The Dust Bowl seemed to justify New Deal policies aimed at reforming American agriculture, and government propagandists exploited the dust storms to build support for new agencies like the Farm Security Administration, the Soil Conservation Service, the Land Utilization Program, and the Agricultural Adjustment Administration, all newly created in the mid-1930s in response to the Great Depression. Skilled promoters created the Dust Bowl story in the American mind, and it has been firmly established there for 75 years.

CONCLUSION

The dust did not stop blowing in 1940. Dust storms continue to be routine on the southern plains, usually in late winter and early spring, sometimes in fall.[32] Lubbock, in the Texas Panhandle, for example, reported thirty-five dust storms in fall 1973 and spring 1974, and surrounding towns more than a dozen.[33] Some years are worse than others. There has not been a series of years to match the 1930s, but then there has not been a drought as deep or as long lasting either. When such a drought returns, as it likely will, perhaps in the coming decade, perhaps in the coming century, we can expect to see serious and persistent dust storms, regardless of human land use.

The use of a GIS-based methodology shifts the scope markedly, from an intense two-county case study to a broad two-hundred-county region at a coarser resolution, but one which allows for systematic analysis and a broad context. The broader spatial scale and the longer temporal scale make the 1930s Dust Bowl look quite different than it does up close in a couple of communities during a couple of decades. It appears that dust storms are a normal part of southern plains ecology, occurring whenever there are extended dry periods. They can originate in unplowed native grassland when it has been diminished by extended drought. Dust storm activity can be exacerbated or locally enhanced by plowing for crops, but that was not the sole and simple cause of the Dust Bowl.

ACKNOWLEDGMENTS

Support comes from grants from the Canadian Social Sciences and Humanities Research Council and from the National Institute of Child Health and Human Development of the U.S. National Institutes of Health (grants HD33554 and HD44889). Colleagues at the Center for Rural and Regional Studies, Southwest Minnesota State University, and in the history department at the University of Saskatchewan contributed valuable comments on early drafts of this chapter. Special thanks go to Charlie Kost, director of the GIS Laboratory at SMSU, and to undergraduate research assistants Carl Pedersen and Lisa Peterson at SMSU who helped assemble newspaper materials and photographs. Anne Kelly Knowles and Amy Hillier provided steady encouragement and long-suffering editorial assistance with good cheer.

NOTES

1. Geoff Cunfer, *On the Great Plains: Agriculture and Environment* (College Station: Texas A&M University Press, 2005), 143–63; Geoff Cunfer, "Causes of the Dust Bowl," in *Past Time, Past Place: GIS for History*, ed. Anne Kelly Knowles (Redlands, Calif.: ESRI Press, 2002), 93–104.

2. For a discussion of New Deal photography as propaganda, see Bill Ganzel, *Dust Bowl Descent* (Lincoln: University of Nebraska Press, 1984), 3–11.

3. Donald Worster, *Dust Bowl: The Southern Plains in the 1930s* (New York: Oxford University Press, 1979).

4. Part of this research was supported by grant numbers HD33554 and HD44889, both from the National Institute of Child Health and Human Development of the U.S. National Institutes of Health, and by a grant from the Canadian Social Sciences and Humanities Research Council.

5. Worster, *Dust Bowl*, 6–7.

6. See William Cronon, "A Place for Stories: Nature, History, and Narrative," *Journal of American History* 78 (March 1992): 1347–76, for an analysis of several Dust Bowl narratives, including Worster's.

7. For introductions to historical methods using GIS, see Anne Kelly Knowles, *Past Time, Past Place: GIS for History* (Redlands, Calif.: ESRI Press, 2002) and Ian N. Gregory, *A Place in History: A Guide to Using GIS in Historical Research* (Oxford: Oxbow Books, 2003).

8. The 208 southern plains counties represented here are bounded by the Rocky Mountains on the west and the line of 700 mm of average annual precipitation on the east. The southern boundary approximates a gradual shift from grassland toward desert, while the more arbitrary northern boundary follows the Colorado and Kansas borders.

9. See Cunfer, *On the Great Plains*.

10. Myron P. Gutmann, Great Plains Population and Environment Data: Agricultural Data, 1870–1997 [United States] [Computer file]. ICPSR04254-v1. Ann Arbor, Mich.: University of Michigan [producer], 2005. Ann Arbor, Mich.: Inter-University Consortium for Political and Social Research [distributor], 2005-06-22.

11. Kansas State Board of Agriculture, *Annual and Biennial Reports* (Topeka, 1877–1973).

12. Climate data comes from two sources. First is T. R. Karl, C. N. Williams, Jr., F. T. Quinlan, and T. A. Boden, United States Historical Climatology Network (HCN) Serial Temperature and Precipitation Data, Environmental Science Division, pub. no. 3404, Carbon Dioxide Information and Analysis Center, Oak Ridge National Laboratory, Oak Ridge, Tennessee. The historical climatology data is stored as point data for weather stations at monthly intervals for 1221 stations in the United States. The second source of climate data is National Climatic Data Center, Arizona State University, and Oak Ridge National Laboratory, Global Historical Climatology Network (GHCN). This dataset includes comprehensive monthly global surface baseline climate data. The Great Plains Population and Environment Project interpolated data from 394 weather stations in the Great Plains to counties for each month between 1895 and 1993 by generating a triangulated irregular network (TIN) with Arc/INFO GIS software. That created 3,492 surfaces, which were then converted to 5 km cell data. The cell data were spatially averaged across each county using a zonal mean function.

13. For more information on the physics of wind erosion, see Myron P. Gutmann and Geoff Cunfer, "A New Look at the Causes of the Dust Bowl," pub. no. 99-1 (Lubbock, Tex.: International Center for Arid and Semiarid Land Studies, 1999).

14. Dust regions come from maps published in the Washington, D. C. *Evening Star,* Dec. 8, 1939, C-7; see also Worster, *Dust Bowl,* 30.

15. "Mills Land Use Adjustment Project, New Mexico Proposal A-4, Final Plan," May 15, 1935; "Land Acquisition Plan (Part One) Mills Land Use Adjustment Project LA-5-38," Feb. 14, 1938, both manuscripts at Kiowa National Grassland Office, Clayton, New Mexico.

16. Dust regions come from maps published in the Washington, D. C. *Evening Star,* Dec. 8, 1939, C-7; see also Worster, *Dust Bowl,* 30.

17. Salina, Kansas, *Journal,* April 1, 1880.

18. James C. Malin, "Dust Storms, 1850-1900," *Kansas Historical Quarterly* 14 (May, August, November 1946): 129-44, 265-96, 391-413.

19. Atchison, Kansas, *Freedom's Champion,* April 7, 1860.

20. Salina, Kansas *Journal,* April 20, 1882.

21. J. T. Lovewell, "Meteorological Report," in Kansas State Board of Agriculture, *Report for the Quarter Ending March 31, 1886,* 16.

22. Topeka, Kansas, *Daily Capitol,* April 7, 1895.

23. Salina, Kansas, *Journal,* April 22, 1880.

24. Salina, Kansas, *Journal,* March 22, 1883; Salina, Kansas, *Herald,* March 22, 1883.

25. Salina, Kansas, *Herald,* April 24, 1880.

26. Salina, Kansas, *Journal,* March 20, 1879.

27. Junction City, Kansas, *Union,* April 15, 1882.

28. Topeka, Kansas, *Daily Capitol,* April 16, 1895.

29. *Monthly Weather Review* 23 (January, 1895), 15, 18-19.

30. Stephen J. Decanio, William N. Parker, and Joseph Trojanowski, "Adjustments to Resource Depletion: The Case of American Agriculture—Kansas, 1874-1936," data archived by the Inter-University Consortium for Political and Social Research, ICPSR file no. 7594.

31. Wichita, Kansas, *Eagle,* April 15, 1880.

32. M. J. Changery, "A Dust Climatology of the Western United States," NUREG/CR-3211(Asheville, North Carolina: National Climatic Data Center, 1983); A. S. Goudie, "Dust Storms in Space and Time," *Progress in Physical Geography* 7 (1983): 502–30; A. S. Goudie and N. J. Middleton, "The Changing Frequency of Dust Storms through Time," *Climatic Change* 20 (March 1992): 197–225.

33. Gutmann and Cunfer, "A New Look at the Causes of the Dust Bowl," 14.

5

"A MAP IS JUST A BAD GRAPH": WHY SPATIAL STATISTICS ARE IMPORTANT IN HISTORICAL GIS

Ian N. Gregory

INTRODUCTION

Good maps produced by professional cartographers are an incredible fusion of the science of measurement and the art of portraying complex information to a reader in an understandable way. GIS rarely produces such maps; instead, it usually produces fairly simple thematic maps, such as choropleths. Too often, the main aim of GIS research seems to be to produce such maps. It should not be. A GIS is a kind of database management system that links each item of data to a coordinate-based representation of its location, such as a point, line, polygon, or pixel. Historical GIS is concerned with taking data in this form and turning it into new knowledge and new scholarship about the geographies of the past. The thematic map is a useful tool for doing this, but a somewhat limited one. This essay contends that spatial statistics are an additional useful tool for describing and understanding spatial patterns. Statistical analysis has a poor reputation among many historians who associate it with crude positivism and the mistakes of the Quantitative Revolution. It need not be. It is simply a way of summarizing the spatial patterns found within and between datasets. These summaries are often best expressed on maps and stress spatial variations rather than eliminating them, a fair criticism of many more traditional techniques.

The first part of this essay critiques thematic maps as a limited way of representing spatially referenced data. The following sections introduce spatial statistics and provide examples of the ways they can advance our understanding of history. Maps, graphs, and statistics are tools to describe patterns in data. Explaining these patterns is an additional step requiring the traditional skills of a historian. There are three main reasons for describing the patterns in data. First, they may confirm relationships that were believed to have existed, thus providing evidence for an existing explanation. Second, the patterns may suggest new relationships that require new explanations. Third, the patterns revealed may challenge an orthodox explanation by showing that the expected pattern is not actually present. Mapping and spatial statistics are, however, simply descriptive; explanation is a further step.

LIMITATIONS OF THEMATIC MAPS

Gail Langran[1] identifies three components of data: space, time, and theme (or attribute). She argues that to represent one, it is usually necessary to simplify a second and fix the third. A thematic map emphasizes the spatial aspects of a dataset. To do this, the attribute component must be simplified. Often only one variable is shown, and it is heavily simplified by subdividing it into arbitrary classes, four or five being the maximum that human visual perception can distinguish effectively.[2] The many approaches to selecting class intervals include quantiles, equal intervals, and nested means.[3] But the choice of which to use remains subjective, and different choices can result in widely different patterns appearing on the map. Time is fixed; the map shows a single slice through time or perhaps the change between two points in time. Animations can be used to attempt to show change over time, but this often involves further simplifying space, theme, or both due to the limitations of human perception. Even space is not handled well on thematic maps, especially not on choropleths, which show data using polygons that usually represent administrative zones. Human perception of a choropleth map inevitably focuses on the larger polygons, which tend to be found in rural areas with small populations. While densely populated urban areas may contain the majority of the population, they can all but disappear from these maps. There are solutions to this perceptual problem, such as cartograms,[4] which distort unit size in proportion to population size or some other attribute, but this approach brings its own problems and is not widely used.

Thematic maps, therefore, are usually capable of showing information about only one of the three components (space, time, or attribute) and often only one variable. They cannot handle time, they arbitrarily simplify attribute, and they tend to emphasize sparsely populated places at the expense of the areas where most people live. In many ways, maps are analogous to graphs. In bar charts, an attribute value determines the length of each bar. In a scatter plot, a pair of attribute values determines the location of each point. Both cases provide a simplified visual summary of patterns in attribute data that may help the researcher understand more about the phenomenon that the attribute represents. The selection of graphing method is subjective, as is the process of interpreting the resulting patterns. It is often desirable to produce statistical summaries such as the mean and standard deviation or a correlation coefficient. These provide objective numerical summaries that complement the information on the graph.

A thematic map uses x,y coordinates to plot the location of a feature and then some other property—usually shade, color, or the size or shape of a symbol—to represent attribute value. Like a graph, a thematic map presents a simplified visual summary of data patterns. Like a graph, it may help the researcher recognize and understand the patterns inherent in the data. Like a graph, it does not explain the processes that form these patterns. And as with graphs, it may be desirable to produce statistical summaries of map patterns to clarify the spatial characteristics of the data.

Spatial statistics thus allow the researcher to go beyond mapping to manipulate, explore, describe, and confirm spatial patterns within and between datasets. Spatial statistics are primarily a quantitative approach but can be used with qualitative historical GIS sources because GIS represents spatial data in the form of coordinates or topology that are inherently quantitative. Thus, just as statistics allow researchers to go beyond graphing, spatial statistics allow researchers to go beyond mapping and gain a better insight into the spatial, thematic, and temporal patterns within a dataset.

SPACE AND SPATIAL STATISTICS: BASIC PRINCIPLES AND LIMITATIONS

The field of spatial statistics predates GIS by decades.[5] It is primarily concerned with finding objective numerical summaries to describe relationships over space. It differs from conventional forms of statistical analysis because the results produced by a spatial statistical technique will vary depending on the location of the data. GIS has reawakened interest in spatial statistics because this approach works well with the GIS data model that links spatial and attribute data.[6] Simple examples can demonstrate their compatibility. In a *univariate analysis,* which is concerned with a single variable, a map may suggest that a point dataset shows evidence of clustering. However, this is a subjective opinion; the pattern may be random. Spatial statistics can provide an objective summary of the likelihood that clusters exist and measure how much it clusters. In a *multivariate analysis,* maps may suggest that two or more variables exhibit a similar pattern. For example, polygons representing areas with high rates of overcrowded housing also may be found to represent areas with high rates of crime. A spatial analysis can demonstrate whether this actually is the case, and if so, can quantify how closely the two variables are related. Ideally, the analysis would also consider whether the relationship remains constant over the study area or varies from place to place.

While providing evidence that a pattern exists, spatial analysis has a key limitation because it can rarely explain what caused the pattern. The univariate analysis can provide convincing evidence of clustering within the dataset, but explaining why this clustering occurs is a separate stage in the analysis. This becomes even more complex with multivariate statistics, raising further questions such as does overcrowded housing lead to crime, is overcrowded housing a surrogate for something else such as poverty, and would crime rates inevitably fall if overcrowding rates decreased? Such questions require further research.

To understand what spatial statistics can and cannot do, consider why space is important and what it represents. It is not the intention here to discuss the philosophy of what space means in detail but to explain why it is important to historical geography. If geography is thought of as the study of places and the relationships between them,[7] then space must be important, as it enables and limits the interaction between people and places. Almost everything that interests a historian—goods and services, capital and labor, ideas and innovations, fashions and epidemics—moves from one place to another; thus space enables and constrains their spread.

This leads us to a limitation of GIS and spatial analysis. People and places interact over complex routes. They involve transport, face-to-face meetings, letters, the telephone, and electronic communications. GIS uses simple representations of space, usually consisting of straight-line distances or, less often, connectivity between areas or over a network. Thus distance and connectivity in a GIS are crude, quantitative approximations for much more complex flows. Having distances is certainly preferable to not having them, but it is a far from perfect representation of how places interact. In this understanding, space can be thought of as a causal variable that represents the costs, in time or money, of two places interacting. This shows how space and time are intrinsically linked, as the cost of crossing space is also likely to be strongly related to the duration of the journey.

Space is also important because it allows us to have different and diverse places. Space allows us to subdivide a place into many different smaller places. Whether the area we are studying is a country, a region, a town, or a village, we need space if we want to subdivide it into smaller places. Once we have space, then states, cultural regions, tracts, and households can be allowed to behave differently from one another. Without space, we have only one place, and it can tell us only one story; with space we have multiple places, and each of these can behave differently.[8] Traditional statistical techniques can be criticized for failing to account for spatial differences. In traditional approaches, if a statistical relationship is found between two variables, it is assumed that this relationship will be constant across the entire study area. This leads to the assumption that the same relationship will be found elsewhere, thus leading to the extreme forms of logical positivism that have given statistical analysis a bad name. Spatial analysis offers alternatives to this. An analysis that does not allow spatial variations is termed a *global* or *whole-map* analysis. GIS has enabled the development of *local* analysis techniques that allow patterns or relationships to vary across a study area.[9] Spatial statistical techniques are either global or local. For example, a global test for clustering would say that a point pattern does or does not cluster; a local technique would say that it clusters in some areas but not in others. Similarly, a multivariate technique would suggest a relationship between overcrowded housing and crime, while a local analysis technique could suggest that the two variables are strongly related in some areas but are not related in others. The results of a local analysis are usually presented in map form to show how the pattern varies.

By including space in analysis, we allow geography to matter even if the reasons why it should matter are not easily quantified or explained. Thus, space can be regarded as a partial solution to the problem of having limited data about the past. We may have similar data for two places but find they behave quite differently. Space allows us to interpret this to see that they are different places in different locations. Local spatial statistical techniques are particularly good at stressing this.

Spatial statistics are well suited to exploratory approaches[10] that attempt to discover what patterns exist within datasets and less well suited to confirmatory approaches that attempt to test predefined hypotheses. This is particularly true with polygon-based datasets such as published census data, which typically provides total populations within predefined administrative boundaries. The boundaries will inevitably affect analytical results and their interpretation for three reasons. First, there are issues regarding the scale of the administrative units. If they subdivide urban areas, they allow us to explore intraurban contrasts. If not, they may allow us to explore rural/urban contrasts but reveal little about the city. If they are even more aggregate, say to the level of U.S. states, they can pose more serious problems for interpretation. Second, the spatial delineation of the units will make a difference. Consider the example of where a single historical area containing a poor and a rich neighborhood is divided into two administrative units. Depending on where the boundary is drawn, this may produce one rich district and one poor district or two districts of the same average wealth. These two issues taken together are termed the *modifiable areal unit problem* (MAUP).[11] The third issue is termed *ecological fallacy*. If areas have high rates of overcrowding and high rates of crime, does this mean that individuals who live in overcrowded houses are more likely to be criminals? We can say the relationship exists at the aggregate level, but it does not explain individual behavior.

EXAMPLES OF SPATIAL ANALYTICAL APPROACHES

All GIS software packages claim to offer analytic functionality. Until recently, this was usually limited to operations that might more properly be described as data manipulation, such as overlay and buffering operations. The challenge for spatial statistics within GIS is to devise appropriate techniques that turn data into statistical summaries that help us identify and interpret the spatial patterns within the data. Recently, limited spatial statistical functionality has been added to some GIS software packages. However, these are a subset of the possible techniques available. Researchers should use imagination and flair in devising new techniques rather than being limited to the functionality offered by software vendors. In particular, researchers should remain focused on the spatial and spatiotemporal patterns within the data and aware of the historical and geographical limitations of their data. Rather than describe the full range of spatial statistical techniques, which are covered in several good textbooks,[12] the following discussion shows how I used spatial analysis to generate new knowledge about two significant historical research topics. One project examined the demographic consequences of the Great Irish Famine. The Irish Famine occurred when the potato crop failed repeatedly in the late 1840s. At this time, the potato was the main foodstuff in a society in which subsistence agriculture still prevailed. The results of the crop failure were catastrophic. The population of Ireland fell from 8.2 million in 1841 to 6.6 million in 1851 and continued to fall to only 5.2 million in 1881.[13] The population of the island of Ireland today is still under 6 million. Although the famine has been extensively studied, there has been little research on its geography. The second project used infant mortality in Victorian and Edwardian England and Wales to explore changes in the north–south divide in England and Wales in the Victorian and Edwardian periods. There is an extensive literature on how health in general and mortality in particular varies geographically. Infant mortality among babies under one year old is seen as a particularly sensitive indicator, because it varies rapidly in response to changing conditions and is closely related to poverty.[14] The north–south divide, or core-periphery divide as it is more correctly known, is a well-established research topic in Britain. Its basic premise is that there are, and perhaps always have been, marked inequalities between the core of England—London and the southeast—and the periphery to the north and west.[15] A major difficulty is how to define the south (or core) and the north (or periphery). Researchers have typically drawn a straight line from the Bristol Channel, an estuary in the southwest of England, to the Wash, a bay in the east. Alternative lines to other rivers in the east have also been suggested to move the core further north on the east side of the country. Such an arbitrary divide is clearly unsatisfactory, so spatial statistical approaches are used instead.

In what follows, the aim is not to present a detailed study of the topic, as these are presented elsewhere.[16] The aim is to show how spatial statistical approaches provide new insights that would otherwise have been concealed by the complexity of the data. The studies used three main types of techniques: areal interpolation, which uses statistics to "redistrict" data from one set of administrative units to another; univariate techniques, which attempt to identify spatial patterns in a single variable; and multivariate techniques, which attempt to identify spatial patterns between two or more variables.

Areal interpolation is a set of techniques that attempt to take data published for one set of polygons, termed the *source zones,* and estimate what the data values would be for another set of polygons, termed the *target zones.* This may sound like an arcane exercise in data manipulation, but it has the potential to be the first stage in greatly enhancing our understanding of many problems in historical geography. Huge amounts of official statistics such as the census are published using administrative units but are frequently incompatible with each other, either because boundaries change over time, or because the data is published using different types of units. The traditional solution to this problem has been aggregation to a common set of larger units. In Britain, this has typically meant counties; in the United States, it has often meant states. This type of massive aggregation removes most of the spatial and statistical detail before the analysis even starts and leads to major problems with the MAUP (page 128). It should thus be avoided. Areal interpolation provides an alternative solution that allows direct comparison over time and provides more reliable analytical results.

The simplest method of areal interpolation, called *areal weighting,* assumes that source data is evenly distributed across source units. The source and target zones are overlaid to give the *zones of intersection* between them. The population of each zone of intersection is then estimated based on the population of the source zone and the relative areas of the zone of intersection and the source zone. Thus, if a source zone is split into two parts, one having 75 percent of the area and the other having 25 percent, then the two zones of intersection will be estimated to have 75 percent and 25 percent of the population, respectively. The estimated populations of the zones of intersection are aggregated for each target zone to give their estimated population. Formally, this can be expressed as the following:

$$\hat{y}_t = \sum_s \left(\frac{A_{st}}{A_s} \times y_s \right) \quad (1)$$

where $\hat{y}_t$ is the estimated population of the target zone, y_s is the population of the source zone, A_s is the area of the source zone, and A_{st} is the area of the zone of intersection between the source and target zones.[17]

This is shown diagrammatically in figure 5.1, where data from the two source units (1 and 2) is to be allocated to three target units (A, B, and C). The first stage is to overlay the two source units to produce the zones of intersection (M, N, O, and P), for which the GIS software automatically calculates new areas. This provides enough data to perform equation 1. For example, target zone B's population is calculated as 30 percent of the population of source zone 1, which gives a population of 15; plus 30 percent of the population of source zone 2, which adds an additional population of 30; resulting in a total population of 45.

However, it is at best suspect and at worst nonsense to assume that a population is evenly distributed across an administrative unit. The resulting data will thus contain large amounts of error, hampering its use in subsequent analyses. A variety of more sophisticated techniques have reduced the reliance on this assumption.[18]

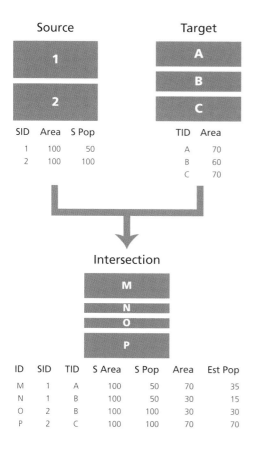

Source

SID	Area	S Pop
1	100	50
2	100	100

Target

TID	Area
A	70
B	60
C	70

Intersection

ID	SID	TID	S Area	S Pop	Area	Est Pop
M	1	A	100	50	70	35
N	1	B	100	50	30	15
O	2	B	100	100	30	30
P	2	C	100	100	70	70

FIGURE 5.1

Areal weighting, a form of areal interpolation. Overlaying the source and target units gives zones of intersection with the attributes shown (for example, source ID [SID], Area, and Pop). The intersection areas' source ID and area are new attributes calculated by the software. Estimated population is then calculated as ((Area ÷ S Area) × S Pop). Summing the values of estimated population for each target unit gives estimated populations of 35 for target zone A, 45 for B, and 70 for C.

Modified from I. N. Gregory and P. S. Ell, Historical GIS: Technologies, Methodologies and Scholarship (Cambridge: Cambridge University Press, in press).

In general, these involve using additional data that provides clues about how the source data is distributed in relation to the target units and statistical techniques to use this information. These techniques usually improve the results of the interpolation but do not completely eliminate error. They also require more complex interpolation. Most techniques are statistically complicated and can be implemented using a variety of approaches. Each approach has its own assumptions and implications for error.[19] The resulting data will include errors, whether the areal interpolation is done well or crudely. Users must address these errors to have any confidence in subsequent analysis. Searching for unusual changes in interpolated time-series data is one way to find errors. Identifying places with suspicious data is a first step toward handling interpolation error.[20]

Despite the difficulties, areal interpolation provides exciting new possibilities to improve our understanding of historical patterns, particularly how they change over time. An example of this is shown in my work with Paul S. Ell on population change during and after the Irish Famine.[21] No accurate figures for famine-related deaths or emigration are available, so researchers such as Joel Mokyr[22] have relied on county-level estimates to perform crude estimates of the geographical variation of mortality and emigration for Ireland's thirty-two counties. Our approach used census data from 1841, 1851, 1861, and 1871 interpolated onto a single set of 163 Poor Law unions. Having interpolated the data, we calculated the intercensal population changes at Poor Law union scale and mapped the results, which are shown in figure 5.2.

The maps show that the geography of population loss changed after the immediate famine years. Over the intercensal period that contains the famine years, 1841 to 1851, population loss was widespread throughout Ireland but concentrated particularly in the west, the midlands, and the south. Only five unions, all of them urban, gained population during this period. In the post-famine decades, population loss remained a major issue but was particularly concentrated in the midlands, rather than the west and the south, which are more commonly highlighted in the literature.

FIGURE 5.2 ▶

Intercensal population change during and after the Great Irish Famine. The legend uses a normalized percentage of population loss, thus the denominator for the rate is the sum of the start and end populations and not just the start population, which would give a more conventional rate.

Modified from I. N. Gregory and P. S. Ell, "Analysing Spatio-temporal Change Using National Historical GISs: Population Change During and After the Great Irish Famine" Historical Methods 38 (2005), 149–67.

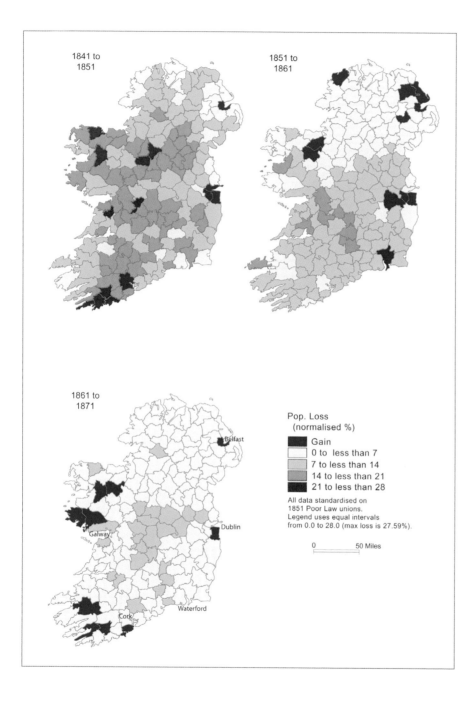

This simple use of interpolation allows a more detailed picture of population loss after the famine than was previously possible to create. The interpolated data does not distinguish between loss due to death, emigration, fertility decline, or a combination of factors. It could not determine whether the famine or internal migration from the countryside had any affect on urban areas where the population grew. Nevertheless, the data provides a more geographically detailed measure of the impact of the famine than previous studies produced.

Figure 5.2 shows a map of the raw data of population loss for the 1840s, 1850s, and 1860s. However, it is difficult to interpret and compare the data patterns over time. To simplify the spatial patterns, a G_i statistic can be used. This gives a local statistic that measures the degree of clustering around each location on the study area. A polygon with high values of G_i has relatively high values found around it, while low values show that relatively low values tend to be clustered around it.[23] This measures another feature of spatial data, *spatial autocorrelation,* the degree to which near values are similar to each other.[24]

Figure 5.3 shows the use of G_i values using the Irish population decline data shown in figure 5.2. The figure reveals that in the 1840s, the highest rates of population decline were found in the west, while in the 1850s and 1860s they were concentrated in the midlands. The lowest rates were found in the north in the 1840s and 1850s but were more dispersed in the 1860s. This univariate technique presents an effective way of simplifying a complex pattern.

When analyzing a dataset, it is important not to limit techniques to those described in the literature or available in the software. Instead, be imaginative and exploratory in attempting to gain a better understanding of the geography inherent in the data. Consider, for example, the changing patterns of infant mortality in England and Wales from 1851 to 1911. Data on infant mortality was published decennially over this period for about 635 registration districts.[25] At this time, infant mortality was very high, about 150 deaths under the age of 1 for every 1,000 live births. There were, however, the beginnings of the large-scale decline that was to last throughout

---

FIGURE 5.3 ▶

G_i statistics for population decline in Ireland, 1841 to 1871. A 70km bandwidth has been used.

*Modified from I. N. Gregory and P. S. Ell, "Analysing Spatio-temporal Change Using National Historical GISs: Population Change During and After the Great Irish Famine" Historical Methods, 38 (2005), 149–67. For (c), the G**statistics were calculated using the Vis Stats program written by Leonidas Housos.*

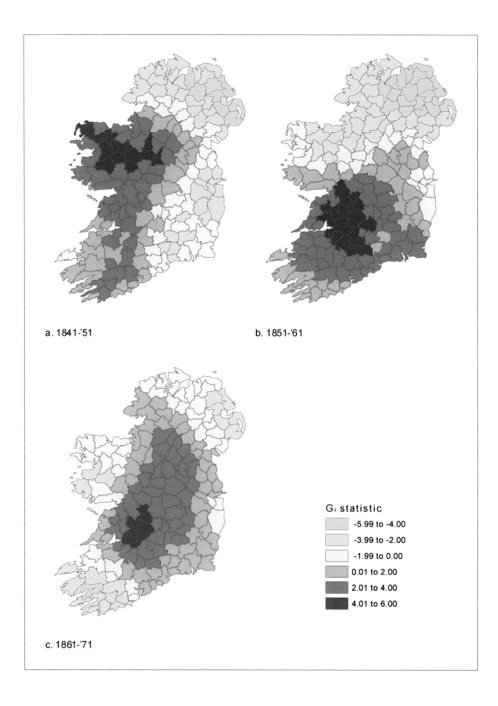

a. 1841-'51

b. 1851-'61

c. 1861-'71

G₁ statistic

	-5.99 to -4.00
	-3.99 to -2.00
	-1.99 to 0.00
	0.01 to 2.00
	2.01 to 4.00
	4.01 to 6.00

the twentieth century. By 1911, it is clear that the national-level decline was underway. In 2001, the infant mortality rate had fallen to only 5.4 deaths per 1,000 live births.[26] The question explored here is whether there was a north–south divide, or more properly a core-periphery divide, in infant mortality in England and Wales from the 1850s to the 1900s and how the start of the decline in rates affected the divide.

Data for infant mortality rates and the registration district boundaries for which they were published are available from the Great Britain Historical GIS (GBHGIS).[27] With this data, it is possible to calculate the straight-line distance from central London to the centroid of each registration district. The calculated values can then be included in a regression analysis where distance from London, a surrogate for how peripheral each place is, is the predictor variable for the infant mortality rate. This is shown for the 1900s data in figure 5.4. Using ordinary least squares (OLS) regression tells us that the overall trend is an infant mortality rate of 95.41 deaths per 1,000 live births in central London, rising by 6.0 deaths for every 100 kilometers in distance from London. This has an r^2 of 5.48 percent and is significant at the 1 percent level.

Performing this analysis for earlier decades gives the results shown in table 5.1. The results suggest that from the 1870s to the 1900s, there was a pronounced and increasing core-periphery divide in England and Wales. This did not exist in the 1860s, and there appears to be the reverse in the 1850s, namely a periphery-core divide with the best rates found well away from the South-East.

This analysis has limitations. OLS regression assumes that the data represents independently random observations, whereas because neighboring values likely influence the data, it can be expected to exhibit spatial autocorrelation. The graph also suggests that the data exhibit *heteroscedasticity,* whereby the error term is not randomly distributed along the trend line—another violation of the assumptions that underlie OLS regression.[28] A third limitation is that all registration districts are treated equally in the analysis regardless of their population size. In 1911, the largest two registration districts had populations of more than 250,000, while the smallest two had populations of less than 2,500. Equal treatment of such disparate districts may overstress the impact of rural areas.

FIGURE 5.4 ▶

Infant mortality rates with distance from central London, 1900s. Nelson's Column is used as the coordinate for central London. Infant mortality data is taken from the *Registrar General's Decennial Supplement* of 1911. The trend line is fitted with OLS regression and has the equation y = 95.41 + 0.06x with an r^2 of 5.48 percent.

Table 5.1 Regression coefficients for infant mortality rates with distance from central London. The table includes the slope (expressed as the increase in rate per 100 kilometers from London), the intercept (the expected rate in central London), the r^2 value, the F statistic, and the level at which the F statistic is significant.

	Slope (100kms)	Intercept	r^2 (%)	F	Significance
1900s	6.00	95.41	5.5	36.64	1%
1890s	4.88	118.50	3.5	22.57	1%
1880s	3.04	115.31	1.7	9.59	1%
1870s	2.72	124.14	1.4	8.75	1%
1860s	1.16	132.30	0.2	1.35	No
1850s	-3.20	143.14	1.7	10.71	1%

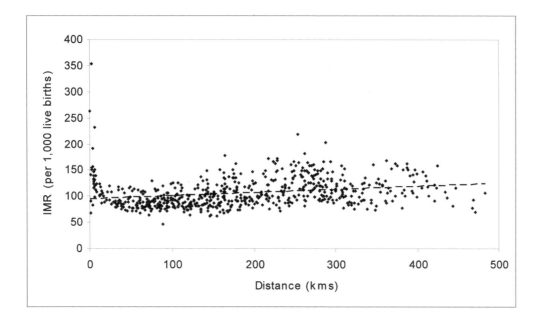

To investigate this further, an alternative approach follows the same logic, namely that the lowest rates should be found near London if there is a core-periphery divide. Rather than the statistical approach used above, a far more graphical method splits the country into buffers 25 kilometers wide, centered on central London. The total number of infant deaths and live births in districts whose centroids lie in each buffer was then calculated to give the infant mortality rate for each buffer. This avoids the problem of different district sizes. Mapping this for the 1850s and 1900s shows the patterns in figure 5.5.

A general pattern of low rates appears around, but not in, London. The worst rates are located in the buffers that contain Liverpool, Manchester, and Leeds. Many of the best buffers are in the far periphery in the 1850s. But by the 1900s, the best rates are

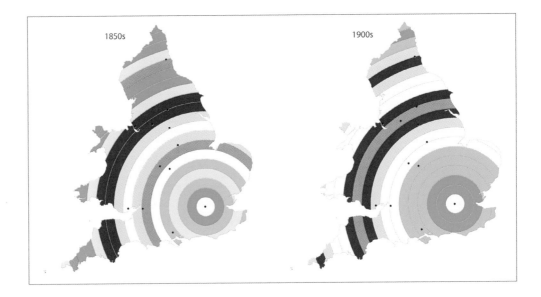

FIGURE 5.5

Infant mortality rates in England and Wales in the 1850s and the 1900s organized by 25-kilometer buffers. Each of the three green class intervals holds 10 percent of the population, with the darkest green representing the lowest rates. The red class intervals hold the highest rates, with the darkest being the highest. The yellow shade holds the middle 40 percent of the population. Major cities are shown as black dots.

Outline of country from Great Britain Historical GIS.

concentrated in the area around London, the worst in the periphery. The exceptions are the three buffers farthest from London, all with very small populations.

To confirm this, data for the 1850s and 1900s was split into deciles such that the buffers' infant mortality rates were ranked and split into classes, with each holding 10 percent of the population. Figure 5.6 shows the result. With one exception during this period, buffers about the distance of Nottingham and Swansea got worse, while those nearer London got better.

One might suggest that high rates of infant mortality in the periphery were largely driven by the growth of large industrial towns and collieries in northern England and South Wales. These populous, unhealthy regions may have pulled down the average value of northern buffers, even though there were still some very healthy areas in

FIGURE 5.6

Changing deciles of infant mortality by buffer from the 1850s to the 1900s. Red buffers have become more than two deciles worse, orange have become worse by one or two deciles, and gray have remained the same. Light blue buffers have become one or two deciles better, while dark blue have shown an increase of three or more deciles.

Outline of country from Great Britain Historical GIS.

the periphery. A final piece of analysis on this topic seems to refute this and suggests that something more fundamental was happening. Taking the eleven districts with the lowest rates in the 1850s[29] shows that the nearest to London was Whitchurch in Shropshire, which was 241 kilometers from central London. The farthest was Belford in Northumberland, which was 468 kilometers away. The median distance for all eleven was 301 kilometers. In other words, these are all very peripheral places. By the 1900s, the farthest district from London of the best eleven was Wareham in Dorset, which was only 168 kilometers from London. Thus in the 1850s, all of the best places were peripheral, while all were significantly closer to the core by the 1900s. Table 5.2 summarizes the distances to the eleven districts with the lowest rates in each decade. It shows the most dramatic declines in the 1860s and 1870s.

This suggests that in the 1850s, the lowest infant mortality rates were found in the rural periphery. Over the next fifty years, there were marked improvements in rural core areas that were not matched in the periphery. As a result, there was a clear move from a periphery-core divide in the 1850s to a core-periphery divide in the 1900s. Although the data used has been available for more than a century, this pattern had not previously been identified, demonstrating that using GIS and simple spatial analysis techniques on a single variable can provide new insights into data.

Table 5.2 Distances from London showing the eleven districts with the lowest infant mortality rates, 1850s to 1900s

	1850s	1860s	1870s	1880s	1890s	1900s
Min	230	57	46	38	46	1
LQ	271	86	72	64	129	73
Median	301	284	88	146	155	146
UQ	436	319	243	243	247	158
Max	468	468	468	469	348	168

Distances are in kilometers; the minimum, maximum, median, and lower and upper quartile values are shown.

Most statistical techniques are not concerned with the patterns within a single variable but are instead concerned with exploring how two or more variables relate to each other. Correlation and regression are typical examples,[30] but few are specifically spatial multivariate techniques. The best developed example of a local multivariate spatial analysis technique is *geographically weighted regression* (GWR).[31] Conventional regression uses a set of *predictor variables* to estimate the value of a *dependant variable.* It involves using known values of the dependant and predictor variables to calculate the *intercept term,* usually the estimated value of the dependant variable when all of the predictor variables have a value of zero, and a *slope term* for each predictor variable that estimates how much the dependant variable is likely to increase by a given unit increase in the predictor variable. These coefficients are assumed to be global. GWR calculates a separate regression equation for each location in the study area by adding a distance decay model to vary the amount of impact that each observation in the predictor variables has on the dependant variable. Thus, near values have more influence than far ones. Having done this, the values of all of the coefficients will vary across the map, as will values of their significance and the r^2 values. This provides an effective exploratory technique to show how spatial relationships may vary across the study area. The results are usually best shown on maps.

The Irish Famine study used GWR to examine the assumption that population loss was concentrated among the poor.[32] There are no variables directly associated with poverty, so two variables from the census were used as surrogates: illiteracy and low-quality housing. We also added two dummy variables representing small and large towns. This resulted in the following model:

$$pop\_dec = b_0 + (b_1 \times s\_town) + (b_2 \times l\_town) + (b_3 \times frth\_clss) + (b_4 \times illit) \quad (2)$$

where *pop_dec* is the population decline, *s_town* is the presence or absence of a small town, *l_town* is the presence or absence of a large town, *frth_clss* is the proportion of houses that are fourth class (the lowest classification in the census), and *illit* is the proportion of the population that is illiterate. The intercept term is b_0, and b_1 to b_4 are the slope terms. The analysis was applied to the 1840s, 1850s, and 1860s.

Table 5.3 shows the global regression parameters. The predictor variables have been offset by their mean. In the 1840s, for example, a Poor Law union with the average amount of fourth-class housing and illiteracy and no town lost 13.5 percent of its population. The presence of a small town reduced this by 2.29 percentage points and a large town by 12.99 points. Every percentage of the population that was illiterate above or below the national average would increase or decrease population loss by 0.17 percentage points. As the value for fourth-class housing is small and not statistically significant, it is not considered to have a noticeable impact on population change.

This last finding shows the proportion of fourth-class housing declining from 36 percent in 1841 to 8.6 percent in 1861. There appears to be no relationship between population loss during a decade and the amount of fourth-class housing at the start of the decade. The pattern of no statistically significant relationship between fourth-class housing and population loss is consistent across the three decades. The GWR results shown in figure 5.7 suggest a possible reason.

In the east of the country, a positive relationship appears to exist between the two variables, as would be expected. In the west, however, the results showed the opposite relationship: high values of fourth-class housing seem to lead to relatively

Table 5.3	Global regression coefficients for Irish Famine regression					
	intercept	s_town	l_town	frth_clss	illit	r^2 (%)
1840s	13.5	-2.29	-12.99	-0.01	+0.17	38
1850s	7.00	+1.51	-3.06	-0.04	+0.18	10
1860s	4.66	-0.33	-6.31	-0.02	-0.04	15

The dependant variable is population decline, so negative values show population gain. The predictor variables are small towns, large towns, proportion of fourth-class housing, and proportion of the population that was illiterate. All predictor variables have been offset by their mean. Figures in bold are statistically significant at the 5 percent level. The r^2 values are also shown.

FIGURE 5.7 ▶

Geographically weighted regression parameters for fourth-class housing as a predictor for population loss, 1840s to 1860s. The other predictor variables are small towns, large towns, and proportion of the population that was illiterate.

Modified from P. S. Ell and I. N. Gregory, "Demography, Depopulation and Devastation: Exploring the Geography of the Irish Potato Famine" Historical Geography 33 (2005), by permission of GeoScience Publications, Louisiana State University.

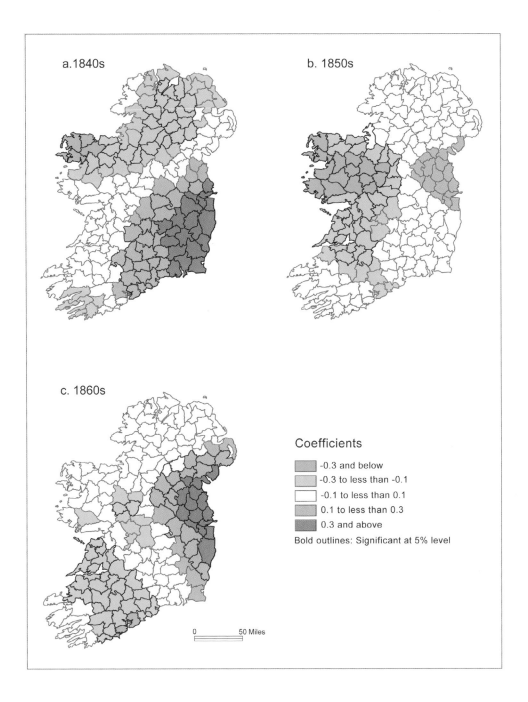

a. 1840s

b. 1850s

c. 1860s

Coefficients

- -0.3 and below
- -0.3 to less than -0.1
- -0.1 to less than 0.1
- 0.1 to less than 0.3
- 0.3 and above

Bold outlines: Significant at 5% level

0   50 Miles

low values of population loss. Explaining this requires further research that may not involve either spatial analysis or GIS. It does, however, provide further insight into the impact of fourth-class housing on population loss and shows that the relationship between poverty and the impact of the famine was more complex than global statistics would suggest.

A final use of GWR is shown in figure 5.8. Here, a more complex model has been created for population loss in the 1850s and 1860s, for which dates more data was available. The model includes a total of nine predictor variables. Rather than map the coefficients, figure 5.8 shows two measures of how effectively the model works at each location: local r^2 values and the number of variables that have a statistically significant t-value.

The patterns between the two measures are broadly similar and show that the model does not work very well, particularly for the south of Ireland in the 1850s. This finding enables us to evaluate to what extent each place was a "typical" place after the famine. Skibbereen, in the south of Ireland, is often used as a case study. However, these results suggest that it is far from a typical place in the immediate post-famine period. This, in turn, suggests that lessons learned from case studies on Skibbereen should be applied to other places with care.

CONCLUSION

GIS databases can be time-consuming and costly to construct. Justifying this investment will require new insights into our knowledge of historical geography. We are only beginning to explore the major challenge of turning spatially referenced data in a GIS into information about historical geography. We risk failing this challenge if we restrict GIS analysis to mapping and publishing data on a Web site.

Describing a map as a "bad graph" is unduly negative. The idea was suggested in passing during a discussion of statistical mapping at a conference some years ago.[33] It stayed with me because that provocative comparison helps counterbalance the dangerous assumption that the map is an objective truth that by itself provides new historical understanding. It is far from this. Mapping simply provides a way of exploring the spatial patterns of the past.

FIGURE 5.8 ▶

GWR and explanation, 1850s and 1860s. The two maps on the left show the local r^2 values; the maps on the right show how many of the nine predictor variables are statistically significant at the 5 percent level.

Modified from P. S. Ell and I. N. Gregory, "Demography, Depopulation and Devastation: Exploring the Geography of the Irish Potato Famine" Historical Geography 33 (2005), by permission of GeoScience Publications, Louisiana State University.

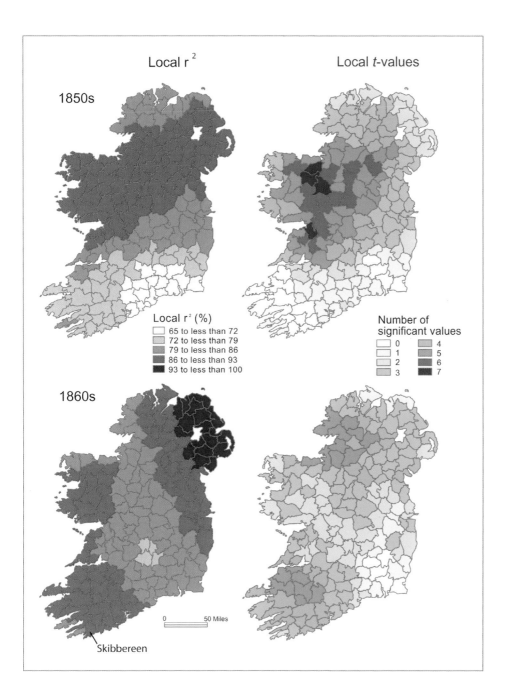

Local r ^{2}

Local *t*-values

1850s

1860s

Local r^2 (%)

- ☐ 65 to less than 72
- ☐ 72 to less than 79
- ☐ 79 to less than 86
- ☐ 86 to less than 93
- ■ 93 to less than 100

Number of
significant values

- ☐ 0
- ☐ 1
- ☐ 2
- ☐ 3
- ☐ 4
- ☐ 5
- ■ 6
- ■ 7

0   50 Miles

Skibbereen

Spatial statistical analysis provides a further step toward understanding. It allows us to summarize the relationships within and between datasets and importantly says where, and perhaps when, these relationships vary. It does not prove relationships and should not be construed as doing so, but it does give insights into *what* is happening *where*. This approach has many limitations. Historians wanting to conduct spatial statistical analysis usually find limited data that is often a poor surrogate for what they want to study. This approach, therefore, tends to be data-led, and the data may not lead us to real-world problems. The interpretation of spatial data also has serious limitations such as ecological fallacy and the MAUP. Any spatial analysis must consider these limitations. This should be done in an imaginative manner that uses distance and connectivity as important concepts in understanding the geography under study. Remember also that the concept of space embodied in GIS is only one of many concepts that make up real-world human geography.

Spatial statistics is an important and underused tool for historical GIS. It allows us to produce summaries of complex patterns that occur in space, attribute, and time. The greatest challenge to the historian is not performing these techniques but interpreting the patterns that emerge from the data. Analytic techniques help in this, but historians must interpret the results within the context of the historiographical questions, the limitations of the data from a historical perspective, the limitations of the data from a geographical perspective, and the limitations and underlying assumptions of the techniques used. If this is done, then spatial analysis techniques will become valuable tools in helping us to understand the geographies of the past.

ACKNOWLEDGMENTS

Ian N. Gregory acknowledges support for research on infant mortality from a Leverhulme Early Career Fellowship (ECF/40115) and for work on the Great Irish Famine from the Economic and Social Research Council's Research Methods Program (H333250016). He thanks Ciaran Higgins for research assistance on this work. The G_i statistics were calculated using the VisStats program written by Leonidas Housos as part of his master's thesis in GIS at the University of Portsmouth. The GWR analysis was performed using GWR 2.0 software provided by Martin Charlton, Stewart Fotheringham, and Chris Brunsdon.

NOTES

1. Gail Langran, *Time in Geographic Information Systems* (London: Taylor & Francis, 1992).

2. Arthur H. Robinson, Joel L. Morrison, Phillip C. Muehrke, A. Jon Kimerling, and Stephen C. Guptill, *Elements of Cartography*, 6th ed. (Chichester: John Wiley & Sons, 1995).

3. Ian S. Evans, "The Selection of Class Intervals," *Transactions of the Institute of British Geographers* 2 (1977): 98-124.

4. Daniel Dorling, *Area Cartograms: Their Use and Creation. Concepts and Techniques in Modern Geography*, 59 (Norwich: University of East Anglia, Environmental Publications, 1996); and Michael T. Gastner and M. E. J. Newman, "Diffusion-Based Method for Producing Density Equalizing Maps," *Proceedings of the National Academy of Sciences* 101 (2004): 7499-503.

5. Anthony C. Gatrell, "Any Space for Spatial Analysis?" In *The Future of Geography*, ed. Ronald J. Johnston (London: Methuen, 1985), 190-208.

6. A. Stewart Fotheringham, Chris Brunsdon, and Martin Charlton, *Quantitative Geography: Perspectives on Spatial Data Analysis* (London: Sage, 2000).

7. Ronald J. Johnston, *Philosophy and Human Geography: An Introduction to Contemporary Approaches* (London: Edward Arnold, 1983).

8. Doreen Massey, "Space-Time, 'Science' and the Relationship between Physical Geography and Human Geography," *Transactions of the Institute of British Geographers: New Series* 24 (1999): 261-76; and Doreen Massey, *For Space* (London: Sage, 2005) both provide detailed explorations of why space is important to geographers.

9. See A. Stewart Fotheringham, "Trends in Quantitative Methods I: Stressing the Local" *Progress in Human Geography* 21 (1997): 88-96; or Luc Anselin "Local Indicators of Spatial Association—LISA" *Geographical Analysis* 27 (1995): 93-115.

10. John W. Tukey, *Exploratory Data Analysis* (Reading, Mass.: Addison–Wesley, 1977).

11. See Stanley Openshaw, *The Modifiable Areal Unit Problem. Concepts and Techniques in Modern Geography,* 38 (Norwich: Geobooks, 1984); A. Stewart Fotheringham and D.W. Wong "The Modifiable Areal Unit Problem in Multi-Variate Statistical Analysis" *Environment and Planning A* 23 (1991): 1025–44; or Robin Flowerdew, Alastair Geddes, and Mick Green, "Behaviour of Regression Models under Random Aggregation," in *Modelling Scale in Geographical Information Science,* eds. Nicholas J. Tate and Peter M. Atkinson (Chichester: John Wiley & Sons, Inc., 2001), 89-104.

12. The most comprehensive are Trevor C. Bailey and Anthony C. Gatrell, *Interactive Spatial Data Analysis* (Harlow: Longman, 1995); Fotheringham, Brunsdon, and Charlton, *Quantitative Geography;* and David O'Sullivan and David Unwin, *Geographic Information Analysis* (Chichester: John Wiley & Sons, Inc., 2003).

13. Liam Kennedy, Paul S. Ell, E. Margaret Crawford, and Lesley A. Clarkson, *Mapping the Great Irish Famine: A Survey of the Famine Decades* (Dublin: Four Courts Press, 1999).

14. See, for example, Sarah Curtis and Ian Rees Jones, "Is There a Place for Geography in the Analysis of Health Inequality?" *Sociology of Health & Illness* 20 (1998): 645-72; and Anthony C. Gatrell, *Geographies of Health* (London: John Wiley & Sons, Inc., 2002).

15. Alan R. H. Baker and Mark Billinge, eds., *Geographies of England: The North-South Divide, Imagined and Material* (Cambridge: Cambridge University Press, 2004).

16. The work on the Irish Famine is a summary of work presented in Paul S. Ell and Ian N. Gregory, "Demography, Depopulation, and Devastation: Exploring the Geography of the Irish Potato Famine," *Historical Geography* 33 (2005): 54-77; and Ian N. Gregory and Paul S. Ell, "Analyzing Spatio-Temporal Change Using National Historical GISs: Population Change during and after the Great Irish Famine," *Historical Methods* 38 (2005): 149-67.

17. Michael F. Goodchild and N. S.-N. Lam, "Areal Interpolation: A Variant of the Traditional Spatial Problem," *Geo-Processing* 1 (1980): 297-312.

18. Ian N. Gregory and Paul S. Ell, "Breaking the Boundaries: Integrating 200 Years of the Census Using GIS," *Journal of the Royal Statistical Society, Series A* 168 (2005): 419-37 provide a review.

19. Ian N. Gregory, "The Accuracy of Areal Interpolation Techniques: Standardising 19th- and 20th-Century Census Data to Allow Long-Term Comparisons," *Computers Environment and Urban Systems* 26 (2002): 293-314.

20. Ian N. Gregory and Paul S. Ell, "Error Sensitive Historical GIS: Identifying Areal Interpolation Errors in Time-Series Data," *International Journal of Geographical Information Science* 20 (2006): 135-52.

21. Ell and Gregory, "Demography, Depopulation and Devastation."

22. Joel Mokyr, *Why Ireland Starved: A Quantitative and Analytical History of the Irish Economy, 1800-1850.* (London: Harper Collins, 1983).

23. Arthur Getis and J. K. Ord, "The Analysis of Spatial Association by Use of Distance Statistics," *Geographical Analysis* 24 (1992): 189-206.

24. Spatial autocorrelation has important implications for many conventional statistical tests. If data exhibits spatial autocorrelation it means that values at one location are influenced by values at other locations. Many

statistical tests use the assumption that the observations under study are independent from each other. If the data is spatially autocorrelated, this assumption is violated. See Andrew D. Cliff and J. K. Ord, *Spatial Autocorrelation* (London: Pion, 1973); or Michael F. Goodchild, *Introduction to Spatial Autocorrelation. Concepts and Techniques in Modern Geography,* 47 (Norwich: GeoAbstracts, 1987).

25. The exact number depends on date.

26. Office for National Statistics. *National Statistics Online,* http://www.statistics.gov.uk/StatBase/Expodata/ Spreadsheets/D6803.xls (accessed on August 22, 2005).

27. Ian N. Gregory, Chris Bennett, Vicki L. Gilham, and Humphrey R. Southall, "The Great Britain Historical GIS: From Maps to Changing Human Geography," *The Cartographic Journal* 39:1 (2002): 37–49.

28. Any good statistical textbook will discuss heteroscedasticity and its implications in detail.

29. Using eleven rather than ten allows us to calculate a median with an actual value rather than being half way between two.

30. See, for example, Gareth Shaw and Dennis Wheeler, *Statistical Techniques in Geographical Analysis* (London: David Fulton, 1994); or Peter A. Rogerson, *Statistical Methods for Geographers* (London: Sage, 2001).

31. A. Stewart Fotheringham, Chris Brunsdon, and Martin Charlton, *Geographically Weighted Regression: The Analysis of Spatially Varying Relationships* (Chichester: John Wiley & Sons, Inc., 2002).

32. Gregory and Ell, "Analysing Spatio-Temporal Change using National Historical GISs."

33. Comment made during discussion in a session titled "The Role of Location in Social Science History: Is There a Spatial Turn?" at the annual meeting of the Social Science History Association, Chicago, November 18, 2001. Thanks to Steven Ruggles for bringing this comparison to my attention.

6

MAPPING HUSBANDRY IN CONCORD: GIS AS A TOOL FOR ENVIRONMENTAL HISTORY

Brian Donahue

Hidden within the voluminous historiography of colonial New England is an unanswered question: how did farmers work the land? Farming and the household production that flowed from it were the main economic activities of this society of yeomen and goodwives—the primary means by which a "comfortable subsistence" was wrested from the earth and modest wealth created. Yet we know surprisingly little about how farming was actually conducted. The purpose here is to describe how historical GIS can be used to uncover the ecological organization of colonial farming and its impact on the land.

For all our ignorance concerning colonial New England farmers, we are certainly not lacking for a prevailing story about them. For two centuries, we have been told that they were bad farmers. They farmed crudely and extensively, mistreating their livestock, wasting their manure, wearing out their land, and moving on. So said the gentlemen who observed the colonial yeomen in their day, and so said nineteenth-century agricultural improvers looking back on their forefathers. Citing these authorities, twentieth-century historians elaborated a theory of environmental decline that led to crisis. By the end of the colonial period, New England towns were overcrowded. After four or five generations, their burgeoning populations caught up with their extensive farming methods. They ran out of land to exhaust. This resulted in a "world of scarcity," of social and economic stresses that contributed to the American Revolution, the Market Revolution, the Industrial Revolution, and migration to the West. Clearly, the relationship of New England farmers to their land has been seen as a matter of historical consequence.[1]

But what was that relationship, exactly? Until recently, our understanding of colonial farming descended almost entirely from that handful of colonial and early-nineteenth-century observers. To get beyond their disdainful remarks, historians turned to a new set of sources: tax valuations, probated estates, court records, diaries, and account books. With a little statistical massaging, this data gave us a better picture of changes in agricultural methods and crop yields. But opening a window on colonial farming requires connecting such information more closely to the landscape. What kinds of land were being put to use for what purposes? Did farmers move about or stay put? *Was* land being worn out? To understand the ecological structure of colonial husbandry better, we need to map it.

In 1980, I began researching and mapping the history of landownership and land use in Concord, Massachusetts. As a farmer and logger in neighboring Weston, I had a strong personal interest in what had happened to land in the Concord area. Thanks to Henry David Thoreau, Ralph Waldo Emerson, and the "shot heard round the world," Concord is a place of unusual historical interest, with abundant primary and secondary sources dating to the first English settlement. GIS mapping for the colonial period was the basis of my book *The Great Meadow* and for this case study on methods. This study will also make occasional comparisons to unpublished work about central Kansas.[2]

Concord was typical of the first generation of white settlement in New England. Some twenty miles northwest of Boston, it started as a grant by the General Court to about fifty proprietors in 1635, the first inland community in Massachusetts Bay Colony. The grant was supposed to have been six miles square but in reality came closer to seven, encompassing nearly thirty thousand acres, although about half of that had been whittled away by the end of the eighteenth century through the creation of daughter towns.

The GIS assembled for Concord included some layers that covered the entire original grant and some that focused on smaller areas within the town. The power of GIS, of course, is its ability to deftly handle many layers of data. Historians can give some of those layers temporal dimension to show change over time. Layers that capture features of interest at critical dates can be stacked in a pile with the oldest on the bottom. This stratigraphic "layer cake" is conceptually satisfying and organizes the material for effective display. But it can be just as powerful to build temporal depth into a single layer, creating master maps that are continuous records of historical change that can then be sliced, examined, and displayed at any date desired.

The bottom layer of my cake was the graded stuff of the earth as dropped by the last glacier (figure 6.1). This map was digitized from U.S. Geological Survey (USGS) surficial geology maps, which exist for some quadrangles and not for others. It was relatively straightforward to group glacial landforms such as eskers, kames, and drumlins into three distinct categories of soil that were actually recognized by the Concord farmers who had to plow through this debris. *Rocky land* was glacial till deposited directly by the ice. *Sandy land* was coarse outwash graded by meltwater streams pouring into glacial lakes. *Moist land* included finer silts that settled at the bottom of those lakes along with more recent deposits in floodplains and wetlands. The distribution of rocky till, sandy outwash, and moist alluvium in Concord influenced the subsequent development of vegetation, native land use, and English farming, for these soil types have strikingly different agricultural capabilities and limitations. In other parts of the world, different geological processes may play similar roles. In Kansas, for example, contrasting soils that formed in successive strata of bedrock that were subsequently exposed by erosion strongly influenced what land was plowed and what was left for range.[3]

A soil map would be an obvious alternative (or supplement) to a surficial geology basemap for a GIS. The Natural Resources Conservation Service (NRCS) has detailed maps designed for evaluating the capabilities and limitations of soils for farming, carving the land into small units of a few acres each. Unfortunately, in Middlesex County, Massachusetts, no soil survey has recently been published, let alone digitized, although an "Interim Soil Survey Report" (now in its fourth edition) is available from NRCS. I used this report to digitize the soil units underlying part of the study area, which was useful for detailed analysis of particular farms. To make sense of the multitude of tiny soil units across a larger region, some scheme of aggregation into broader categories is necessary. In Kansas, "soil capability subclasses" worked well because they captured key aspects of soil texture and slope.[4]

The basemap shown in figure 6.1 also includes a hydrology layer. Watercourses and how people used and manipulated them were important to the story in their own right. They also provide the viewer with orientation and continuity from

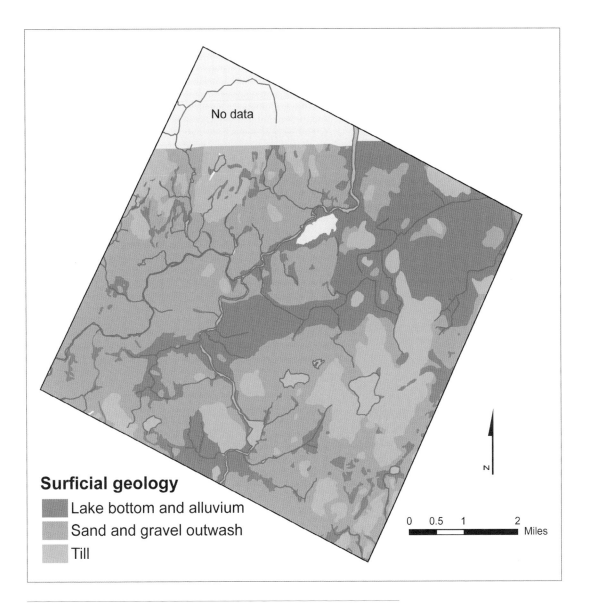

FIGURE 6.1

Surficial geology of Concord aggregated into rocky till, sandy outwash, and moist alluvium. The top corner is blank because the geology has not been mapped by USGS.

one map to the next. The Sudbury and Assabet rivers meet to form the northward flowing Concord River near the center of the town. In the south central area lies the familiar shape of Walden Pond, flanked by Flint's (or Sandy) Pond to the east and Fairhaven Bay to the west. The waters of Concord were subject to historical change, so I made several versions of the hydrology layer to use on successive maps of the town's development, draining swamps, ditching brooks, and filling ponds.

The next map in the series depicts land use in the place the native people called "Musketaquid" (figure 6.2). This is necessarily a tentative, impressionistic map because so little evidence remains of how the people of this place lived, or even who they were. The map was informed by the many artifact collections made in Concord during the past two centuries (beginning with Thoreau) and compiled by archeologist Shirley Blancke. It was also informed by descriptions of land and vegetation found in early town records or in local lore and by pollen cores from Walden Pond. Guided by these slender clues, I took a high estimate of precontact native population in the Concord River valley and distributed familiar anthropological categories of native land use in southern New England across this section of countryside, keyed to surficial geology. The map shows a cultural landscape of four broad land management zones, all with some evidence of burning. The five areas marked as horticultural (HP1–HP5), located on light sandy soils, correspond to the documented sites of abandoned planting fields and heavy concentrations of artifacts from the late Woodland period. A swath of open, frequently burned scrub oak and pitch pine forest was found across coarser sand and gravel outwash soils throughout the valley. Denser, less frequently burned closed-canopy forest was found on the rocky till uplands. Finally, extensive grassy meadows lay interspersed with several kinds of swamps on low-lying, moist soils.[5]

The existence of these zones is highly speculative and the location of boundaries between them even more so. But even such a hypothetical mapping allows one to visualize what native land-use practices might have looked like over a real stretch of the earth's surface, moving us beyond the abstraction of words. For example, this map shows vividly that even a high native population would have been unlikely to clear more than a small percentage of the upland forest for shifting cultivation. Native New England may have been a cultural landscape, but it was hardly the intensely cultivated, open landscape that has sometimes been suggested.[6] Forest

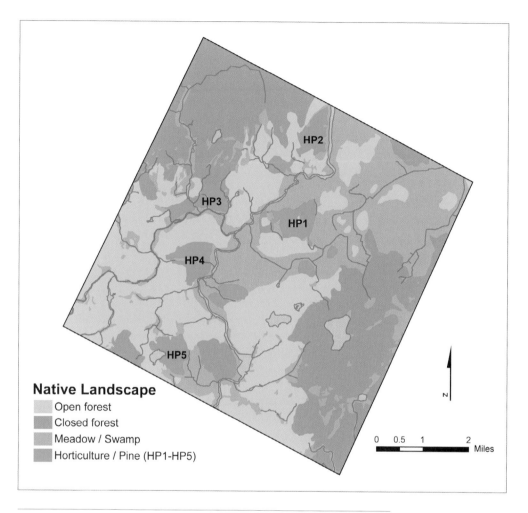

FIGURE 6.2

Concord native landscape, circa 1600. Soils, disturbances, and native land use
combined to order the ecosystems of Musketaquid into a working landscape.
This map shows five tracts devoted to shifting cultivation, an open pine/oak forest
across the sandy plains bordering the river, a denser forest on the rocky highlands,
and wetlands that graded from grassy meadows to wooded swamps.

generally prevailed, even if burning may have modified its species composition and structure. Yet a large part of the wetlands may have been in a grassy state. If there were extensive open areas in the native landscape, they may have been here. Once such a hypothetical pattern of land use has been mapped, we can target new research to refine or refute it. A transect of strategically located pollen and charcoal cores across this landscape mosaic would sharpen the picture. Were the meadows burned, keeping them open and grassy? Were orchards of hickories and chestnuts deliberately managed? Were hilltops frequently torched to encourage blueberries? The map suggests where to look.

Onto this landscape in 1635 came about fifty families of English Puritans. We have a better idea who they were, and much of what they did with the land can be traced. The Massachusetts Bay Colony granted Concord plantation to these families to use largely as they saw fit. In 1636, they also formally purchased the land from a handful of native people who had survived devastating epidemics. What the English put in place marks a startling change from what had gone before: a common-field village set down in what they experienced as the American wilderness (figure 6.3). This map was constructed from the land division records of the town—about eight hundred parcels distributed among fifty or so proprietors over a period of about forty years. The map is not 100 percent correct for the location of every parcel, but the overall *pattern* is reasonably close to what actually existed.

The map in figure 6.3 shows only "First Division" parcels granted prior to 1653, when some three-quarters of the town was still held undivided in common. We see the tightly clustered house lots of the village, the tillage lots spread among several large general fields, the stream-side meadows subdivided into mowing lots—all surrounded by the undivided commons, which is shown as a white background. We are used to thinking of the "common" as a small patch of green at the center of a New England village or city, but it began life as a great swath of land *encompassing* the village, its plow lands, and meadows. The common land in Concord, which was largely forested, was devoted to grazing the common herd and supplying timber and firewood. This pattern of landownership and use was radically different from the native arrangement of the same landscape. It was also a long way from the nucleated freehold farms that became the norm in later towns.

How was land held in this commons system, and how and when did the system change? We can move in closer and take a look at the land grants of William Hartwell,

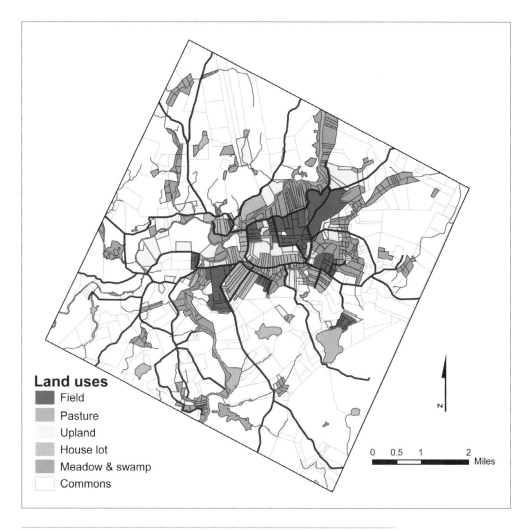

Land uses
- Field
- Pasture
- Upland
- House lot
- Meadow & swamp
- Commons

0   0.5   1   2
                          Miles

N

FIGURE 6.3

Concord "First Division," circa 1652. About fifty house lots clustered around the meeting house and mill pond. Most plow land was grouped within several general fields, although a few detached parcels of upland were granted. Meadow lots flanked the brooks and rivers. There were a few small enclosed common pastures, while about three-quarters of the town was left open to provide common grazing and woods.

a man of middling means (figure 6.4). The GIS can display the distribution of land-holdings for any of the Concord proprietors. Hartwell's holdings were fairly typical. His First Division grants before 1653 are outlined in red. He owned a house lot in the village; dispersed tillage lots in the Great Field, the Brickiln Field, and the Chestnut Field; and even more widely dispersed mowing lots in the Great Meadow, Elm Brook Meadow, and Rocky Meadow. This wide scattering of small lots indicates these husbandmen were spreading their bets, as you would expect in a common field system. The remote Chestnut Field was located on such unworkable, rocky soil that it may have been devoted not to grain, but to chestnuts. A pollen core from a boggy spot within the field might determine whether this was a descendant of an ancient native nut orchard. The map also suggests the critical importance of meadows, from which the husbandmen mowed native hay—much more than they had mowed in mild old England, where livestock could graze most of the year. New England winters were long and hard, so hay production moved quickly to the center of New England farming. Low-lying meadows of native grasses would remain the principal source of hay, and thereby of manure for the corn fields, in most Massachusetts towns throughout the colonial period.

As Concord's second generation came of age in the 1650s and began looking for land of its own, the proprietors decided to divide most of the remaining commons among themselves. Several early towns did the same thing at about the same time, and most towns established after that point distributed land quickly to private owners, rather than holding and managing much of it as commons. Many towns made their divisions in large, regular blocks, but not Concord. Concord proprietors, like William Hartwell, mostly received their Second Divisions in irregular, dispersed pieces—often, but not always, as upland adjoining some of their far-flung meadow lots (figure 6.4). These divisions are shown in green on the Hartwell map. Again, mapping these lists of land grants dramatized this wide scattering and provided a few clues to explain it. Many of the smaller parcels look like minute subdivisions of key resources. For example, Hartwell received one in a range of a dozen small woodland lots running up a narrow valley toward Flint's Pond, and there were several similar clusters throughout the town. These were likely stands of particularly

FIGURE 6.4 ▶

William Hartwell First and Second Division grants, circa 1652–1670. The First Division grants made up Hartwell's working landholding. The Second Division divided the commons into private parcels that would provide homesteads for the coming generations.

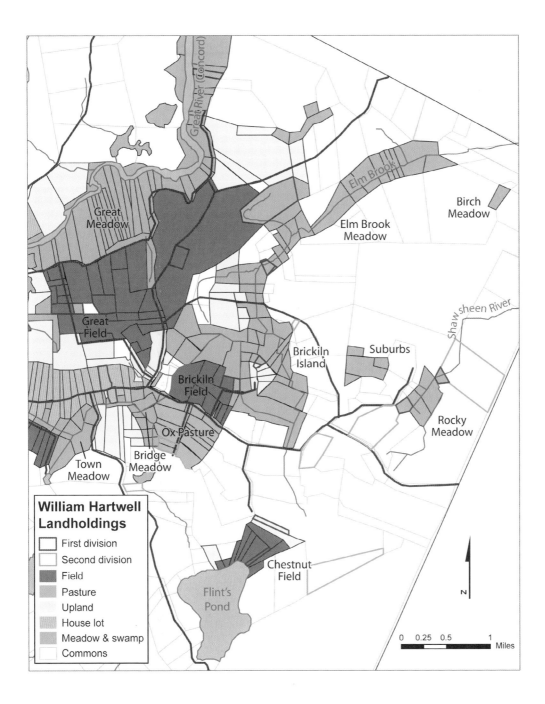

William Hartwell Landholdings

- First division
- Second division
- Field
- Pasture
- Upland
- House lot
- Meadow & swamp
- Commons

Great River (Concord)

Elm Brook

Great Meadow

Great Field

Brickiln Island

Brickiln Field

Ox-Pasture

Town Meadow

Bridge Meadow

Elm Brook Meadow

Birch Meadow

Shawsheen River

Suburbs

Rocky Meadow

Chestnut Field

Flint's Pond

0   0.25   0.5   1
Miles

N

attractive timber such as white oak, which was in high demand in New England for building frames, cooperage, and ship timbers; and white cedar, which resisted rot.[7]

Most Second Division grants, however, were intended less for immediate use and more as a land bank for future settlement. All but a few hundred acres of the town became private in this sweeping division. A few proprietors moved out to a large Second Division grant at once, but most stayed put. For most, these grants would serve as the nuclei of homesteads for sons and grandsons. Older sons moved to new lands, and sometimes to new towns, as they came of age and married. One son (typically the youngest) inherited the family homestead and the bulk of the old cluster of First Division holdings around the village, along with the duty of caring for his parents. The steady growth of New England towns (driven by a population that doubled every twenty-five years) was simultaneously expansive and highly conservative of its core community and family structure. There was no contradiction between these two seemingly opposing tendencies.[8]

To follow this orderly process of farm development across a highly diverse landscape through several generations, I mapped a two-mile stretch of country along the Bay Road, running from Meriam's Corner east to the old Cambridge town line (figure 6.5). In general, the second generation settled the second mile from the village; the third generation settled the third mile; and by the fourth generation Concord was full. But what did these farms look like, and how were they run? Determining this meant reconstructing the changing pattern of landownership and then getting inside landownership to discern land use. This generated a map of more than three centuries of land transactions covering about two thousand acres.

Assembling such a map was a straightforward task of running the title chain for each parcel from the current owner back to the First or Second Division land grants. The current owner for much of the study area is the National Park Service, because this is the Battle Road section of Minute Man National Historical Park. Knowing who owned what in 1775, and how it was used, helps in the interpretation of the April 19 battle and also in the stewardship of the park today, so the mapping had a practical as well as a scholarly purpose. In general, once the earliest land grants had been connected to modern town assessor's maps, information about all the ownerships in between could be firmly placed.

In New England, parcels tend to be irregular in shape and are described by metes and bounds. Reading a deed is like taking a walk. The boundary is traced around the perimeter by direction and distance (with great precision in some deeds, and almost none in others), and by neighboring owners upon whom it abuts. For example, "begin at the country road by a stake and stones, run northeast 17 rods

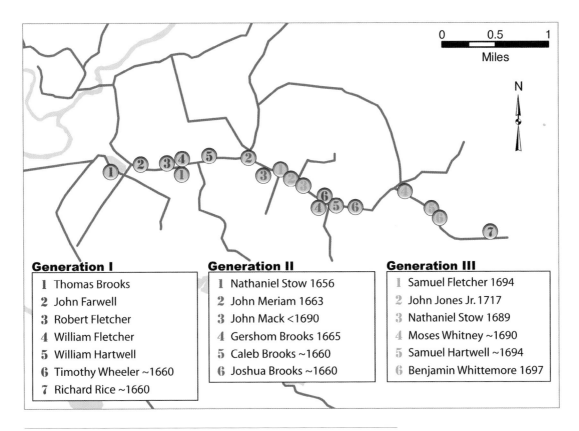

FIGURE 6.5

Concord East Quarter settlement along the Bay Road. The first generation stayed mostly within a mile of the meeting house, with a few exceptions. Members of the second generation moved out another mile but skipped past the Brickiln Field. The third generation settled the Brickiln Field and the third mile to the town bounds.

bounded southeast by Josiah Meriam to the corner of the stone wall, thence 36 rods northwest by several angles bounded northeast on the said Meriam and on land now or formerly of Thomas Brooks on the wall and on another wall to the white oak, marked,…" and so forth to the bounds first given. Before the twentieth century, it was rare to see a more exact survey with compass bearings, let alone a plot plan. At the Registry of Deeds and Probate, I abstracted deeds and filed them into notebooks according to landowner—one copy for the grantor, one for the grantee. This provided the raw material for mapping and analysis. Most chains contained fuzzy boundaries and a few gaps where ownership was uncertain. I noted these uncertainties in the database and continued mapping by approximations.

Doing similar work in Kansas was simple by comparison, partly because that state was not settled by whites until about 1860, and because land was surveyed and sold according to the rectangular public land survey system. One could map a whole prairie county in a few months and be accurate to within a single blade of bluestem.

The object of the Concord research was to construct a map of landownership in three dimensions: two dimensions for the surface of the earth, and the third dimension for the passage of time. The finished map was like a solid brick, made up of many small adjoining and interlocking blocks. Each block represented a single ownership. Building such a map meant focusing on one small chunk of countryside at a time—a half dozen or so neighboring parcels—until its history of ownership through centuries was grasped, then drawing stacks of overlapping polygons. Each record in the database included the owner, the date at which the parcel was acquired (and from whom), and the date at which it was sold or passed by inheritance (and to whom). If an owner sold part of a parcel, I drew two polygons with a new start date: one enclosing the land purchased by the new owner and the other enclosing the residue retained by the old owner. When one stack was finished, the next piece of ground could be mapped. The result was a perfectly filled brick made up of blocks of varying shape and thickness, each abutting precisely and interlocking with its neighbors on every side, above, and below.

Anyone looking at the completed layer on the flat screen cannot see its temporal thickness, only a flattened mish-mash of all property boundaries at all times—looking down through the brick, if you will. The same little piece of Concord was often divided, reconsolidated, and redivided in many ways over twelve generations. To follow how landownership developed, slice the brick at each generation and display the slices side by side. Two clusters of homesteads along the Bay Road are shown in figure 6.6.

FIGURE 6.6 ▶

Landownership patterns in Concord. At Meriam's Corner, a kin neighborhood of fragmented, intermixed landholdings developed from generation two through generation four, and then stabilized. The Brickiln Field was maintained as a general tillage field through the second generation and then developed into a neighborhood of four intermixed family landholdings.

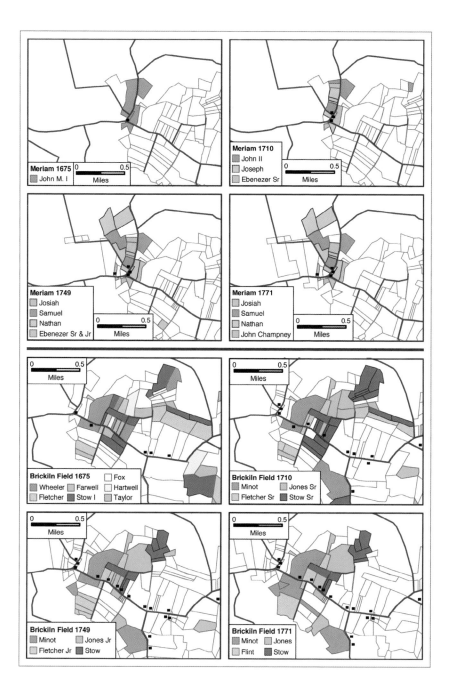

Meriam 1675
John M. I
0   0.5
Miles

Meriam 1710
John II
Joseph
Ebenezer Sr
0   0.5
Miles

Meriam 1749
Josiah
Samuel
Nathan
Ebenezer Sr & Jr
0   0.5
Miles

Meriam 1771
Josiah
Samuel
Nathan
John Champney
0   0.5
Miles

0   0.5
Miles
Brickiln Field 1675
Wheeler   Farwell   Fox
Fletcher   Stow I   Hartwell
Taylor

0   0.5
Miles
Brickiln Field 1710
Minot   Jones Sr
Fletcher Sr   Stow Sr

0   0.5
Miles
Brickiln Field 1749
Minot   Jones Jr
Fletcher Jr   Stow

0   0.5
Miles
Brickiln Field 1771
Minot   Jones
Flint   Stow

John Meriam of the second generation settled at what became Meriam's Corner about 1664, and his holdings are shown in 1675. In the third generation, the homelands were divided among John's three sons, Ebenezer, Samuel, and Joseph. Their tightly clustered houses and intermixed home fields and meadows are shown in 1710. By the fourth generation in 1749, these homelands had been augmented by the purchase of more land, but now they were divided among four Meriam households: three sons of Joseph, and the joint holding of old Ebenezer and his son. There was no further fragmentation during the colonial period, as the 1771 map demonstrates. In fact, if the series were continued, we would see the trend of subdivision to accommodate more family members reversing to one of consolidation and loss of family continuity during the early Republic.

A similar story, but with its own twists and turns, unfolded half a mile east of Meriam's Corner at the Brickiln Field. Here, a general tillage field was maintained through the second generation, with the owners living a mile away in the village. Consolidation into three homesteads did not start until the third generation, between 1690 and 1720. Consolidation was never completed, however, and a pattern of intermixed holdings among these neighbors crystallized and persisted throughout the colonial period well into the nineteenth century. This cluster of farms didn't start out as a kin neighborhood but did become one as the Stow and Jones families intermarried. Moving farther east another half mile, the Brooks neighborhood showed a pattern of intricate family subdivision similar to the Meriams but on a larger scale (figure 6.7). Farther east again, on the uplands near the Cambridge bounds, larger, more consolidated farms were assembled by the third and fourth generations of the Hartwell family referred to earlier. It may be that those with a preference for such holdings were drawn to the town's periphery, where there was more room to assemble consolidated farms.

Returning to the pattern of intermingling found at Meriam's Corner in figure 6.6, GIS mapping makes vivid a process of land settlement and inheritance that might otherwise be only vaguely sensed. These family members deliberately chose to cluster their houses and scramble their land. Implications of social and economic priorities call to us across the centuries. The closeness of the households was doubtless a comfort and convenience to women in their cooperative labor exchange and

---

FIGURE 6.7   ▶

More Concord landownership patterns. Development of the Brooks family cluster was quite similar to the Meriams, though on a larger scale. On the uplands to the east, settled by Samuel Hartwell and Benjamin Whittemore of the third generation, a pattern of larger, more consolidated farms prevailed.

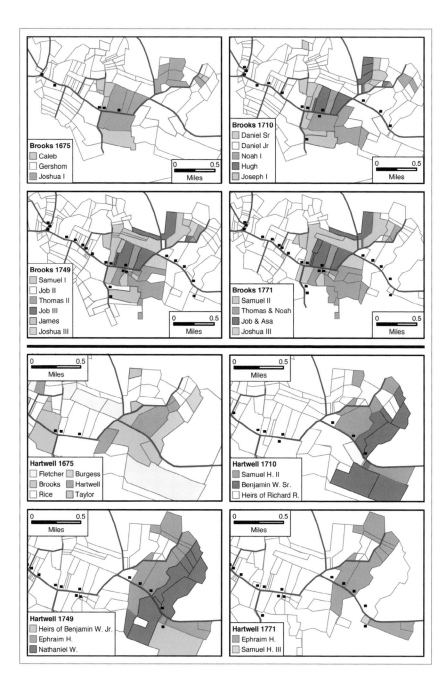

Brooks 1675
- Caleb
- Gershom
- Joshua I

0   0.5
Miles

Brooks 1710
- Daniel Sr
- Daniel Jr
- Noah I
- Hugh
- Joseph I

0   0.5
Miles

Brooks 1749
- Samuel I
- Job II
- Thomas II
- Job III
- James
- Joshua III

0   0.5
Miles

Brooks 1771
- Samuel II
- Thomas & Noah
- Job & Asa
- Joshua III

0   0.5
Miles

0   0.5
Miles

Hartwell 1675
- Fletcher
- Burgess
- Brooks
- Hartwell
- Rice
- Taylor

0   0.5
Miles

Hartwell 1710
- Samuel H. II
- Benjamin W. Sr.
- Heirs of Richard R.

0   0.5
Miles

Hartwell 1749
- Heirs of Benjamin W. Jr.
- Ephraim H.
- Nathaniel W.

0   0.5
Miles

Hartwell 1771
- Ephraim H.
- Samuel H. III

support networks: gardening, spinning and weaving, birthing and caring for children, visiting. Perhaps there are ways to get at that female realm from the data available for these families—deeds, probated estates, and tax valuations—and to add a map layer that interlocks with the male world of husbandry.

These mixed-up homelands were not all the land the Meriams owned and farmed. The organization of their system of husbandry is suggested by a map of the complete landholdings of the three Meriam brothers at the height of their careers about 1735, shown in figure 6.8. Because most of these parcels fell outside the area of detailed property mapping, they were placed approximately in the surrounding countryside and represented with symbols. Here we see the working landscape of these men: nearly forty parcels averaging only five acres in size, scattered over three miles of country! Like most of their neighbors, the Meriams also owned backcountry pastures for their beef cattle in younger towns to the west—lands that

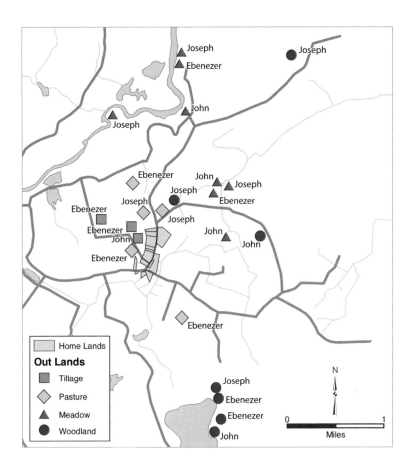

FIGURE 6.8

Meriam land holdings, 1735. Between them, the three Meriam brothers owned some three dozen small parcels of land scattered over three miles of countryside. This was their working landscape.

were eventually settled by several of their sons and grandsons and their wives—often the daughters of Concord neighbors. The same pattern was repeated and intensified in the next generation. The Meriams lived near the village, so their holdings were perhaps more dispersed than many of those on the outskirts of town. But almost all Concord farmers were willing to travel several miles to their hay meadows and wood lots well into the nineteenth century. The Meriams almost certainly worked these entangled holdings cooperatively, and they were blacksmiths and locksmiths besides—they joined a family trade with their husbandry. They were not wealthy, but they were solid and comfortable. We are not looking at a partible inheritance fragmentation debacle like pre-famine Ireland but at a deliberately embraced way of life. After four generations, the system may have been reaching its limits, but it worked.

This pattern of intentionally scattered landholdings can only make us wonder what lay behind it. How did it function as a working landscape? Understanding this evolving system of husbandry, the challenges it overcame and the limits it encountered, required mapping that could reach inside the boundaries of landownership to the patterns of land use. This was taking a plunge, but at least there were clues about where to jump. Colonial tax valuations, deeds, and probated estates employed a consistent terminology for the elements of husbandry found in Massachusetts: tillage (or plow land), orchard, pasture, meadow, English mowing, woodland, and (the wild card) "unimproved." Mapping these elements across a representative swath of Concord's topography and soils might provide a clearer picture of how husbandry was organized.

Ideally, such a map would have covered three miles, from the river meadows at the town's center to the woodlands at the border—the two poles that the Meriams visited at different seasons. Many other Concord farmers owned land across a similar wide arc. Even village men who planted their corn in the Great Field often cut their fuel in Walden Woods, while many farmers who lived on the far edge of town still cut part of their hay on the Great Meadow alongside distant village cousins—the inheritors of adjoining portions of a single First Division meadow grant, perhaps. That map is still under construction. This study employs a land-use map for the two thousand acres of the Minute Man study area in 1749, the date of the province's first comprehensive tax valuation listing each farmer's land holdings, livestock, and crop production (figure 6.9). By comparing land-use information supplied by deeds and probated estates with the information recorded in the tax valuation, I could take an educated guess at the use of every parcel on the landowners' map and subdivide parcels in a plausible manner. If a man returned ten acres of tillage on the 1749 valuation, for example, and his probated estate a few years later indicated that he had a six-acre "home field," I might draw four additional acres of tillage within an eight-acre parcel described as "pasturage and plowland" in a deed. This map starts with core parcels backed by strong evidence and builds the pattern out to a complete picture of the entire landscape that is at least *consistent* with all the available evidence. It is not simply a visual display of data—it combines evidence and argument like a piece of historical writing.

Houses

1749 Land Use

Tillage
Pasture
Orchard
Meadow
Farm yard
Woodland
English Mowing

0   0.25   0.5
Miles

This merging of hard and soft information on a single map layer is invisible to the reader who cannot look behind the layer at the supporting database. That database includes a "Notes" column explaining the land-use designation of each polygon, but this can't easily be displayed in standard print publications. You don't know, looking at the map, whether that is definitely where the farmer put the orchard or just where the author put it. When maps mix evidence and interpretation in this way, it is important to warn map readers what is going on and to make the underlying data available to the scrutiny of other scholars. The plan is to post all of these maps and data on a Web site for this purpose. In the meantime, makers of historical maps, like all scholars, have a responsibility to extrapolate cautiously from incomplete data and to understate their conclusions. The map shown in figure 6.9, if anything, oversimplifies the agricultural landscape of Concord. The arrangement of fields, pastures, meadows, and wood lots becomes even more intricately molded to minute differences in soil and topography where information about a farm is complete and certain, such as from an exceptionally detailed estate inventory or survey.

With that caveat, figure 6.9 presents colonial agroecology as it was practiced in Concord after four generations. A few features stand out. One is the concentration of prime tillage lands, the "home fields," on light sandy soils surrounding each cluster of houses. Homesteads were consistently located adjacent to these ideal tillage soils, probably for convenience in carting manure from the barnyard. Many of these plow lands remained in production for generations. Manure was essential to the practice of husbandry in Concord. Another feature is the placement of many of the orchards on rocky slopes of glacial till—excellent soils for apples because they hold water but are too bony to plow. Another is the survival of so much woodland in a crowded agrarian landscape. There were even more woods farther away from the road and off the map, generally on the most marginal land for farming. Above (or beneath) all, on display here is the comprehensive improvement of meadows to produce the all-important hay. Every wetland was carefully ditched and drained. This map depicts a remarkably well-adapted, stable form of husbandry—a far cry from the wasteful, improvident neglect of cultivation of which these farmers have long been accused.[9]

◄ **FIGURE 6.9**

East Quarter Land Use in 1749. Homesteads were clustered near patches of tillable land except on the more dispersed eastern uplands. Orchards were strung along the roads, and small meadow lots flanked every brook. Pastures were spread throughout the landscape, and woodlots were found mostly on rocky hills and in remote swamps.

GIS proved particularly useful in reconstructing the complex pattern of meadow drainage, which involved a thorough reworking of the flow of brooks through the landscape as shown in figure 6.10. Farmers improved the meadows and made them accessible for mowing and carting hay by channeling brooks, and by cutting narrow lateral drains with a tool called a ditching knife. When ditches were periodically cleaned, the muck was dried and spread on the cornfields or mixed with dung (itself ultimately derived mainly from meadow hay) in the barnyards to form manure. The meadows supplied the bulk of nutrients that drove the entire system of husbandry in Concord. They required careful planning and painstaking management.

Figure 6.10 illustrates the lengths to which these husbandmen would go to improve their meadows. In 1695, the four Brooks brothers, Daniel, Joseph, Job, and Noah, diverted the flow of Elm Brook west through their meadows into Mill Brook to get better drainage. In 1715, Nathaniel Stow diverted Elm Brook west at a second point, north of Brickiln Island, through a ditch later maintained by his son Joseph. The object was not only to improve drainage, but also to deliberately flood and fertilize downstream meadows along the Mill Brook, such as one called the Dam Meadow, during the winter. Stow's diversion did not sit well with meadow owners farther down Elm Brook, who were cut off. They diverted the water back to the north, precipitating court battles in the 1760s and again in the 1790s. This protracted struggle over a piddling flow of water illuminates the importance of the meadows and of GIS mapping. The full meaning of the information recorded in a handful of deeds and legal depositions would have remained obscure without the map to make sense of the locations and relationships of these contested meadow lots and ditches.

Much the same claim can be made concerning our understanding of colonial New England husbandry in general. What mapping uncovered in Concord looked very different from the widely accepted picture of an unstable world of careless husbandry. Here were cornfields plowed for generations without being worn out, woodlands that survived despite intense pressure to clear more farmland, and hay meadows that were carefully maintained. This was a town where the destiny of every drop of water and plop of dung seemed to be arranged before it fell. It is true that Concord was an early town with a common field origin and a large expanse of river meadows, yet a glance at tax valuations from other towns in Massachusetts suggests that the fundamental agroecological organization of mixed husbandry was similar. Even many hill towns, incorporated late in the colonial period, relied heavily on meadow hay until well into the nineteenth century. It will be interesting to see what can be discovered about how such towns were settled and farmed. These maps offer a new way of looking at colonial farming, working from the basic documents of husbandmen themselves—

their deeds, wills, and tax returns. The picture that emerges calls into question the jaundiced comments of outside observers and recollections of nineteenth-century improvers, whose vision of agricultural progress began by denouncing yeoman husbandry. It is a world that would have remained hidden without GIS.

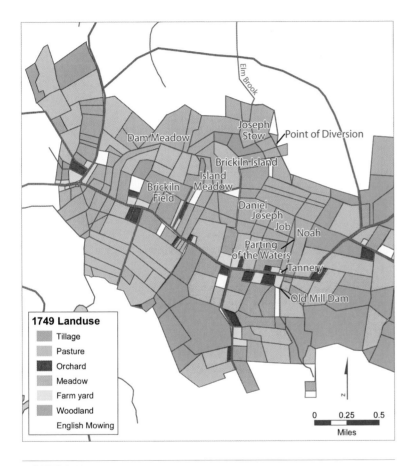

FIGURE 6.10

Elm Brook drainage, showing the "parting of the waters" where the four Brooks brothers turned Elm Brook west into Island Meadow and the Mill Brook in 1695, and the contested point where Nathaniel and Joseph Stow diverted it west again into the Dam Meadow.

CONCLUSION

This leads to some concluding thoughts about future directions for GIS research into land-use history at the local level. The research continues in Concord, and perhaps others will take it up elsewhere, so that these findings can be tested. Despite the labor required, it would be great to see these parcel-mapping techniques used in conjunction with field investigations, including pollen cores, soil studies, and vegetation surveys such as those pioneered by historical ecologists at Harvard Forest in western Massachusetts.

Across the country, communities, land trusts, conservation organizations, and state agencies are working to protect and care for land and the historic buildings upon it. Based on experience, historical GIS mapping can be of great service to these efforts. In addition to scholarly interest, the work described in this essay was done so that the Park Service could lay out an interpretive trail and take better care of land in Minute Man National Historical Park. Campaigns to protect other pieces of land in Concord, and elsewhere, have made use of historical GIS to raise awareness. Harvard Forest has done similar work to inform conservation land management throughout the state of Massachusetts. This research provides insight into past ecological changes that can help guide current stewardship. It also connects people to the land around them in compelling ways by revealing the story of the land and the people who have lived on it. Widespread historical GIS mapping might be undertaken not only by lone academics but by scholars working with broader communities in the preservation and stewardship of cultural landscapes.

For me, scholarship and stewardship have always been intimately connected. The historical questions that most interest me are to what degree a culture's relationship with the environment was sustainable and to what degree it was ecologically degrading and how and why that changed over time. GIS mapping has helped make a case that colonial farming in New England was more environmentally sound than is generally supposed. Continued research and mapping may demonstrate a dramatic rise in ecological degradation caused by the expansion of fully commercial farming in the nineteenth century as the rate and scale of deforestation, pasture depletion, and nutrient extraction in Concord exceeded sustainable bounds. The question of sustainability remains a central concern in the stewardship of the same land today. Historical insight is an important part of contemporary conservation.[10]

Historical ecologists aim for a practical understanding of how the sequence of past events influenced New England ecosystems. How is the structure and composition of forests we see today a product of their history, what is their ecological trajectory, and what should we do to protect biological diversity and ecosystem health into the future? For all that scholars and government agencies may devote themselves to these questions, the bulk of land protection and stewardship in New England is being done by local conservation groups. Given this context, the wide application of historical GIS mapping can serve as a useful tool to help guide and inspire grassroots conservation efforts. We need a unifying vision of the ecological character of the land we are striving to protect and of how it has emerged from our history. GIS mapping can help build a complex, productive engagement between people and the places they inhabit. It can pull together the layers of environmental history to inform how we care for our land today.

ACKNOWLEDGMENTS

Brian Donahue wishes to acknowledge the work of Carl Koteff, Arthur Nelson, and Wallace Hansen, whose U.S. Geological Survey quadrangles provided the original base for the map of surficial geology. The maps of landownership and land use in chapter 6 were originally drawn from manuscript records at the Concord Free Public Library and the Middlesex County Registry of Deeds and Probate. Donahue created the maps in this chapter with the able assistance of Michael Law at ESRI; however, the author would also like to thank Yale University Press, which published earlier versions of the maps in *The Great Meadow.*

NOTES

1. Harry J. Carman, ed., *American Husbandry* (New York: Columbia University Press, 1939); Timothy Dwight, *Travels in New England and New York,* Vol. 1 (Cambridge, Mass.: Harvard University Press, 1969), 76; Percy W. Bidwell, "The Agricultural Revolution in New England," *American Historical Review* 26 (1921); William Cronon, *Changes in the Land: Indians, Colonists, and the Ecology of New England* (New York: Hill and Wang, 1983); Carolyn Merchant, *Ecological Revolutions: Nature, Gender and Science in New England* (Chapel Hill: University of North Carolina Press, 1989); Robert Gross, *The Minutemen and Their World* (New York: Hill and Wang, 1976).

2. Brian Donahue, *The Great Meadow: Farmers and the Land in Colonial Concord* (New Haven, Conn.: Yale University Press, 2004).

3. Carl Koteff, *Surficial Geology of the Concord Quadrangle, Massachusetts* (Washington, D.C.: USGS Map GQ-331, 1964); Arthur E. Nelson, *Surficial Geologic Map of the Natick Quadrangle, Middlesex and Norfolk Counties, Massachusetts* (Washington, D.C.: USGS Map GQ-1151, 1974); Wallace R. Hansen, *Geology and Mineral Resources of the Hudson and Maynard Quadrangles Massachusetts* (Washington, D.C.: USGS Geological Survey Bulletin 1038, 1956). For a Concord-farmer's-eye view of these soils, see William Jones, "A Topographical Description of the Town of Concord, August 20th, 1792," *Collections of the Massachusetts Historical Society, 1792, vol. 1,* 237.

4. "Soils and Their Interpretation for Various Land Uses, Town of Concord, Massachusetts," (Soil Conservation Service, USDA, 1966).

5. Shirley Blancke, "Survey of Pre-Contact Sites and Collections in Concord," report for Massachusetts Historical Commission Survey and Planning Project, 1980; Gordon G. Whitney and William C. Davis, "Thoreau and the Forest History of Concord, Massachusetts," *Forest History* 30 (1986); Peter A. Thomas, "Contrasting Subsistence Strategies and Land Use as Factors for Understanding Indian-White Relations in New England," *Ethnohistory* 23 (1976), 1-18; Dean R. Snow, *The Archaeology of New England* (New York: Academic Press, 1980), 101-56; William A. Patterson and Kenneth E. Sassaman, "Indian Fires in the Prehistory of New England," in *Holocene Human Ecology in Northeastern North America,* ed. George P. Nicholas (New York: Plenum Press, 1988); Kathleen J. Bragdon, *Native People of Southern New England, 1500-1650* (Norman, Okla.: University of Oklahoma Press, 1996), 38, 88–97. For a similar approach to reconstructing a patchy mosaic of native land

use zones, see Julia E. Hammett, "Ethnohistory of Aboriginal Landscapes in the Southeastern United States," in *Biodiversity and Native America,* ed. Paul E. Minnis and Wayne J. Elisens (Norman: University of Oklahoma Press, 2000), 249-93.

6. See, for example, Diana Muir, *Reflections in Bullough's Pond: Economy and Ecosystem in New England* (Hanover, N.H.: University Press of New England, 2000), 4-23; or Charles Mann, *1491: New Revelations of the Americas before Columbus* (New York: Alfred A. Knopf, 2005), 36-61, 312-23.

7. Classic works on generational dispersion of early New England towns include Sumner Chilton Powell, *Puritan Village: The Formation of a New England Town* (Middletown, Conn.: Wesleyan University Press, 1963); Philip J. Greven, *Four Generations: Population, Land, and Family in Colonial Andover, Massachusetts* (Ithaca, N.Y.: Cornell University Press, 1970); Richard Bushman, *From Puritan to Yankee: Character and the Social Order in Connecticut, 1690-1765* (New York: W.W. Norton, 1967).

8. Similar conclusions have been reached by David Jaffee, *People of the Wachusett: Greater New England in History and Memory, 1630-1860* (Ithaca, N.Y.: Cornell University Press, 1999); and Joseph S. Wood, *The New England Village* (Baltimore: Johns Hopkins Press, 1997).

9. Seeing the relationship between land use and soil types requires consulting the underlying soil or surficial geology layers. This is easy to do in GIS, but very hard to *display* because the resulting maps are so busy.

10. For a similar argument, see David R. Foster, "Thoreau's Country: A Historical-Ecological Perspective on Conservation in the New England Landscape," *Journal of Biogeography* 29 (2002), 1537-56.

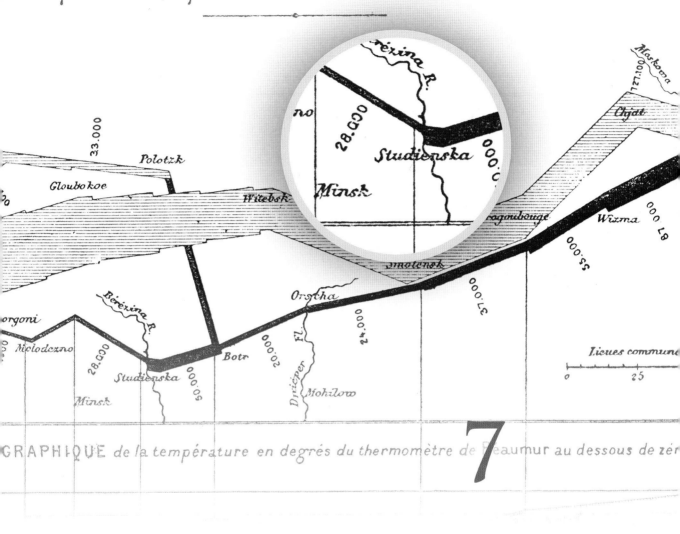

7

COMBINING SPACE AND TIME: NEW POTENTIAL FOR TEMPORAL GIS

Michael F. Goodchild

INTRODUCTION: THE MAP METAPHOR

Humans have always needed to share information about their surroundings, whether as members of a band of hunter-gatherers or as European traders exploiting new routes to the Orient. From the earliest times, the preferred method of representing geographic information was the analog model, in which the true dimensions of the earth's surface were scaled or proportioned so they could be fitted on an easily handled sheet of paper or onto a globe. By the nineteenth century, the technology of gathering, collating, interpreting, and printing maps had developed to a fine art, and detailed maps of much of the earth's land surface were readily available from national mapping agencies and commercial firms.

Despite their elegance and efficiency, paper maps have always suffered from fundamental inadequacies as media for storing what is known about the surface of the earth. Most obviously, they require that the earth be flattened, a trivial requirement in the case of local areas but increasingly problematic when maps must cover large proportions of the earth's surface. The earth is not flat, and in principle no flat map can ever show aspects of the earth's surface in constant proportion, so over the years humans have become used to the inherent distortions of the paper sheets of atlases. Maps are also expensive to create and only become financially viable when they can be produced and used in large numbers; as a result, maps tend to show those features of the earth's surface that are of the widest interest, such as coastlines, roads, and topography. For the same reason, they must also be valid for as long as possible, so maps tend to emphasize features that are fixed and constant, a point that is particularly relevant to this chapter. As two-dimensional models, maps cannot show information that is truly three-dimensional, such as the configuration of an underground mine or cave system. Finally, the devices used to make measurements of distance or area from maps—rulers, dividers, planimeters—are inherently imprecise and tedious to use.[1]

The widespread adoption of digital technology has revolutionized the process of sharing geographic information during the past four decades. Instead of an analog model, in which the features of the earth's surface were (imperfectly) proportioned, a digital computer stores information in coded form, allowing it to be copied, manipulated, transmitted, and edited at electronic speed. But the earliest computers were designed to solve problems in numerical analysis and cryptography. It was not obvious that one could store the contents of a map in a computer, or that doing so would have any valid purpose.

In the mid-1960s, a number of visionaries working under contract with the Canadian government created what became known as the Canada Geographic

Information System (CGIS).[2] The primary driver for this project was the Canada Land Inventory, a major effort to assess the actual and potential uses of land in a portion of the Canadian landmass extending north from the U.S. border. Because measures of area were essential and could be derived from maps only by a tedious manual process, groundbreaking processes were devised for converting the content of maps to digital form, calculating area, and reporting the results. While maps were the primary input, there was no intention in the original design to produce them as output, in part because computer-driven plotting devices had not yet been invented.

Over time, the vision of a geographic information system (GIS) evolved and grew, based primarily on the notion of a GIS as a computerized mapping system—a container of maps. A number of methods were devised for creating efficient and economical representations of the contents of maps in digital form. The concept that geographic reality could be separated into a number of distinctly different themes, or layers, represented a natural extension of the practice of printing color maps from different plates using distinct inks. This concept became one of the icons of GIS. By the late 1990s, geographic information systems were capable of capturing the important information from maps and performing virtually any conceivable operation on the results, including display, measurement, and advanced forms of analysis and modeling.

However, the map metaphor continued to dominate thinking. Various methods used to represent geographic data in GIS essentially began with the contents of maps. The raster option is analogous to the methods used to create digital images: a map is captured as a rectangular grid of cells and stored as an ordered sequence, typically row by row from the top left. The vector option first identifies all of the features on the map, classifies them as points, lines, or areas, and creates a digital representation using coordinates. Each point is captured as a single set of coordinates (normally two, but possibly three in some applications that involve elevation); each line is captured as a *polyline,* an ordered sequence of points assumed to be connected by straight segments; and each area is captured as a *polygon,* with a similar ordered sequence of points that returns to the first point to close the area. Not surprisingly, a GIS was explained as a digital map container. It inherited many of the conventions and practices of cartography, including the concept of scale or representative fraction. Like mapmakers, GIS designers continued to struggle with concepts that were problematic for maps, including time and the third dimension.

One of the unfortunate consequences of this heritage concerns uncertainty. No map can perfectly replicate the real world, since it inevitably generalizes, abstracts, and approximates the complexity of reality. Thus a GIS database created from maps similarly leaves its user uncertain about the real world that the databases supposedly represent. While paper maps are obviously approximate, there is an unfortunate tendency to believe that because a computer works to seven or even fourteen significant digits, its outputs must be as accurate as its precision would suggest. GIS designers have tended to encourage rather than dispel this misconception by largely ignoring the basic scientific principle that results should be reported to a precision that matches their inherent accuracy rather than the internal precision of any calculations. Moreover, cartographers generally lack methods for displaying the uncertainty associated with maps. GIS tends to have inherited this legacy.[3]

MAINSTREAM CONCEPTS: OBJECT ORIENTATION

As a concept, information is notoriously difficult to define. In practice, information takes an enormous variety of forms, from printed text to spoken instructions to the equations of mathematics. Nevertheless, any information processing system must make assumptions about the nature of information, and a GIS is no exception. As we have seen, early GIS assumed that the information to be captured and stored in its database would be contained in maps. Early GIS had problems capturing anything that could not be represented using the paper and pen of the cartographer.

Since the 1960s, the computing industry has developed and produced a number of types of *database management systems.* Each system has attempted to provide a general solution to the task of storing data and has similarly made assumptions about the nature of data. By the 1970s, the *relational* database management system had become dominant.[4] Its basic assumption is that all information can be expressed in the form of tables, with common keys providing the links between tables. This model proved ideal for a wide range of applications, from airline reservations to banking, and the database management industry flourished accordingly. Moreover, several visionaries in the GIS industry recognized that this model could be usefully applied to the contents of maps. Figures 7.1A, B, and C show three maps, one of county boundaries, one of city streets, and one of soil classes. In each case, the map can be regarded as a collection of *nodes* (the points where lines come together or end), *arcs* (the lines connecting nodes and separating areas), and *faces* (the areas bounded by the arcs).

Moreover, each arc is connected to two nodes, and each arc bounds two faces (the two faces will be the same for arcs representing dead ends in a street network, and one node will have no connections to other arcs). So these maps could be represented by three tables—of nodes, arcs, and faces. The common keys of the relational model could keep track of the relationships between the elements.

FIGURES 7.1A, B, and C

Three types of data readily accommodated in early hybrid GIS databases: (A) a county boundary map, (B) a street map, and (C) a soil map.

ESRI Data & Maps 2006. State and County layers courtesy of ArcUSA, U. S. Census, and ESRI; Major Roads layer courtesy of TeleAtlas; Interstate Highways and Railroad layers courtesy of U. S. Bureau of Transportation Statistics. All other data courtesy of ESRI.

One problem remained, however, in applying the relational model to map content. The arcs that connect nodes are generally curved and must be represented as polylines with multiple segments. But the number of segments per arc varies, whereas the tabular structure of the relational model requires a constant number of entries per row. If polylines were stored in a table, the number of columns would have to be sufficient to accommodate the polyline with the largest number of segments, and a large proportion of the table would be empty. Instead, GIS designers adopted what became known as the *hybrid* approach, in which polylines and their coordinates were stored outside the relational model. While awkward, this solution survived in the leading GIS products from 1980, when the relational model was first introduced, well into the 1990s. It meant that only part of the database could be stored in relational tables and required GIS developers to maintain in effect two databases, one for the tabular information on arcs, nodes, and faces, and one for polylines and their coordinates.

The solution preserved the map metaphor. Just as certain types of information could not be displayed on maps, so the same types of information were problematic for GIS. Many authors have commented on the inability of 1990s GIS to store information on change through time,[5] information about three-dimensional structures,[6] and information about hierarchical relationships in geographic information.

This situation changed dramatically in the late 1990s after a new data model emerged to address many of the deficiencies of the relational approach. The *object-oriented* model begins with the assumption that any application is based on well-defined objects that can be organized into classes—everything in the world is an instance of a class. Thus geography consists of mountains, cities, buildings, trees, and so forth. Each class has certain attributes: mountains have heights, names, and locations; trees have heights, girths, and ages. In the object-oriented model, classes are organized into hierarchies through the concept of *inheritance.* For example, the class *male human* could be represented as a specialization of the more general class *human;* every male human has all of the attributes associated with humans, plus specific attributes associated only with male humans. *Human* could be represented as a specialization of the class *primate,* which could itself be a specialization of the class *mammal,* and so forth.

This concept of inheritance turns out to be very useful in the design of GIS databases. A county, for example, could be modeled as a specialization of the more general class *administrative unit,* which could in turn inherit all of the general properties of the class *polygon,* one of the fundamental concepts of any GIS and one defined and made operational by the GIS designer. An object-oriented design for a GIS database

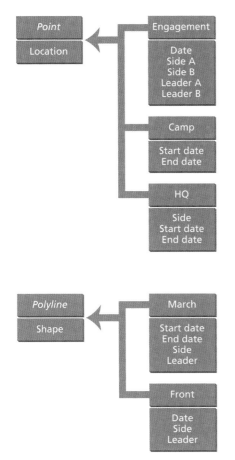

FIGURE 7.2

A simple design for a database representing military campaigns, showing the concept of specialization. The point and polyline classes are shown in italics, indicating that they are provided by the GIS and will have no instances of their own in this application. The design could be simplified further by identification of Side and Leader classes associated with Front, March, Camp, and Engagement classes. Since these classes would not have locations, they would have no inheritance from the GIS classes.

thus resembles a tree. At the top are the classes defined by the GIS designer and valid for all applications: the polygons, polylines, points, and other classes for which the designer has implemented various procedures for capturing, editing, displaying, storing, and analyzing each respective data type. Below in the tree are increasingly specialized classes relevant to the application. For example, figure 7.2 shows a design that might be appropriate for a GIS application in military history. Points are specialized to *engagement, camp, headquarters,* and polylines are specialized to *march* and *front*. In addition, polygons could be specialized to *country* and *terrain type*, though these are not shown in the figure.

The object-oriented model represents a substantial advance on earlier thinking. In addition, the two decades that had elapsed since the development of the earlier hybrid approach based on the relational model had seen massive improvement in processing speed and the costs of data storage. Developers of database management systems had vastly improved the flexibility of their products, particularly what could be stored in the cells of tables. While earlier versions had allowed only single numbers or fixed-length strings of characters to be stored, by the late 1990s it had become possible to store a wide range of information types, including images and variable-length strings. Today, it is straightforward to store an entire polyline or polygon in a cell, obviating the need for the separate storage system of the hybrid approach.

The earlier model had stored the relationships between the arcs, nodes, and faces of figure 7.1, in part to enable faster access to such properties as adjacency and connectivity. With the increased computing power of the late 1990s, however, it became easy to compute such properties as and when needed. These *topological* properties could now be omitted from databases, leading to much simpler designs. The county boundary map shown in figure 7.1A, for example, could be represented simply as a single class of polygons, with each polygon's coordinates stored as a single attribute termed *shape,* rather than the much more cumbersome hybrid approach of three tables (nodes, arcs, and faces) and a separate database of polyline coordinates.

All of these advances succeeded in moving substantially away from the map metaphor, allowing GIS databases to store things that were fundamentally not mappable. Classes could be time-dependent, with attributes and locations that changed through time. Areas could overlap, and lines could cross without forming nodes. The only requirement was that the geographic world be conceived as populated by discrete, identifiable, and countable objects in an otherwise empty space. This *discrete-object* model coincides substantially with the way humans think about the geographic world, but it conflicts fundamentally with the approach often taken in science, in which the world is characterized by continuously varying *fields* of such properties as elevation, population density, or rainfall. Moreover, concepts of continuous variation may be the only way of dealing with uncertainty about the locations of objects or events, or about the locations of object boundaries, whether they are definite or indeterminate.[7] The GIS community is still struggling with how to achieve efficient representation of such continuous phenomena within the object-oriented approach that now dominates the industry.

Two more concepts of the object-oriented approach have particular value in GIS. Besides the generalization and specialization associated with inheritance, the object-oriented model allows classes to be related hierarchically through *aggregation* relationships, in which the instances of one class are aggregations of two or more component classes. Such hierarchical relationships are impossible in the relational model but are commonly found in geographic reality. For example, a military *campaign* might be modeled as an aggregation of the classes *engagement, troop movement, camp,* etc. A geographic region might be modeled as an aggregation of its components *city, village, road,* etc. These relationships allow the properties of aggregates to be related to the properties of the components through simple rules such as addition, counting, or averaging.

Second, the object-oriented approach recognizes *associations* between classes, much as the relational model supported the notion of common keys. These might be used to represent associations between cities and the nations that contain them, or between lakes and the rivers that flow into them, or between roads and the intersections where they join. But the object-oriented approach goes one step further than the relational model in this area. In addition to recording the existence of relationships between objects, it is possible to create *association classes* and to use them to give attributes to relationships. Thus, two cities might be linked with data on the historic flow of migrants between them, or the number of newspaper stories that originated in one city and were published in the other, or the time taken to travel between them in historic periods.

Figure 7.3 shows the full set of these relationships and the symbols commonly used to represent them in graphic depictions of object-oriented database designs. The examples later in this chapter illustrate each of these types of relationships.

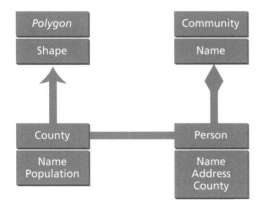

FIGURE 7.3

The graphic symbols used to depict inheritance, aggregation, and association relationships between classes in UML. Each county is a kind of polygon, each person lives in a county, and each community is an aggregation of people.

In summary, the object-oriented model provides a much more flexible and general approach to the representation of geographic information, which is much less limited than its predecessors by the map metaphor. In this new approach, it is easy to represent time-specific events, objects that move or change properties through time, and other aspects of geography that were similarly difficult to represent on maps. A single database has replaced the cumbersome hybrid design. Numerous tools are now available to assist in the design process, including computer-assisted software engineering (CASE) tools. It is common to create designs for databases using the standard conventions of Unified Modeling Language (UML)[8] and graphics packages such as Microsoft Visio. Modern GIS includes tools to bring such designs into the GIS and to create the necessary tables and relationships automatically, so that they are ready to accept data.[9] Object-oriented designs allow for inheritance, aggregation, and association classes, none of which was supported by previous data models. In essence, GIS has moved from a technology heavily dominated by the map metaphor to one that provides a comprehensive, efficient, and flexible approach to the representation of phenomena in space and time.

MOVING OBJECTS: LIFELINES AND TRACKS

One of the commonest examples of moving objects is the tracks formed by humans as they move through daily activities, travel to work and on vacations, and relocate during a lifetime. At the daily scale, such tracks are of great use to transportation planners as they struggle to understand the patterns of trips made by individuals and their vehicles and to plan better for future demands on the transportation system. Figure 7.4 shows an example, the result of tracking a sample of individuals in Lexington, Kentucky, during a short period.

At the scale of years or a lifetime, such tracks or *lifelines* can be valuable contributions to the historical record, as they show the meetings that occur between individuals, the routes followed by explorers, and patterns of travel and migration from one place of residence to another. They can also be invaluable records of the exposure of individuals to environmental contaminants, particularly

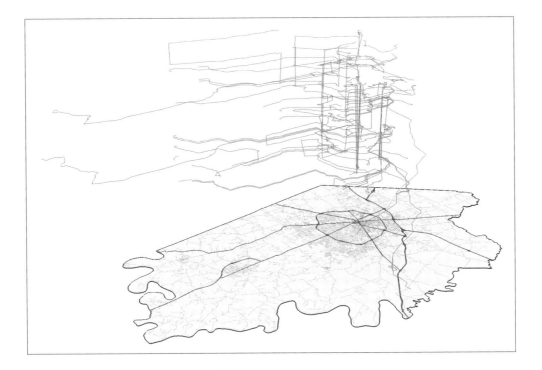

FIGURE 7.4

A visualization of tracks of individuals in Lexington, Kentucky. The horizontal axes denote position, and the vertical axis time.

Created and provided by Mei-Po Kwan. Used by permission. Copyright Mei-Po Kwan 2007.

in relation to diseases with long latencies, such as cancer. Torsten Hägerstrand formalized many of the basic concepts of such tracks,[10] and there have been several recent efforts to extend his framework. Today, large volumes of tracking data are becoming available as a result of the widespread use of the Global Positioning System (GPS), and geographers and others are developing interesting ways of analyzing and modeling such data.

Figure 7.5 shows an object-oriented database design for storing tracking data. The fundamental element of a track is the observation of an individual's position at some point in time. GPS data might produce such points as often as every second, whereas tracks compiled from diaries, such as those of the Lewis and Clark expedition, might record locations only a few times per day. A *track* is composed of many observations of position and carries attributes of the individual who made the track, which are inherited from the *individual* class. A track also is a type of polyline and inherits from this basic GIS class. When a *meeting* occurs between individuals, their tracks coincide for a period of time equal to the duration of the meeting. Such meetings might be observed and recorded directly or inferred from the spatial and temporal coincidence of tracks.

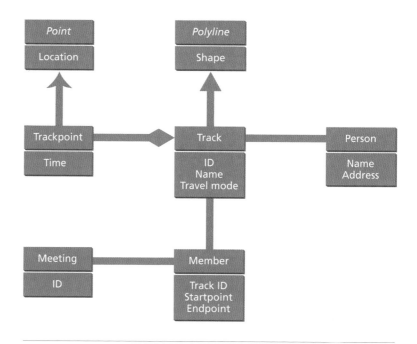

FIGURE 7.5

A simple design for storing tracking data, showing person, location, track, and meeting classes. Persons and meetings do not have locations, and thus do not inherit from GIS classes.

In his analysis of the visual display of information, Edward Tufte identifies the map made by the French statistician and engineer Charles Joseph Minard of Napoleon's Moscow campaign, reproduced in figure 7.6, as a particularly effective representation of the events and conditions of the campaign.[11] The map shows the route taken by the army, major events along the route, the size of the army, and the temperature during the return from Moscow, all factors important in understanding this military and humanitarian catastrophe. Alan Glennon and I used this as a working example to develop a general data model for capturing information on flow-like phenomena—a *use case* in the terminology of database design. In principle, we looked for a design in the form of classes, attributes, and relationships that would succeed in capturing the objects shown on the map and their characteristics and allow the map

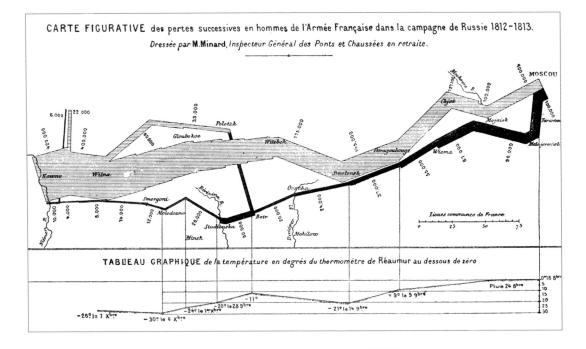

FIGURE 7.6

A reproduction of Minard's original map of Napoleon's Moscow campaign.

Etienne-Jules Marey, La Méthod Graphique (Paris: G. Masson, 1885), fig. 37. Courtesy of Rare Books Collection, University of Chicago Library, Special Collections Research Center.

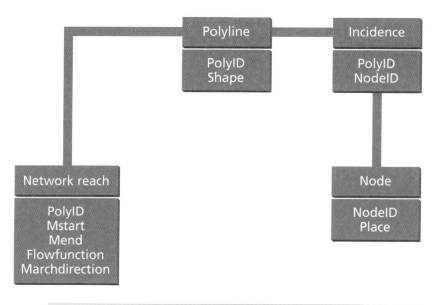

FIGURE 7.7

A simplified design for a database containing the primary contents of the Minard map.

to be regenerated from the database using the cartographic rendering tools of GIS. The test of such a design is satisfied when some location exists within the database to store every fact portrayed on the map and when the full content of the map can be regenerated from the database. The cartographic styles used by Minard are not generally available in today's GIS, so the regenerated map will appear somewhat different and lack the grace of the historic styles.

Figure 7.7 shows our design, which was informed by several additional examples or use cases of flow-like phenomena. It has been simplified to accommodate only the major features of the Minard map. Polylines provide the underlying geometry. Reaches are sections of polylines with consistent patterns of attributes that start and end at defined distances along the polyline. The volume of flow on a reach can vary along the reach, defined by a flow function. Polylines start and end at nodes, which are identified with place-names. A full representation of all of the content of the map would require a significantly more elaborate design, but this one serves to illustrate the basic principles involved.

A generic design such as this can provide the basis for storing, analyzing, and displaying numerous examples of flow-like phenomena. In addition to the Minard map, we used use cases based on historic migration between U.S. states and underground flows in a region of central Kentucky to develop the design. But now that it is established, the same basic design can serve to store geographic information on flow-like applications as diverse as the Lewis and Clark expedition, the movement of armies prior to the Battle of Waterloo, and the invasions of Italy during the collapse of the Roman Empire. All of these examples are difficult to display in map form because of their temporal complexity, but a generic object-oriented design can provide the basis for storing all of the information relevant to their study and for extracting, studying, and visualizing different aspects. The necessary tools to implement this design as an extension to ESRI ArcGIS software are available for download at http://dynamicgeography.ou.edu/flow/index.html.

CHANGING BOUNDARIES

Agencies such as the U.S. Bureau of the Census provide abundant data on the socioeconomic and demographic characteristics of the population, and similar agencies perform the same function in other countries. To maintain confidentiality, results are necessarily aggregated to standard units, such as counties, ZIP Codes, or census tracts. Unfortunately, each of these standard units has a tendency to shift through time, making it notoriously difficult to obtain longitudinal perspectives on social patterns. In some historic cases, it may even be impossible to determine the exact boundaries of certain administrative areas. While that is rarely the case in the United States, boundary changes have sometimes been much more extreme than most researchers realize. For example, Portage County, Wisconsin, changed its geographic location between two census years, the same name being assigned to two separate areas in two succeeding enumerations.[12] In other cases, reporting zones have been split or merged, and boundaries have been shifted. Historians interested in geographic patterns of Chinese society face even more daunting problems, since there may be no maps whatever to define the boundaries of a certain named reporting zone in some past period.

Several attempts have been made to overcome these problems by making census data available for a consistent set of geographic units. Typically, past data is adjusted to match the boundaries of the latest census, providing a single longitudinal series since the first census. The largest, most recent, and likely most successful of these is the National Historical Geographic Information System (NHGIS) project, funded by the National Science Foundation and housed at the University of Minnesota (www. nhgis.org). It aims to provide high-quality digital boundaries for each census year and estimates of population of any year based on any year's boundaries.

Early GIS database designs created great difficulty for this type of application because the map metaphor implied that any layer would be a single snapshot, making it impossible to organize multiple snapshots into a coherent database. A common workaround employed a concept often termed the *region,* consisting of an aggregation of parts of a reporting zone assembled to match the definition of the zone at a specific time. Consider, for example, all of the maps of census reporting zones since the first census year. Superimposing all of these maps creates a single map. Each face in this composite map represents an area that has never been divided by the reporting zones of any year. This map will contain many thousands of faces. Moreover, it will be affected by a problem that is universally encountered in GIS. Each of the maps will have been digitized independently, so that if two maps contain the same boundary, it will appear slightly different because of random errors and distortions introduced by the digitizing process. Thus when the two versions of the boundary are overlaid, a large number of small slivers will be produced. The complete overlay of all maps will contain a vast number of such slivers. GIS software commonly attempts to remove such slivers based on a user-defined tolerance, but this solution is in many ways imperfect.

Having prepared the composite, it is possible to recreate each census year's boundary map by dissolving boundaries between faces in the composite that were part of the same reporting zone, or *region.* This is achieved by preparing a table indicating which faces belonged to which reporting zones in each year.

Modern GIS designs solve the problem in a much simpler way and do so because of the enormous increases in computing power and storage capacity during the past decade. Figure 7.8 presents a simple design that links the names or other identifying attributes of zones to their polygonal shapes through associations. Again, such designs are fundamentally incompatible with the map metaphor and enabled because of the adoption of object-oriented approaches.

ASSESSMENT AND CONCLUSION

Early GIS was dominated by the problem of creating digital representations of the contents of maps, a valuable exercise as we saw in the case of CGIS and one that sustained the rapid growth of GIS applications that occurred prior to the 1990s. But the inability to deal with dynamics and other inadequacies of the early approach,

FIGURE 7.8

A simple design for a longitudinal database of census reporting zones. Each name may be associated with more than one boundary, and boundaries may exist for varying lengths of time.

including the need to create two databases—one to store the nodes, arcs, and faces of networks, and the other to store coordinates—eventually led to a dissatisfaction with the relational database approach. Since the 1990s, the field has seen enthusiastic adoption of the object-oriented model, because of its ability to deal with events in time and other aspects of geographic data incompatible with cartographic practice and with the early data models. This process has relied on massive increases in computing power and storage capacity, largely removing the constraints that in part necessitated the earlier approach. Today, GIS databases can readily deal with objects that move, objects that change shape, and other phenomena that cannot be portrayed on paper maps.

As with other innovations, this one is being adopted slowly by a GIS community of users and GIS industry that have grown used to earlier approaches and are committed to them in many ways. Thus a historian approaching GIS is still tempted to think of this as a technology of maps and to assume that one cost of adopting GIS will be an inability to deal with time—that GIS is the toolkit of geographers who look at the world as essentially static and focus on understanding cross-sectional rather than longitudinal variation. In reality, this view is no longer valid—GIS has been dealing successfully with space and time for many years. But other factors serve to preserve the legacy of a space-only approach. We still lack good tools for the analysis of dynamic data in GIS, because such data have only recently appeared. While researchers have made much progress in developing such tools, it will be some time before they are fully deployed. Demand drives the GIS software industry, and static applications still dominate the community, so tools inevitably will first appear in the research community and will be implemented only slowly in commercial products.

Dynamic, three-dimensional data is also still comparatively scarce, particularly for historic periods, despite the efforts of such projects as NHGIS.

These comments lead to some fairly confident predictions about the future of GIS, at least as far as historians are concerned. First, tools for analysis of dynamic data will appear at a steadily increasing rate in the coming years. These will include methods for visualization, analysis of real data against simple models and hypotheses, and such basic operations as clustering similar tracks and preparing longitudinal series. The latter will require improvements in current methods of areal interpolation,[13] which has become the key technique for estimating attributes of hypothetical reporting zones. Researchers will develop specialized data models for dynamic data, and there is every reason to believe that a data model designed specifically for the needs of historians will be added to the list of existing models.[14] In short, the transition to object-oriented data modeling in GIS has solved some basic problems, allowing a rapid expansion of interest in the use of GIS to improve our understanding of historical and other time-dependent phenomena. After many years, we are finally able to examine data in full spatio-temporal perspective.

NOTES

1. D. H. Maling, *Measurements from Maps: Principles and Methods of Cartometry* (New York: Pergamon, 1989).

2. T. W. Foresman, ed., *The History of Geographic Information Systems: Perspectives from the Pioneers* (Upper Saddle River, N.J.: Prentice Hall, 1998).

3. J.-X. Zhang and M. F. Goodchild, *Uncertainty in Geographical Information* (London, New York: Taylor & Francis, 2001).

4. C. J. Date, *An Introduction to Database Systems* (Reading, Mass.: Addison-Wesley, 2000).

5. G. Langran, *Time in Geographic Information Systems* (London: Taylor & Francis, 1992); D. J. Peuquet, *Representations of Space and Time* (New York: Guilford, 2002).

6. J. Raper, *Multidimensional Geographic Information Science: Extending GIS in Space and Time* (New York: Taylor & Francis, 2000).

7. On indeterminate boundaries, see P. A. Burrough and A. U. Frank, eds., *Geographic Objects with Indeterminate Boundaries* (London: Taylor & Francis, 1996).

8. G. Booch, J. Rumbaugh, and I. Jacobson, *The Unified Modeling Language User Guide* (Upper Saddle River, N.J.: Addison-Wesley, 2005).

9. D. Arctur and M. Zeiler, *Designing Geodatabases: Case Studies in GIS Data Modeling* (Redlands, Calif.: ESRI Press, 2004).

10. T. Hägerstrand, "What about People in Regional Science?" *Papers of the Regional Science Association* 24 (1970): 7.

11. E. R. Tufte, *The Visual Display of Quantitative Information* (Cheshire, Conn.: Graphics Press, 1986).

12. See Gordon DenBoer, *Wisconsin, Atlas of Historical County Boundaries,* ed. John H. Long (New York: Charles Scribner's Sons, 1997), 238–42.

13. M. F. Goodchild, L. Anselin, and U. Deichmann, "A Framework for the Areal Interpolation of Socioeconomic Data," *Environment and Planning A* 25 (1993): 383.

14. Arctur and Zeiler, *Designing Geodatabases.*

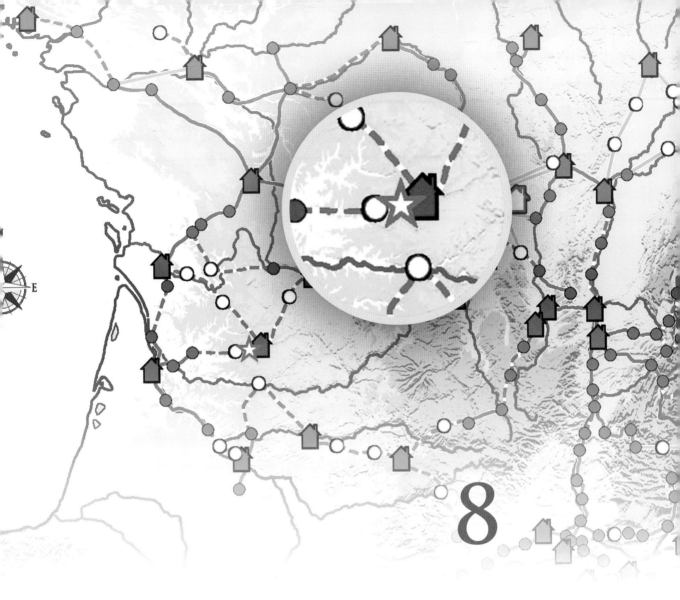

NEW WINDOWS ON
THE PEUTINGER MAP OF
THE ROMAN WORLD

Richard J. A. Talbert and Tom Elliott

The object of this chapter is a unique survival, often called the Peutinger Map, from Conrad Peutinger, who acquired it not long after it mysteriously surfaced somewhere in Germany about 1500.[1] Engravings of it were published about a century later, and it has remained well known. Since the mid-eighteenth century, it has belonged to the imperial (today, national) library in Vienna, Austria.[2] The format comprises eleven pieces of parchment pasted together to form a roll, each piece approximately 33 cm high and on average 62 cm wide. Even so, the design is a single, cohesive composition. What survives is a copy made around 1200. Although proof is unattainable thus far, there seems insufficient reason to dispute the traditional view that the original—from which a succession of copies must stem—was Roman work, possibly of about AD 300.[3]

The map as it survives is incomplete. In all likelihood, the original was intended to represent the world as the Romans knew it, spanning the Atlantic coast of Europe and North Africa to Sri Lanka. Before the surviving copy was made, however, the western end somehow fell away. Despite this loss, there is every reason to believe that the city of Rome was intended to be the center of the whole composition. The complete map could have extended to about 850 cm in width (180 cm longer than the surviving copy),[4] although nowhere does it exceed more than about 33 cm in height. This is a choice of dimensions manifestly deliberate, though puzzling.

No other map remotely comparable to this astonishing one has survived from antiquity, and its uniqueness has hindered understanding. It values land above sea, and land routes are a distinctive component of the design. Typically, these are marked as horizontal lines in red, all of the same weight. In consequence, scholarly opinion has been content to interpret the map as just an outsize "route diagram," comparable in nature to those developed for modern subway systems in London and elsewhere. It was based, so the argument goes, on the type of written route itinerary found in many Roman examples preserved in manuscript and as inscriptions.[5]

This is the interpretation reflected in the sole modern edition of the map, the work of a gifted amateur, Konrad Miller, published in 1916.[6] Miller hardly considers the map as a piece of cartography. His prime concerns are the date of the original map and how well the land routes and accompanying distance figures accurately match conditions on the ground as determined by survey, inscriptions, and archaeology. To investigate this latter aspect is a legitimate and appropriate quest, which dozens of scholars have continued to pursue, although usually with no more than a localized focus. It is disappointing that for nearly a century, this approach, along with ill-founded efforts to fix the date of the original map, has eclipsed all others. No one has yet initiated other lines of inquiry into the map as a whole rather than some part of it.

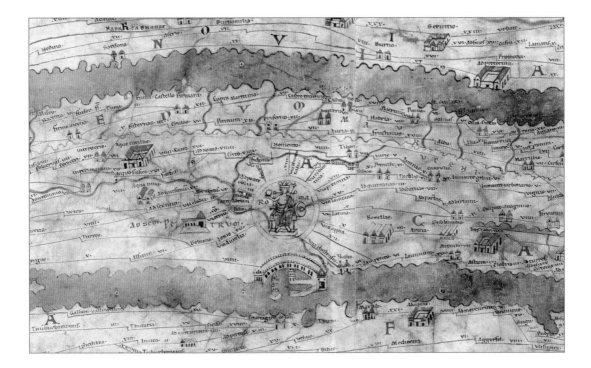

FIGURE 8.1

Composite of Peutinger Map segments 4 and 5 featuring the city of Rome.

Detail from the Peutinger Map, by permission of the Austrian National Library, picture archive, Vienna: Cod. 324, Segm. IV and V.

Our current long-term goal is to prepare a complete fresh edition of the map using digital images of all eleven parchments supplied from Vienna. We expect the result to be an e-book, because only electronic publication offers a suitably versatile and economical format to accommodate the nature and range of necessary approaches to this unwieldy object.

The case study below will show that digitization is invaluable in separating the map into its component parts for the first time. This process reinforces our conclusion, likely to be endorsed by any experienced cartographer, that the basis of the map's design was *not* its network of land routes (as has always been assumed)[7] but rather the shorelines and principal rivers and mountain ranges, together with the major settlements marked by pictorial symbols.

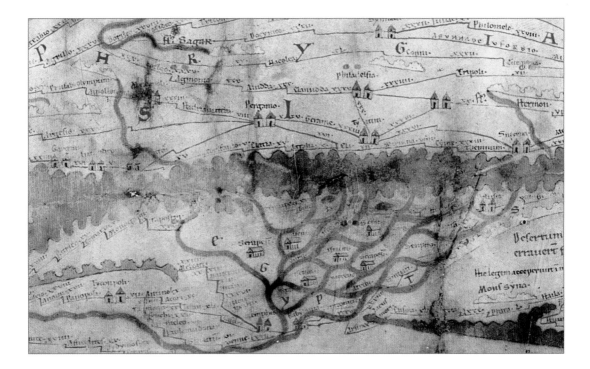

FIGURE 8.2

Detail from Peutinger Map, segment 8. Note the Nile Delta, other named rivers, and region names for Phrygia and Aegyptus.

Detail from the Peutinger Map, by permission of the Austrian National Library, picture archive, Vienna: Cod. 324, Segm. VIII.

This issue aside, close examination of the route network is vital to establish whether it really is as comprehensive, accurate, and useful a component as it may at first appear. Here, we can exploit digitization to pursue questions never previously asked about the map. Moreover, we can now match its presentation of routes against a reliable, detailed, modern rendering of known routes across the entire Roman Empire as furnished for the first time since the late nineteenth century by the *Barrington Atlas of the Greek and Roman World.*[8]

Miller's edition creates a notably misleading impression by presenting the map's route network in the form of 141 distinct "journeys" (say, from Boulogne to Milan), which form the framework for his commentary. It would indeed prove awkward for a printed book to do otherwise, but the fact remains that Miller requires his readers to follow the network along lines that he alone has more or less arbitrarily determined. One benefit of a commentary presented digitally, by contrast, is its ability to dispense with filters and instead maintain the mapmaker's neutrality in this important respect. Accordingly, for each of the three thousand places that are part of the map's route network, the digital edition of the Peutinger Map now in development will provide an individual digital "page" that includes pointers to all preceding and following stretches. At the many junctions in the network, users alone must choose where to proceed next, as the mapmaker evidently intended, without any intervention by a modern editor.

Our appraisal of the route network finds that the mapmaker was not primarily concerned with creating a serviceable resource for travelers. This view in turn challenges prevailing assumptions. It also reopens the fundamental question of what the map *was* seeking to achieve. The present case study does not pursue that aspect beyond underlining the need for more sensitive appraisal of content, design, and context; however, the full edition now under preparation will address these issues in detail. The case study demonstrates that digital separation of the map into its individual components highlights the sheer amount of physical geography presented. Scholars fixated on the route network have dismissed the physical geography as mere decoration. However, the inclusion of about 130 named islands, as well as a comparable number of rivers, proclaims that the mapmaker had more than decoration in mind.

Our efforts to reexamine and reinterpret the Peutinger Map have drawn on a range of joint experience: creation of the maps for the *Barrington Atlas,* interest in how Romans conceptualized their surroundings,[9] and admiration for the History of Cartography project's reappraisal of the maps of premodern societies in more inclusive and more respectful ways.[10] Last but not least, digitization has provided a way to tackle questions that demand investigation if we are to recognize and understand the Peutinger Map's various layers of meaning and purpose.

We used two digital approaches in our analysis. The first approach required deconstructing the map into a series of thematic layers. This process, which depends on the use of industry-standard illustration software and countless hours of painstaking tracing work, enables us to view the thematic components of the map's composition singly or in groups. The "deconstructive approach" mirrors the composition methods used for the production of modern maps and for the integration of thematically different data in the construction of a GIS. We concluded as a result that the first step of the original cartographer was not—as had always been assumed—the drafting of the route network. Viewed alone, the route network resembles no more than a bewildering mass of red spaghetti, even with the major symbolized reference points added (figure 8.3).

Instead, if one establishes first (surely following the original mapmaker) the broad physical outlines of the land masses, major rivers, and mountain ranges, then formation of the map proceeds in a logical and comprehensible fashion. Shorelines, together with the mountains and major drainage features, had to be selectively adjusted and drawn to fit the constraints of the map's elongated format.

Once that difficult task was accomplished, the mapmaker could add settlements marked by pictorial symbols, with due attention to their appropriate placement relative to major physical features. Only thereafter would it make sense to add the route network, which was in all likelihood derived from an assemblage of written itinerary documents collated in advance. This step evidently involved first writing the name

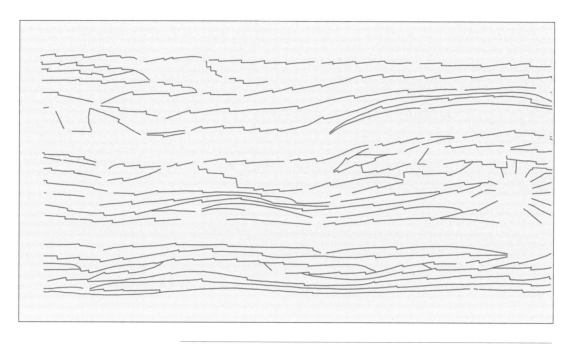

FIGURE 8.3

Route network on Peutinger Map, segment 4.

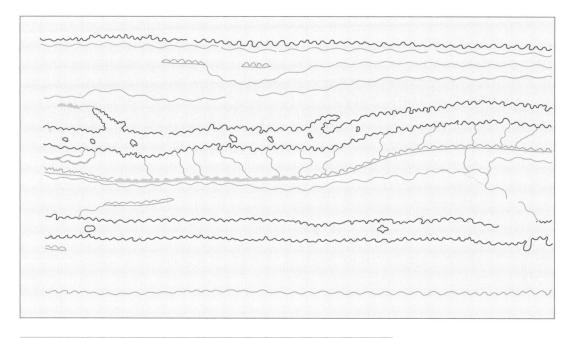

FIGURE 8.4

Physical features on Peutinger Map, segment 4.

and onward distance figure for each stopping point between symbols and then connecting these linkages by adding the distinctive red linework. The governing constraint at this point was not geospatial accuracy but simple graphic composition. The mapmaker fitted the names and distance figures between pairs of pictorial symbols as best he could, sometimes rotating them, staggering them, or even arranging them in an arc.

The analytical deconstruction outlined above was vital in helping us to grasp the map's compositional underpinning and to appreciate its maker's achievement as a cartographic artist. For all its value, however, this deconstruction does not advance several major interests of modern scholars, such as the accuracy of the routes shown or the identification of named settlements with archaeologically attested remains. For these and other related questions, ways must be found to bring the full range of material culture and toponymy depicted on the map into a geographic information system, the second of our two digital approaches.

Several challenges emerged as we sought to develop a GIS-aided approach to studying the Peutinger Map. Chief among them is the inapplicability of "rubber sheeting" (or warping), the standard process for mathematically stretching or shrinking a portion of a map to align its coordinates with known control points. It is impossible to scan the Peutinger Map, load it into ArcGIS software, georegister it, and begin an analysis. It is an idiosyncratic map that lacks anything remotely resembling a consistent system of coordinates against which to build a set of control points. Scale, aspect ratio, and even the cardinality of the compass points shift from one part of the map to the next as the design struggles to accommodate the competing pressures imposed by its extreme shape.

To solve this major problem, we began the process of feature extraction first, preserving the topology of the route network as depicted on the map, and then adding the spatial coordinates for the nodes in that network (settlements, road-stations, spas, and other places marked) on the basis of modern research and survey. In this way, the physical geometry of the map's layout is bypassed, while its content and internal, semantic linkages are preserved. The development of methods for this work and its subsequent completion have taken more than two years. An example of the information taken from the map may best illustrate the methodology.

One example of information captured from the map is the route *Forum Iulii* (modern Fréjus in France) eastward along the Mediterranean coast through the Maritime Alps. On the map, this route exits the symbol for *Forum Iulii* to the right (figure 8.5).

The map represents point features in two ways. One, as here for *Forum Iulii,* is a pictorial symbol (in various styles), accompanied by the name itself and by a figure for the distance to the next stopping point on each onward route. The other limits itself to the name (with no symbol), again accompanied by a figure for the distance to the next stopping point. The route topology linking these symbols and names is represented by red lines that typically incorporate a chicane (or zigzag) at each transition from one stretch of route to the next.

Observe that the lengths of these stretches, or line segments on the map, bear no relation to the distance figure accompanying each name, nor—consequently—to the real distance on the ground. Instead, the length of any stretch between two chicanes is largely determined by the combined length of the name to be marked there and its accompanying distance figure. The role of the red lines is to highlight the route linkages and the order in which they unfold.

Thus, proceeding to the right from *Forum Iulii,* we travel seventeen units (here, Roman miles) to *Ad Horrea.* Normally, the beginning of the label for *Ad Horrea* would

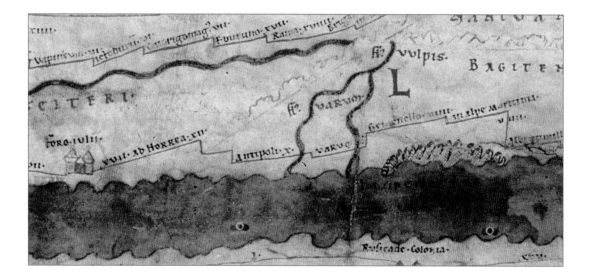

FIGURE 8.5

Detail from Peutinger Map, segment 2, *Forum Iulii* to *In Alpe Maritima*.

Detail from the Peutinger Map, by permission of the Austrian National Library, picture archive, Vienna: Cod. 324, Segm. II.

have been offset sufficiently from the preceding distance figure for the red lines to manifest its customary chicane immediately before the label. In this case, however, the two elements have been run together, with the result that the stretch intended for *Ad Horrea* can only be short and blank. From *Ad Horrea,* we traverse a symbol for a mountain range, arriving at *Antipoli* after twelve more miles. Ten more miles bring us to *Varum,* perhaps a road station, which shared its name with the river depicted just before the chicane and its associated label. A short way beyond *Varum* on the stretch to *Gemenello* is another river crossing (over the *Vulpis*). The distance figure associated with the stretch has been damaged but may have indicated an additional six miles. Beyond *Gemenello,* it is nine miles to *In Alpe Maritima,* and so on.

Our procedure for transferring such data to the GIS is as follows. Elliott constructed a database that permitted Talbert to create a detailed record for each geographic feature on the map and for each route stretch. These records include all names and distance figures. They also classify all symbols, and they tag geographical features (islands, lakes, mountains, rivers, etc.) with a number for identification. Space is provided for references to ancient geographical texts and itineraries and to modern scholarship. Talbert's commentary is accommodated here too. Where a name or feature can be matched with one shown in the *Barrington Atlas,* its placement in the latter is recorded. Figure 8.6 presents the two primary data entry forms devised for the purpose.

Uniting this information with spatial coordinates derived from the *Barrington Atlas* allowed us to plot the Peutinger Map's sites on a modern physical basemap of the corresponding area using today's cartographic symbology. We chose a test area spanning southern France and adjoining areas of Italy and Switzerland. To be sure, the Peutinger Map's overall coverage is far more extensive, but we deliberately chose this smaller region to develop and test our methodology. Our next step was

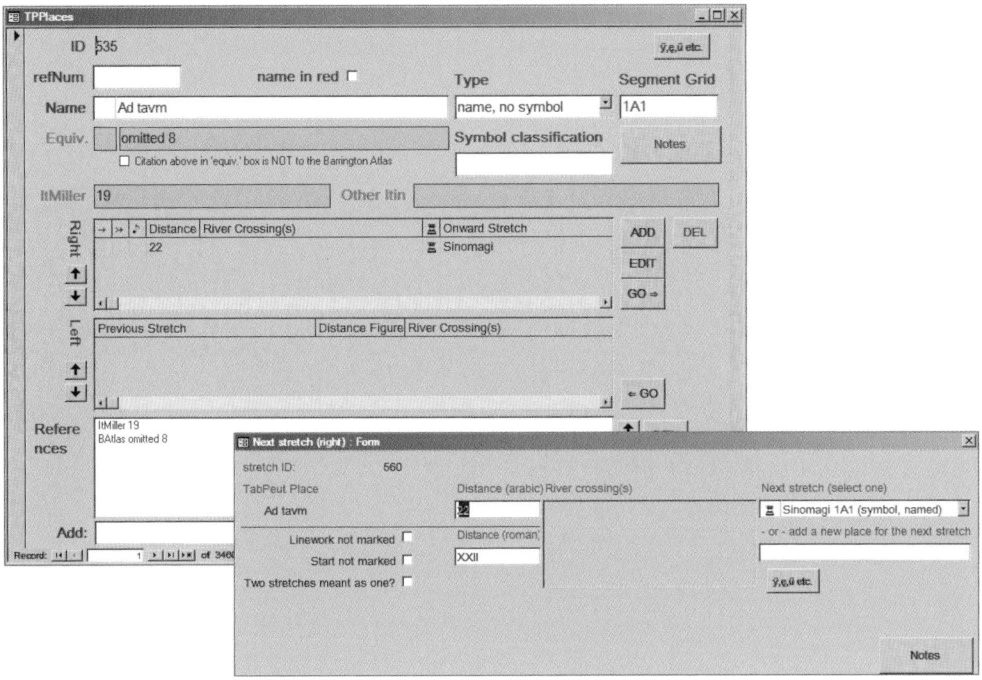

FIGURE 8.6

Data-entry forms for Peutinger Map database.

Data entry form from custom database developed by the authors.

to transfer the route linkages to the GIS. We combined Talbert's records for each stretch with the endpoint data to produce a set of straight line segments, one representing each stretch. Special care was exercised to capture all relevant attribute data, including the associated distance figures. We also remained alert to problems of interpretation presented by incompletely preserved linework, damage to the parchments, and similar factors. In addition, attribute data was checked to differentiate between those stretches whose two endpoints can be securely located and those with one endpoint more or less uncertain.

Figure 8.7 illustrates the results of this process in our test area. Red dots correspond to those sites that appear only as names on the Peutinger Map; red

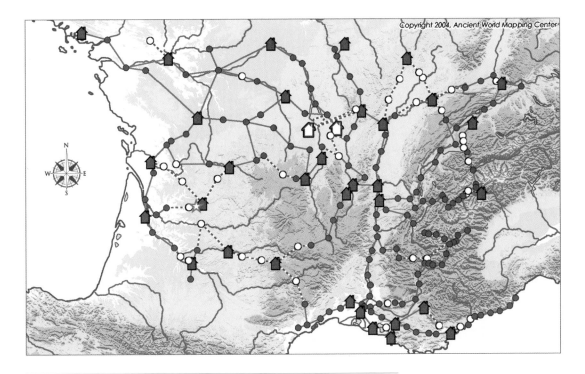

FIGURE 8.7

Map of sites and routes extracted from Peutinger Map, test region.

Original map by the authors. Topographic base developed from GTOPO30 DEM. Peutinger Map feature locations interpolated from materials compiled by the Classical Atlas Project and the Ancient World Mapping Center.

"houses" indicate sites marked by a pictorial symbol. Hollow dots and houses indicate sites whose coordinates cannot be precisely determined, either because the name remains otherwise unattested in any ancient source or because it is as yet impossible to match the name with any appropriate site on the ground identified by archaeology or survey. A hollow five-pointed star (as in the lower left-hand quadrant of figure 8.7) signifies a junction or group of stretches in the route network that presents some unresolved problem, such as the absence of a name or a copyist's slip. Route stretches whose endpoints can be securely located are rendered with a solid red line. A dashed red line is used for stretches with less reliably located endpoints.

Even this relatively simple representation permits an important spatial observation about the Peutinger Map's route network. The distance intervals between junctions differ significantly, and these differences seem to be grouped regionally. Note the apparent higher frequency of junctions in the southeast portion of the test region by comparison with the northwest.

Moving beyond this initial impression required more work on the data. In particular, it was impossible to begin gauging the accuracy of the preserved distance figures or the rationale of the routes recorded without attempting to equate these notional routes to Roman highways attested on the ground. The *Barrington Atlas* may again serve as the basis for making this comparison, because it traces the routes of the major imperial and regional highways insofar as they can be reconstructed from modern archaeology and survey. Where the actual path of a highway is established and where the Peutinger Map demonstrably follows such a path, we traced the physical geometry of the highway and then substituted it for the straight line segments in our dataset. The results of this step are illustrated in figure 8.8.

Solid pink lines indicate stretches for which a route on the Peutinger Map seems to correspond indisputably to the path of a highway attested on the ground. Dashed pink lines signal less confidence, most often because of uncertainty about the course of a highway's path or the location of nodal points named on the Peutinger Map. Straight orange lines signify either our inability to identify an appropriate highway, or such a high proportion of insecurely located junctions as to warrant special caution.

With this dataset in place, we began assessing the information preserved on the Peutinger Map in the context of landscape realities. Our findings to date cannot be presented in detail here, but we offer concise examples.

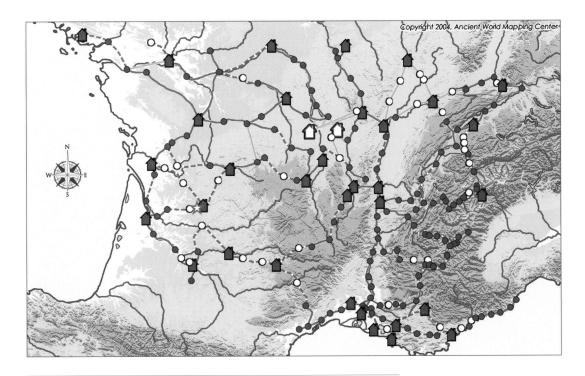

FIGURE 8.8

Test region showing probable physical geometry of Peutinger Map routes.

Original map by the authors. Topographic base developed from GTOPO30 DEM. Peutinger Map feature locations interpolated from materials compiled by the Classical Atlas Project and the Ancient World Mapping Center.

Roman milestones were placed along many imperial highways in accordance with a variety of regional measurement systems. In Italy, for example, the Roman mile predominated, whereas distances in Gaul were often measured in Gallic leagues. Highways in Greek-speaking provinces might be measured in the standard Greek unit, the *stadion*. The Peutinger Map seldom specifies the unit it is employing, and there are no discernible differences in how it represents distance figures from region to region. Yet examination of reliably established route stretches in our test region confirms the presence of distance figures calculated in both Roman miles and Gallic leagues. While this is far from being a novel observation, no statistical analysis of the map's figures and units based on consistently reliable geographic information had been conducted before. Figure 8.9 summarizes the results for our test region in histogram form.

We can calculate the ratio between the ground distance (in meters) and the map's readable distance figures for the 105 stretches in the test region that may be reliably correlated to locatable highways. If, for a given stretch, this ratio corresponds closely to the known number of meters in a given ancient unit of measurement, then we can argue that the distance asserted by the Peutinger Map was measured in that particular unit. The majority of the results fall between approximately 1,200 m/unit and 2,600 m/unit, with two subordinate concentrations. One set of figures is clustered around 1,480 meters, equivalent to a Roman mile. The other set is less well defined, but seems centered on 2,200 meters, the length often theorized for the Gallic league (whose precise length is unattested).

The significant variance detectable in the data is unsurprising. It seems that many distances in the sources used for the map were not measured by survey. Rather, we can imagine that figures extrapolated from travel times may stand beside those computed from markers or estimated by other means. Nonetheless, the amount of "noise" apparent in the data is striking. Nearly one third of the measured stretches produce ratios that fall outside even a fifteen percent "error bucket" around the expected values. At least the wide spread of these anomalous figures makes it improbable that they represent distances cited according to yet another system of measurement. It is more likely that the most widely divergent figures either result from miscopying or have an even earlier origin in the inaccurate transmission of documents from which

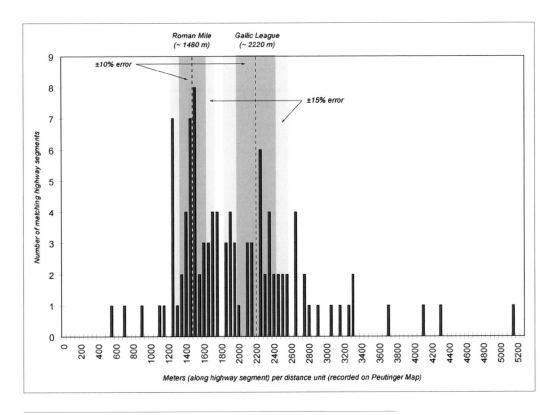

FIGURE 8.9

Histogram of the ratio between distance figures and ground distances for securely established highway segments in the Peutinger Map test region.

Original calculations by the authors on basis of data underlying the map presented here as figure 8.8.

the map's route information was originally compiled. At any rate, we now have the makings of a statistical test for probable corruption in the transmission of distance figures on the map.

Despite such variation in the distance ratios, the data nonetheless exhibits regional concentrations when viewed spatially. Figure 8.10 classifies the reliably locatable stretches by defining a ±10 percent "error bucket" around the nominal expected values for Roman miles and Gallic leagues. The stretches considered in this calculation are marked in black. Stretches with distances likely to be in Gallic leagues are colored orange; those in Roman miles are red. Figure 8.11 presents the results of the same calculation using a ±15 percent "error bucket."

As expected, these calculations confirm a spatial element to the use of a given system of measurement: the closer the location to the Italian peninsula, the stronger the likelihood that the unit in use is the Roman mile. But problems are immediately apparent. Route stretches with erroneous distance figures are widely distributed

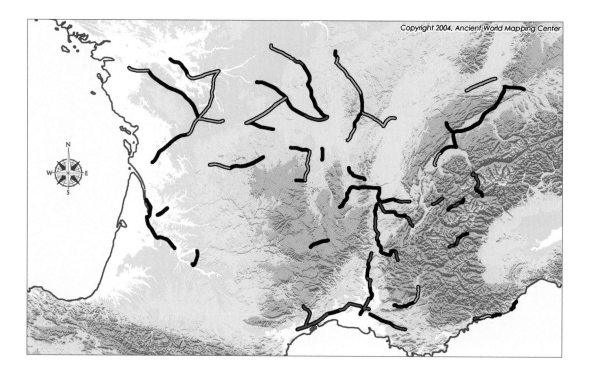

FIGURE 8.10

Classification of distance ratios for reliably locatable stretches (± 10 percent error).

Original map by the authors. Topographic base developed from GTOPO30 DEM. Peutinger Map feature locations interpolated from materials compiled by the Classical Atlas Project and the Ancient World Mapping Center.

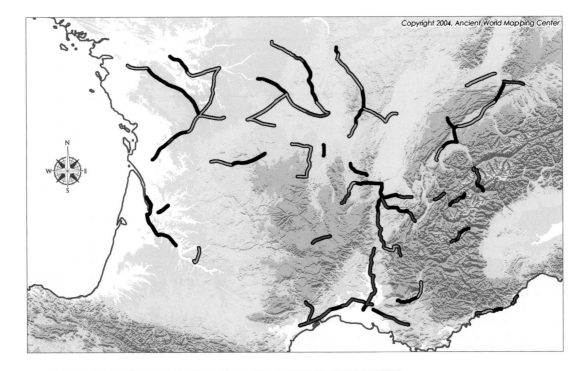

FIGURE 8.11

Classification of distance ratios for reliably locatable stretches (± 15 percent error).

Original map by the authors. Topographic base developed from GTOPO30 DEM. Peutinger Map feature locations interpolated from materials compiled by the Classical Atlas Project and the Ancient World Mapping Center.

throughout the test region. Even with the more stringent ±10 percent "error bucket," route stretches where use of a particular unit could be expected (based on usage for adjacent stretches) are misclassified. There are several potential explanations for this phenomenon. These misclassified stretches may point to the existence of further copying slips. Or they may suggest so large a degree of inaccuracy in the original distance measurements that our simple approach to their classification proves inadequate (i.e., wherever the error distribution around a given unit value is greater than half the difference between the two). Equally, the conventional supposition of 2,200 meters to the Gallic league may be too low. Moreover, the mapmaker may have introduced, or been forced to use, individual figures drawn from one work in order to make up deficiencies in another preferred source text. While it seems fair to imagine that itinerary sources will typically have preserved the units of distance in use on a given road and reflected in its markers, there is no guarantee this was the case. The mapmaker (or an earlier compiler of itineraries) may have indiscriminately combined figures recorded in different units. Since the map mostly does not specify units of distance at given points, we need not assume that the units were controlled during research and compilation.[11]

CONCLUSION

We plan several steps to test these possibilities. Wherever feasible, we intend to calibrate the map's distance figures against corresponding figures preserved in other Roman itineraries. A more involved approach, requiring collaboration with ongoing scholarly projects in Europe, would be the calibration of distance figures (and estimation of units used) on the basis of preserved highway milestones. This valuable milestone data can be further refined by comparison with the locations of Roman road stations, which were often named for their distance along a highway (for example, *Ad Decem,* meaning "at the tenth milestone"). Such efforts should enable us to detect original measurement variations from one highway to another. A more sophisticated classification algorithm—one that gives weight to the classification of nearby stretches—might allow us to cope better with the evidently high variance in our original numbers.

Finally, among other useful consequences of applying GIS to the study of the Peutinger Map, two of particular importance merit mention. First, the fixing of all verifiable sites and route stretches makes it possible to consider the nature of anomalous unnamed stretches, extra (or missing) chicanes, and even apparent repetition of names on the map. Study of this data superimposed on accurate physical bases reflecting the known cultural geography of a region can help to determine whether an apparent extra route stretch has been mistakenly introduced or whether the possible slip comprises no more than the omission of the name and distance figure for the stretch. Moreover, discontinuities or anomalies in route topology, which may originate from deficiencies in the original compilation of the map, are immediately visible when mapped on accurate bases. Without the benefit of spatial visualization, a comprehensive effort to identify such problematic instances would be, at best, prohibitively cumbersome.

Second, it is a common and justifiable practice for archaeologists and others to search the Peutinger Map, along with related ancient testimony, in hopes of identifying an attested name to associate with a newly discovered ancient site. Such searches are liable to be foiled, however, by inadequate appreciation of the shifts in the map's orientation and scale. But now, with the map's data transferred to GIS and pinned wherever possible to accurate spatial coordinates, the range of possible results can be much more reliably demarcated.

The endeavors outlined in this chapter represent only the first stage of a larger enterprise aimed at harnessing the new technology to bring a variety of Greek and Roman geographic materials into GIS formats.[12] To this end, the methodology explained above permits the assessment and comparison of a range of important primary sources for ancient toponymy, not least among them itineraries, inscriptions, and other documents. The resulting datasets will facilitate inquiries and approaches that have hardly been feasible till now; the realities and constraints of physical geography in particular will be given their due weight. Hence, we gain the capacity to uncover the degree to which the Peutinger Map's route data may derive from common sources no longer extant and to determine the character of its relationship to truth on the ground.

ACKNOWLEDGMENTS

Richard J.A. Talbert and Tom Elliott wish to acknowledge the substantive and essential contributions to the research presented in their chapter by Ancient World Mapping Center employees Nora Harris, Andy Hull, and Graham Shepherd.

NOTES

1. For an overview of the map's history to c. 1600, see Patrick Gautier Dalché, "La trasmissione medievale e rinascimentale della *Tabula Peutingeriana*," in *Tabula Peutingeriana: Le Antiche Vie del Mondo,* ed. Francesco Prontera (Florence: Olschki, 2003), 43-52.

2. Reproductions of the map since 1753 are the subject of an appendix (pp. 132-41) to Richard Talbert, "Cartography and Taste in Peutinger's Roman Map," in *Space in the Roman World: Its Perception and Presentation,* ed. Richard Talbert and Kai Brodersen (Münster: LIT, 2004), 113-41. The reproduction preferred above all others is Ekkehard Weber, *Tabula Peutingeriana: Codex Vindobonensis 324* (Graz: Akademische Druck-u. Verlagsanstalt, 1976), which furnishes a full-size color photograph of each parchment.

3. A Carolingian origin is urged by Emily Albu, "Imperial Geography and the Medieval Peutinger Map," *Imago Mundi* 57 (2005): 136-48, with dissent by Benet Salway, "The Nature and Genesis of the Peutinger Map," ibid., 119-35.

4. On these issues, see further Richard Talbert, "Konrad Miller, Roman Cartography, and the Lost Western End of the Peutinger Map" in *Historische Geographie der Alten Welt. Grundlagen, Ertäge, Perspektiven: Festgabe für Eckart Olshausen aus Anlass seiner Emeritierung,* ed. Ulrich Fellmeth, Peter Guyot, and Holger Sonnabend (Hildesheim: Olms, 2007), 353-66.

5. See, for example, discussion by Benet Salway, "Travel, *Itineraria* and *Tabellaria*," in *Travel and Geography in the Roman Empire,* ed. Colin Adams and Ray Laurence (London and New York: Routledge, 2001), 22-66.

6. *Itineraria Romana: Römische Reisewege an der Hand der Tabula Peutingeriana Dargestellt* (Stuttgart: Strecker und Schröder, 1916).

7. See further Talbert, op. cit. in n. 2, 124-25 and n. 30.

8. Richard J.A. Talbert, ed., *Barrington Atlas of the Greek and Roman World* (Princeton: Princeton University Press, 2000).

9. See now, for example, Richard Talbert, "Rome's Provinces as Framework for World-View," in *Roman Rule and Civic Life: Local and Regional Perspectives,* ed. Luuk De Ligt, et al. (Amsterdam: Gieben, 2004), 21-37.

10. Visit www.geography.wisc.edu/histcart.

11. The authors are grateful to the unnamed reviewer who suggested this latter possibility.

12. This effort is now organized as the AWMC's Pleiades Project, with initial funding from the National Endowment for the Humanities. See http://pleiades.stoa.org.

9

HISTORY AND GIS:
IMPLICATIONS FOR THE
DISCIPLINE

David J. Bodenhamer

"Historians begin by looking backward; they often end by thinking backward."[1] So claimed Friedrich Nietzsche after surveying the amateur scholars of his day. Modern critics reach similar conclusions when considering the slow dawning of new technologies within the discipline: Many historians are still using the tools and methods of earlier, pre-chip generations. Computers may be ubiquitous in history offices, but they serve primarily as communication, writing, and search devices. Despite a flurry of interest in quantitative history in the 1960s and 1970s, historians as a group have remained more comfortable with manuscripts than databases. It comes as no surprise, therefore, to discover that most members of the profession lack any meaningful acquaintance with geographic information systems (GIS), much less possess sufficient knowledge to judge the technology's usefulness to historical scholarship.[2]

Even when historians know about GIS, few rush to embrace it, much to the puzzlement of its advocates. The technology is complicated, costly, and at times cumbersome, but its ability to integrate multiple phenomena occurring with a given geography and to visualize results as maps makes its rarity in historical research even more curious. After all, history is about time and space, and GIS is ideal for handling spatial information and is becoming more adept at managing temporal data. Should not this technology be foremost in the methodological grab bag of historians?

Posing the issue this way suggests assumptions about the nature of history that do not always resonate with its practitioners. Arguments about the role of GIS in history often begin outside the discipline and proceed from considerations that may not echo the concerns of historians themselves. If GIS is ever to become central to historical scholarship, it must do so within the norms embraced by historians and from a sophisticated understanding of the philosophy of history and not simply its methods.

History as a discipline comes with definitions advanced in countless books, articles, and ephemera by persons great and obscure. These definitions range from the puerile (Henry Ford: "History is bunk") to the cynical (Voltaire: "History is a pack of tricks we play on the dead") to the mystical and confessional (Carl Becker: "History is an act of faith") to the lyrical conundrum (William Faulkner: "The past is not dead; it is not even past"). Even though every historian likely will cite a different epigram, collectively they would agree that history is a reasoned argument about the known past. It is an inevitable consequence of our human nature, and its purpose is to learn who we are and what we may become as individuals, groups, and societies.

The past, of course, is irretrievable, which is why historians draw a sharp distinction between the past and history. We understand the past's value: it is our source of evidence; without it, we would know nothing or have any sense of who we are. But the past escapes us as soon as it becomes past. We cannot recapture it; we can only represent it. In representing the past, we seek perspective, the point of view that allows us to discern patterns among the events that have occurred. We are not so much trying to transmit accumulated knowledge—culture and tradition do this, among other means—as to understand the significance of our experience.

In its essence, history seeks to generalize from the particular, not for the purpose of finding universal laws but rather to glean insights about cause and effect from a known outcome. Here, history differs from social science, which attempts to reach a generalization that holds true in any similar circumstance.[3] This difference is significant and influences the way the two groups of scholars create knowledge. For many social scientists, the search for trustworthy generalization focuses on the isolation of an independent variable—the cause that has a predictable effect on dependent variables or ones that respond to the stimulus or presence of a catalyst. They believe it is possible to discover such a variable, given sufficient resources, because the world is not yet lost to them. Historians must contend with fragmentary evidence and are painfully aware that the past is incomplete and irretrievable. They also are skeptical of prediction. The past is fixed: in it the intersection of patterns and singular events can be discovered. Not so in the future, where continuities and contingencies coexist independently of one another. Historians view reality as web-like, to use philosopher Michael Oakeshott's phrase, because they see everything as related in some way to everything else.[4] Interdependency is the *lingua franca* of historians.

This sense of interrelatedness plays out within two dimensions—space and time. Although the past is always bound by these two elements, historians often treat them as artificial, malleable constructs. Time especially is a complicated concept for historians, who well understand T. S. Eliot's sense of

Time present and time past
Are both present in time future
And time future in time past.[5]

In landscapes and timescapes, we impose divisions—eras and epochs, cultural footprints and spheres of influence—that allow us to manage complexity. We move freely across these grids, ignoring issues of scale as we compare and contrast one place or one time with another in an effort to recapture a sense of the whole, to illuminate differences, to discover patterns. We go to great lengths to verify and analyze evidence, but we pay little critical attention to its temporal and spatial attributes.

Such casual use of time and space may seem odd for a discipline that, in so many ways, refers to these terms continually. An explanation lies in recognizing that historians seek to portray a world that is lost, not to re-create it precisely. The scholars' goal is not to model or replicate the past; a model implies the working out of dependent and independent variables for purposes of prediction, whereas replication suggests the ability to know the past more completely than most historians would acknowledge is possible. Rather, the goal is to simulate or illustrate a specific set of events. Historians, in a sense, are abstractionists: they have the "capacity for selectivity, simultaneity, and the shifting of scale" in pursuit of the fullest possible understanding of the past.[6] Traditionally, historians have used narrative to construct the portrait that furthers this objective. Narrative encourages the interweaving of evidentiary threads and permits scholars to qualify, highlight, or subdue any thread or set of them—to use emphasis, nuance, and other literary devices to achieve the complex construction of past worlds.

All of these elements—interdependency, narrative, and nuance, among others—predispose the historian to look askance at any method or tool that appears to reduce complex events to simple schemes. The computer, of course, is a technology that does not tolerate ambiguity, expressing all matter as zeroes and ones and demanding mutually exclusive categories in its data structures. Its insistence on precision does not fit the worldview of historians; indeed, the discipline appears at times to embrace an uncertainty principle—the more precisely you measure one variable, the less precise are other variables. Given this stance, it is no accident that GIS, the tool initially of engineers and earth scientists, has made few inroads into history. Yet of all modern information technologies, GIS may have the most potential for breaching the wall of tradition in history for at least two reasons: it maps information, thus employing a format and a metaphor with which historians are conversant; and it integrates and visualizes information, making it possible to see the complexity historians find in the past.

Representation of the past, John Lewis Gaddis has suggested, is a kind of mapping where the past is a landscape, and history is the way we fashion it. The metaphor, one consistent with disciplinary traditions, makes the link between "pattern recognition as the primary form of human perception and the fact that all history…draws upon the recognition of such patterns."[7] In this sense, mapping is not cartographic but conceptual. It permits varying levels of detail, not just as a reflection of scale but also of what is known at the time. Like the map, history becomes better and more accurate as we continue to accumulate more detail and refine our knowledge.

Gaddis's metaphor is apt for historians. Using maps to display information and aid understanding is an ancient practice. Populated with mythical as well as physical features in their earliest forms, maps always have symbolized what was known or believed about the world. Their usefulness for more than navigation and warfare became well established in the nineteenth century with the "map that changed the world," as Simon Winchester labeled William Smith's geologic masterwork, and with John Snow's pioneering use of spatial analysis to pinpoint the cause of a cholera outbreak in 1854.[8] Historians of this period often opened their narratives with maps and lengthy descriptions of the landscapes they portrayed. For generations, history teachers have used maps to illustrate the movement of people and the spread of empires. Today, hardly a year passes without the publication of another four-color atlas to help communicate how and where its subject developed. Few types of presentation could be more familiar to chroniclers of the past.

At its core, GIS is a mapping technology with properties that should appeal to historians. Its fodder is physical space—location—and all attributes that coexist with it. Though historians may conceptualize space in flexible terms, the evidence we use comes from some place, no matter how loosely defined. This spatial tag, of course, is the key to GIS in relating one piece of evidence to another from the same geography. Historical data typically has better spatial than temporal markers, though not always, so GIS is equipped to handle most of our evidence. If the evidence has a known location—and the degree of granularity may vary widely—it may be used profitably within a GIS.

The spatial integration of information makes GIS attractive as a platform for history. Many scholars use the technology primarily to manage evidence of different types of data—qualitative, quantitative, and visual—based on the common space they share.[9] This mixing of formats is nothing new to historians, who always have taken evidence in the form they find it. What is different is the technology's ability to parse large amounts of disparate data quickly and to keep it in relationship with all other information from the same place. Even the geographic uncertainty associated with historical artifacts—some come from known locations; for others, provenance is much less certain—is manageable within the technology.

This integrative ability means that historians can construct multiple perspectives, much as we might in our verbal descriptions of the past. We can shift scales quickly, zoom in and out, and view levels of detail. Spatial relationships can prompt questions we might otherwise ignore; we can intuit connections for further exploration.

We can treat these multiple perspectives literally or figuratively. For some scholars, the ability to re-create a literal view can be instructive. Military historians can place opposing commanders in known locations on a battlefield and determine what they might have seen from their vantage point, or they can use evidence from a hundred soldiers to represent the chaos of war. Urban scholars can simulate the vistas and even the voices of a cityscape, using a map and multimedia with great economy to do what James Joyce took hundreds of pages to do for 1904 Dublin.

Multiple perspectives and shifting scales may cause problems for the cartographer but not necessarily the historian. Students of the past use well-honed methods for critically examining historical evidence. Their methodological toolkit is remarkably large, employing techniques and insights sharpened by a number of disciplines. Reasoning by analogy is part of the historian's approach to evidence, as is comparison of events across time and culture. Both advance the scholar's impulse to understand an event by reference to a similar event, regardless of origin or circumstances, at least initially. Both also invite the development of multiple views, from local to global, for the same problem. Such multiplicity is inherent in the nature of events. An observation, British historian Thomas Carlyle wrote in 1830, is successive in its recounting: one thing follows another in historical accounts, but in fact the events "were often simultaneous" in their occurrence.[10] Since the discipline's goal is an objective representation of reality, a singular view, no matter how precise, inevitably misrepresents the past and can become the enemy of comprehension. In his famous lectures on the nature of history, E. H. Carr implied that multiple perspectives promote the search for an objective past, a valid aim even in the postmodern world of scholarship. "It does not follow," he wrote, "that, because a mountain appears to take on different shapes from different angles of vision, it has objectively no shape at all or an infinity of shapes."[11]

Multiplicity is inherent in the word-narratives used to communicate history. Words are complex forms of information; they have "halos of meaning," making them wonderfully evocative but imprecise and slippery.[12] The word "holocaust" carries certain dictionary definitions, but capitalized it also labels a horrific period and calls to mind images and emotions ranging from trains to Auschwitz and death camps to the Warsaw ghetto and the cinematic figure of a small girl in a red coat. Historians embrace this range of meanings. We prefer the medium of words and narratives because it permits us to represent the past as multidimensional, complex, and nonlinear, even though structurally our prose and our logic are sequential.

A preference for words suggests that visualization, a key feature of GIS, is perhaps more problematic for historians than for practitioners of other disciplines, even though it too offers great potential for our work. Images are the accumulation of detail: they allow us to find patterns we might miss by other means of analysis. Ultimately, the shape and size of the forest commands our attention, not the nature of each tree. Maps represent the past in ways we deem helpful because they let us see events in large scale. But we historians rely on maps infrequently because, like other humanists, we are logo-centric. We are far more comfortable with words and narratives than with images. Our evidence usually comes to us wrapped in words. We parse these texts critically to extract the cause-and-effect relationship that feeds our argument and our narrative, the word products of our craft. The problem is not a lack of appreciation for visual communication. We all live in a visual information age, and increasingly turn to photographs, moving images, and the like for evidence to analyze. Our difficulty comes when we seek to communicate visually. We construct textual images that we embed in our story, but we struggle to create visual images that convey our interpretation.[13]

Our difficulty with visual communication stems partly from the training we receive and partly from a disciplinary emphasis on print publication as the preferred expression of our work. Few graduate programs in history offer coursework in visual methods. Most books or articles on historical method fail to address the subject. Our journals and monographs carry densely packed prose; we take it for granted that scholarly history is written history. But the issue goes far deeper than technical training and publication standards: most of us do not understand how to use images to construct narrative. It simply is foreign to our culture.

As a technology, GIS is not yet a facile visualization tool, at least not as experienced by most historians who have used it. This circumstance inhibits its use in history except as a mapping engine. The result is ironic: more than most computer-based technologies, GIS seems well suited to history. Through integration, GIS permits the use of multiple perspectives. Its mapped display of information facilitates the recognition of patterns, and its concept of spatial proximity prompts intuitive inference in much the same way that other proximate relationships do. In sum, its ability to integrate disparate information drawn from the same place and at the same time allows scholars to simulate the complexity of history.

Given its potential for the discipline, why have most historians not embraced GIS? Certainly, some exemplary projects exist. Many of them, such as those noted in *Past Time, Past Place* (2002),[14] involve extensive data collection and creation within a historical GIS, including major national historical GIS projects in Great Britain, Taiwan, China, and the United States, among others. An international consortium, the Electronic Cultural Atlas Initiative, begun in 1997, has sought to speed the development of such compendia for cross-cultural research. Indeed, much of the so-called spatial turn in social sciences involves such resource development. A major research center, the Center for Spatially Integrated Social Science at the University of California–Santa Barbara, has devoted considerable effort to creating tools and methods of use to historical GIS. Handbooks on GIS for historians are now appearing, as are dedicated workshops and professional journals and networks.[15] The *American Historical Review*, the discipline's major journal, recently experimented with a new article format that included a printed summary with reference to a Web site containing an array of data and views, including some spatial analysis.[16] Still, spatial analysis has yet to make major contributions to historiography.

The nascent literature on historical GIS notes problems with the technology that have slowed its adoption as a tool for historians.[17] One of the most cited impediments is the technology's awkwardness or inability in managing ambiguous, incomplete, contradictory, and missing data. Historians traffic regularly in evidence tinged with uncertainty, if not replete with it. Missing data is a larger problem: the record of the past often reads like a book with only a word or two on every page. Even if we had a full record, scholars understand that artifacts derive their meaning from the culture and circumstances that produce them, which adds another layer of complexity to problems of evidence. History as a discipline has wrestled with these issues for a long time. Researchers have developed numerous methods to create useful generalizations out of evidentiary scraps, though Mark Twain's assessment of nineteenth-century science at times seems to fit historical scholarship: "one gets such wholesale returns of conjecture out of such trifling investments of fact."[18]

From its origins, GIS has dealt with objects and events that can be measured, verified, and tested. As with any technology, it requires precision, perhaps not completely, but far exceeding what historians find in their evidence. History comes with a variety of spatial and temporal indicators, the stuff of GIS, but most are general and imprecise even when expressed in language that suggests geographic certainty. Consider land deeds from early colonial America, some of the most precise documents of their day. In an age when surveyors were scarce, the law accepted boundary markers in the landscape—rivers, rock outcroppings, and the like—which it assumed, incorrectly, were sufficiently permanent to assure undisputed ownership and generational transfer of property. When moving outside of legal records, our spatial and temporal indicators become murky in terms of GIS: close to the river, a day's ride from the capital, near the cathedral, on the battlefield. These are difficult concepts to express in a technology that requires polygons to be closed and points to be fixed by geographical coordinates.

Another problem of evidence arises with the lack of GIS-compatible strategic or contextual datasets. Strategic data includes statistical resources, such as censuses, that provide a common framework for large geographies, thus allowing useful comparisons among and across locations. With few exceptions, such as the Great Britain and Irish Historical GIS, we still do not have enough GIS-enabled datasets to frame the international, national, or regional comparative context in which most scholars work. This circumstance is quite unlike what occurs in traditional history, where national and regional narratives form the backdrop for countless local studies. Until strategic data exist in sufficient quantity, it is difficult to imagine the emergence in historical GIS of the "general to particular, particular to general" cycle that animates scholarship about the past. More likely in the near term is a case-study approach in which GIS is a tool in local tests of generalizations reached by other methods.

Accurate historical basemaps form a special subset of the strategic or framework data required for effective use of GIS within the discipline. Creating them presents numerous problems. Many older maps do not have known coordinate systems, which defeats the technology's ability to reproject them. More important is the instability of historical boundaries. Boundaries change continually as societies expand and contract, governments create new functions and jurisdictions, and wars or disputes make boundaries uncertain. Some boundaries are never established formally but are inferred, for example, cultural, linguistic, or conceptual boundaries such as frontiers. GIS can handle the overlap among known boundaries at any given point in time but it currently cannot deal efficiently with continually shifting or vaguely defined boundaries. At one level, we can manage this problem through arbitrary assignment based on the best available information. This practice may be acceptable, since any map, digital or otherwise, is an abstraction. Another solution is standardization of spatial units over time, as Ian Gregory has demonstrated with the Great Britain Historical GIS. While not insurmountable, these barriers must be addressed for historians to feel comfortable using this technology. Maps carry the impression of certainty and, especially in easily manipulated digital formats, may remove us further from the circumstances the map represented originally.

How to handle time, an essential variable in history, is another widely recognized obstacle to adoption of GIS within the discipline. For historians, time is epiphenomenal and causal. As epiphenomenon, time is a secondary characteristic of an event and results associated with it; for example, the Battle of Hastings occurred in 1066. Here, time is a static marker, denoting a point on the calendar when something happened. But time is also dynamic and sequential, linking events in a cause-and-effect statement: William the Conqueror's victory at Hastings began the redefinition of English society and culture. In GIS, time is fixed as part of the event; it is not dynamic.

One problem relates to the nature of GIS visualization, which traditionally has focused on 2D data, where the vertical dimension and time are attributes rather than inherent parts of the data structure. More recently, the technology has developed better ways of displaying time—time-series animations and rotating views, for example—and new modules make 3D displays much easier. It also is not necessary to cast all geographic visualizations in the form of a traditional map. Time-space cubes, for instance, allow the visualization of information integrated by space but without reference to a map. For most historians, however, GIS manages time inadequately, requiring us to remain within an artificial 2D or 2½D world that does not adequately represent the complexity of the contemporary world, much less the rich tapestry of the past.[19]

Other impediments relate less to the nature of data or tools and more to the culture of GIS. Mastering spatial methods and software is, in effect, learning another discipline, another way of thinking. It also means developing expertise in a complicated technology that is continually evolving. GIS uses programming logic and language, second nature to the engineer perhaps but not to historians. The concept of modeling, so necessary to spatial scientists, seems alien to historians. Also, we are statistical impressionists given to the use of categories that have no easy correspondence to ones employed in spatial technologies. Even metadata, the part of GIS most recognizable to historians, exists in a format quite different from the documentation required in humanities scholarship.

The scarcity of financial and technical resources within the humanities presents another obstacle to the development of historical GIS. The technology requires time and money, often lots of it. Users must develop data models and databases, create or locate framework data and get it into GIS-compatible formats, locate or create suitable basemaps, process the data and secure the outputs, decide on the appropriate cartographic form and elements, and interpret the results. Many of these steps must be taken for each data source, which historians develop continuously throughout their projects, thus making it difficult to use GIS as a set piece. For many projects, this process means collaboration with technical and domain experts. Working in a team, itself an act foreign to historians, places a premium on management skills. The cost of this GIS process is high and can only be justified by the analytical benefit performed with the data. Most historians would be hard pressed to make this calculation in their favor at present.

A more significant barrier, perhaps the largest one, is the absence of spatial questions in history. As historians, we understand the importance of place. Former Speaker of the U.S. House of Representatives Thomas P. (Tip) O'Neill's famous dictum, "All politics are local," can be applied to history with equal force. Yet for all our allegiance to contextualization, we still treat space and the events associated with it primarily as cultural markers. This lack of interest in spatial problems is largely a product of the last half-century. Earlier historians typically began their narratives with spatial descriptions, judging that human interaction with the physical world partly shaped the resulting societies. Discussions of proximity, topography, and other spatial concepts informed the work of historians from Herodotus to Braudel. But as the modern world collapsed our notion of distance, space became less visible to students of the past. With few exceptions—the Annales school of France, for instance—we long ago ceased to raise spatial questions, and the ones we do pose rarely admit measurement, except in the most elemental sense. While not the fault of its developers, GIS does not strike many historians as a useful technology because we are not asking questions that allow us to use it profitably.

Fortunately, recent advances in GIS may mitigate some of the burdens of adapting spatial technologies for historical research. As evidenced by the efforts of collector David Rumsey, among others, historic maps promise to be become more readily available for use in GIS.[20] Digital gazetteers are rapidly emerging as one answer to issues surrounding uncertainty, at least as it relates to the location of places, many of which have gone by a variety of names over time. GIScientists are creating new methods of spatial analysis—geographically weighted regression (GWR) and multilevel modeling, for example—to address some of the problems faced by historians who seek to understand local variation as well as the relationship among individual and aggregate data within a defined geography. Some techniques developed for other purposes hold potential for new approaches to historical questions, such as spatial interaction modeling, used primarily in retail and marketing studies, as a tool for counterfactual history.[21] The Open GIS Consortium and other groups of information scientists are addressing the issue of geo-spatial ontology to allow comparison of data from widely disparate sources, cultures, and times.[22] Considerable effort is going into creating spatiotemporal browsers and other tools for managing time more effectively, a quest that has importance for fields far beyond history. Similarly, new visualization techniques and strategies are the object of numerous research initiatives. Once we have ways to visualize the integration of different types of sources, including multimedia, then we can imagine cartographic narratives, historical life maps, spatial stories, and other means of helping historians weave stories that represent the complex past they are interpreting. All of these developments hold great potential for making GIS more compatible with the needs of historians, at least for a new generation of scholars who, as members of a post-computer age, eagerly take up new tools and methods.

What is the future of GIS in history? Assuming continued progress in making the technology more complete and easier to use, it is possible to construct at least two views—one of GIS as a means and one as a medium. In the first scenario, historical GIS is a powerful tool in the management and analysis of evidence, contributing primarily by locating historical exegesis more explicitly in space and time. It aids but does not replace narrative: it finds patterns, facilitates comparisons, enhances perspective, and illustrates data, among other benefits, but its results ultimately find expression primarily in traditional word forms. In this view, historians employ GIS to give geographical context and depth to their interpretation of the past. As a tool, we can imagine wide utility for GIS in many genres of history, such as the following:

- *Religion history:* Do patterns of adherence conform to other geographical or cultural patterns?
- *Immigration history:* Do patterns of migration, typically understood in terms of groups, have a different expression when traced individually and aggregated spatially? What about patterns of demographic or cultural diffusion?
- *Political history:* Do patterns of political affiliation and behavior have an underlying geographical or spatiocultural explanation that is not readily apparent from the socioeconomic analyses typically used by scholars?

Undoubtedly, our treatment of the past would be greatly enriched by answers to these questions and others, although it will remain uncertain for some time if the results shift interpretations, thus providing clear vindication of the significance of historical GIS.

In the second scenario, historical GIS offers the potential for a unique postmodern scholarship, an alternate construction of the past that embraces multiplicity, simultaneity, complexity, and subjectivity. Postmodernist scholarship has sharply challenged the concept of objectivity in history, which has been the lodestar of so-called scientific history since the late nineteenth century.[23] It rejects the supremacy of empiricism, an Enlightenment concept, in favor of knowledge based on all the senses. Postmodernism also has called into question the primacy of texts and logic as the foundation of knowledge. In its epistemology, history is not a grand narrative—an authoritative story of a society's past—but instead a fragmented, provisional, contingent understanding framed by multiple voices and multiple stories, mini-narratives of small events and practices, each conditioned by the unique experiences and local cultures that gave rise to them. Methodologically, postmodernism emphasizes reflexivity, or lived connections among the researcher, the research topic, and the research subject; the importance of giving voice to research subjects; positionality; the non-neutrality of the researcher; the situatedness of all knowledge; and the importance of diversity and difference.

Historians in general have not embraced postmodernism, but it has influenced us, as evidenced by the rise of new genres of history. Many people see this development as further fragmenting a past that already is too splintered. Any notion of a comprehensible, unified past based on a discoverable objective reality was unrealistic, but it also seems clear that we will benefit from some way to meld diverse approaches to the past. GIS may offer a path to this goal, at least in part, because of its ability to integrate information and to make it visual.

Perhaps historical GIS ultimately makes its contribution not as a positivist tool but a reflexive one: integrating the multiple voices and views of our past, allowing them to be seen and examined at various scales; creating the simultaneous context that historians accept as real but unobtainable by words alone; reducing the distance between the observer and the observed; and permitting the past to be as dynamic and contingent as the present.[24] In sum, historical GIS offers an alternate view of history through the dynamic representation of time and place within culture. This visual and experimental view fuses qualitative and quantitative data within real and conceptual space. It stands alongside—but does not replace—traditional interpretive narratives, inviting participation by the naïve and knowledgeable alike. Historical GIS is not yet at this point, but some day it could be. It is a vision worth pursuing.

NOTES

1. Quoted in David Hackett Fisher, *Historian's Fallacies: Toward a Logic of Historical Thought* (New York: Harper & Row, 1970), 131.

2. For example, a recent book by two prominent practitioners of digital history on the Internet fails to mention GIS or other spatial technologies, much less consider how they might be used (or are being used) by historians. Daniel J. Cohen and Roy Rosenzweig, *Digital History: A Guide to Gathering, Preserving, and Presenting the Past on the Web* (Philadelphia: University of Pennsylvania Press, 2006). The omission is altogether too common.

3. This discussion owes much to John Lewis Gaddis, *The Landscape of History: How Historians Map the Past* (New York: Oxford University Press, 2002), chapter 4. It is easy to overdraw the distinction between social scientists and historians, of course, and the use of social science methods by historians confuses the issue even more. The basic distinction cast here relates more to epistemology than practice. Although practitioners of historical GIS overwhelmingly use the methods of social science, they do so for purposes that go the nature of history, not social science.

4. Oakeshott, as cited by Gaddis, *Landscape of History,* 64.

5. "Burnt Norton" in T. S. Eliot, *The Complete Poems and Plays, 1909-1950* (New York: Harcourt, 1952).

6. Gaddis, *Landscape of History,* 22.

7. Gaddis, *Landscape of History,* 33.

8. Simon Winchester, *The Map that Changed the World: William Smith and the Birth of Modern Geology* (New York: HarperCollins, 2001). Edward R. Tufte, *The Visual Display of Quantitative Information* (Cheshire, Conn.: Graphics Press, 1986), 24, cites Snow's map as a classic graphical analysis.

9. Ian N. Gregory, Karen Kemp, and Ruth Mostern, "Geographical Information and Historical Research: Current Progress and Future Directions," *History and Computing,* 13 (2001), 7-22.

10. Thomas Carlyle, "On History," in *The Varieties of History: From Voltaire to the Present,* ed. Fritz Stern (New York: Vintage Books, 1972), 95.

11. Edward Hallett Carr, *What Is History?* (New York: Random House, 1961), 30.

12. "Halos" is the term of mathematician Douglas R. Hofstadter, *Le Ton beau de Marot: In Praise of the Music of Languages* (New York: Basic Books, 1997), 305.

13. An excellent introduction to visual thinking in history may be found in David J. Staley, *Computers, Visualization, and History: How New Technology Will Transform Our Understanding of the Past* (Armonk, N.Y.: M.E. Sharpe, 2003).

14. Anne Kelly Knowles, ed., *Past Time, Past Place: GIS for History* (Redlands, Calif.: ESRI Press, 2002).

15. The best primer on historical GIS is Ian N. Gregory, *A Place in History: A Guide to Using GIS in Historical Research* (London: Oxbow Books, 2003). *History and Computing,* the official journal of the association by that name, publishes frequent articles on historical GIS, including a recent issue dedicated to the subject (vol. 13, September 2001).

16. William G. Thomas III and Edward L. Ayres, "An Overview: The Differences Slavery Made: A Close Analysis of Two American Communities," *American Historical Review,* 108 (2003), 1299-1308.

17. Gregory, et al., "Geographical Information and Historical Research."

18. Mark Twain, *Life on the Mississippi* (New York: Bantam, 1983), 156.

19. A good discussion of the problems associated with visualizing humanities data within a GIS can be found in Martyn Jessop, "The Visualization of Spatial Data in the Humanities," *Literary and Linguistic Computing,* 19 (2004), 335–50. Also see William Goran, "Multiple Dimensional Visualization and Spatial Analysis Technologies," http://www.geoplace.com/gw/2003/0312/industryoutlook/goran.asp.

20. http://www.davidrumsey.com.

21. The reemergence of counterfactual history is discussed in Gavriel Rosenfeld, "Why Do We Ask 'What If?' Reflections on the Function of Alternative History," *History and Theory,* 41 (December 2002), 90–103.

22. Ontology is the development of information hierarchies that categorize how meaning is captured, represented, and communicated across a variety of users so that we can know the synonymous and parallel relationship of terms and concepts across disciplines and cultures (e.g., trunk and boot have the same meaning when applied to the luggage space of a car, although one usage is American and the other English).

23. Although the attack on objectivity is a centerpiece of postmodern criticism, historians have fought bitterly over this issue for decades, as Peter Novak discusses in his prize-winning monograph, *That Noble Dream: The "Objectivity" Question and the American Historical Profession* (Cambridge: Cambridge University Press, 1988).

24. In geography, much of the critical discourse on postmodernism and GIS occurs in the subfield known as Public Participation GIS. A useful critique from the perspective of feminist research is Mei-Po Kwan, "Feminist Visualization: Re-envisioning GIS as a Method in Feminist Geographic Research," *Annals of the Association of American Geographers,* 92 (2002), 645–61. This potential path for GIS parallels the proposed applications of virtual reality (VR) and its application to the humanities and social sciences. See, for instance, the *Journal of the Association for History and Computing,* 6 (September 2003), for several articles about the possibilities in history for VR and other immersive environments.

10

WHAT COULD LEE SEE
AT GETTYSBURG?

Anne Kelly Knowles
with Will Roush, Caitrin Abshere, Lucas Farrell, Andrew Feinberg,
Thom Humber, Garrott Kuzzy, and Charlie Wirene

At key moments during the battle of Gettysburg on July 1–3, 1863, commanders paused to assess the ground, consider their own and the enemy's positions, and observe the course of battle (figure 10.1).[1]

One such moment came at 1:00 PM on July 2, when Confederate Major General Lafayette McLaws halted the long column of soldiers following him down a narrow valley about two miles west of the Union line. A ridgeline had concealed their movements until they turned east toward Bream's Hill, a short rise above the Black Horse Tavern. Lieutenant General James Longstreet rode ahead to discover the cause of the delay. He immediately perceived that the planned route for his corps' march toward the federals' left flank would be dangerously exposed to the view of enemy signalmen visible on the rocky prominence that lay ahead, a hill called Little Round Top. Longstreet ordered his men to countermarch along an avenue of approach that would better conceal their movements. Several hours later, just as Longstreet's corps was almost ready to launch its assault, the chief of topographical engineers for the Union army, Gouvernour Kemble Warren, happened to climb Little Round Top to view the surrounding area. He saw gray-coat soldiers in battle lines and urgently called for troops to defend the Union's exposed left flank. That same day, Confederate commander-in-chief Robert E. Lee watched events unfold from the cupola atop the Gettysburg Lutheran Seminary. And on the third and final day of the battle, Lee watched from the rear of the Confederate line as his men walked, then trotted and ran across open fields into the slaughter that became known as Pickett's Charge.

Over the years, almost everything about the battle of Gettysburg has been closely scrutinized. As the battle considered variously the high tide of the Confederacy or the turning point that tipped the Civil War in favor of the Union, it is the most intensely studied of all Civil War engagements.[2] Historians have given a great deal of thought to what happened as the result of each of the moments when commanders paused to look and consider their situation. What McLaws, Longstreet, Warren, and Lee actually saw, however, has received little attention. Scholars have basically accepted the participants' written statements about what they saw at key moments as recorded in official reports and personal correspondence.[3]

FIGURE 10.1 ▶

Gettysburg battlefield, showing Union and Confederate positions and major lines of engagement on July 1–3, 1863. The curving "fishhook" of the Union line along a series of hills and ridgelines gave federal forces a strong defensive position.

Frederick Tilberg, Gettysburg National Military Park, Pennsylvania (Washington, D. C.: National Park Service Historical Hardbook Series No. 9, 1959), 30–31. Used by permission of the Gettysburg National Military Park.

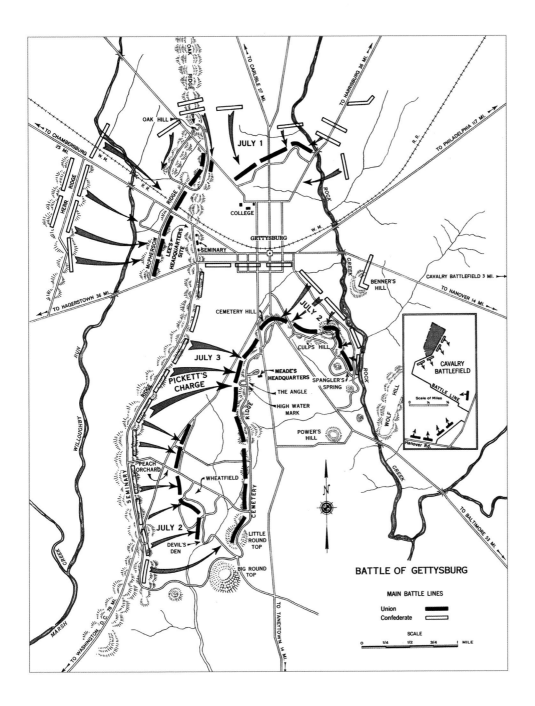

BATTLE OF GETTYSBURG

MAIN BATTLE LINES

Union ▬▬▬
Confederate ▭▭▭

SCALE

0   1/4   1/2   3/4   1 MILE

The sense of sight has figured more prominently in tourists' understanding of the battle's major events and of the battlefield itself. American tourists steeped in the lore of Gettysburg feel a tremor of fear looking across the fields where Pickett's Charge took place as they realize that Confederate soldiers could not see the enemy line when they began their deadly march; the undulating swales before them hid the low rise of Cemetery Ridge and the fences behind which federal rifles awaited them. On the rocky crest of Little Round Top, another obligatory stop, tourists gaze across a shallow valley imagining the legendary rebel yell echoing off the rock-strewn landscape as they size up the margin of safety provided by the boulders and hastily built stone walls where Union troops found shelter. Tours led by battlefield guides often give more particular attention to commanders' lines of sight at key moments of the battle.

Using the landscape to enhance visitors' ability to visualize scenes of battle has become an important part of historical interpretation at Gettysburg National Military Park, which encompasses much of the battlefield in southeastern Pennsylvania. Since 1999, the park has been rehabilitating the physical landscape as it was in 1863. Park personnel are planting trees and bushes in historically correct locations, removing dense vegetation elsewhere, and rebuilding fences in the materials and manner recorded at the time of the battle. The plan aims to give tourists the same lines of sight commanders had and to help visitors imagine soldiers' difficulties as they crossed exposed ground, dodged through underbrush, and struggled to dismantle worm fencing. Gettysburg National Military Park, already the most popular Civil War battlefield in the country, is striving for a new level of physical and visual verisimilitude.[4]

The title of this chapter was the basic question that inspired this study: What could Lee see at Gettysburg? That question soon gave rise to many others. To what extent did commanders rely on their quick reading of the ground as opposed to information on maps or from advance scouts? Can the evidence of sight be used to test the credibility of generals' post-hoc justifications, such as Longstreet's explanation of his long countermarch on July 2? Did the Union's possession of Cemetery Ridge give Major General George G. Meade and his intelligence officers superior knowledge of the battlefield and enemy movements in addition to providing them more defensible positions? How might visual obstructions have affected battlefield communications? Historians have noted that the rudimentary state of communications in the mid-nineteenth century meant that visual awareness and visual reconnaissance were vital during the Civil War, so much so that Lee determined the size of a corps by the number of men a commanding general "can properly handle & keep under his eye in battle."[5]

Social historians have recently become interested in the history of the senses, particularly aurality.[6] Most evidence for studies of sensual perception has come from manuscript records such as diaries and correspondence. In the search to understand the role that sight may have played at Gettysburg, the landscape itself became a source of evidence. Visibility analysis, a common method for analyzing terrain and landscape perception in GIS, uses a digital model of the terrain to determine points and areas that are, or are not, theoretically visible from a known viewpoint. Visibility analysis is routinely used today in computer simulations of battles. It is also used to site ski resorts and luxury homes to maximize the splendor of breathtaking views. Before addressing the technical questions of how to create a terrain model of the Gettysburg battlefield, however, it was important to know how Civil War military commanders perceived terrain and what they knew about Gettysburg before the two armies converged there in July 1863. The keener their ability to read the landscape and the less they knew of the battlefield in advance, the greater the consequences of what they could and could not see during the battle itself.

GEOGRAPHICAL KNOWLEDGE AND SIGHT AT GETTYSBURG

Of all the ways geography served as the "handmaiden of power" in the nineteenth century, none was more important than the role of topographical mapping in military campaigns. French mapping and engineering techniques, developed largely at the state-sponsored École Polytechnique, provided superior logistical and tactical support for Napoleon's conquests at the beginning of the century. French methods of topographical mapping became a required subject at military institutes in the United States, just as Napoleon's tactics became models for waging war.[7] Lee and Meade, who faced each other as commanders-in-chief at Gettysburg, learned topographical mapping and engineering at West Point, as did the many other West Point graduates in both armies. Some of the Civil War's leading figures spent decades working as Army topographical engineers ("topogs" in the parlance of the day). Lee honed his topographical skills surveying the Mississippi River and building water-control projects at St. Louis in the late 1830s. During the Mexican-American War, he conducted reconnaissance missions that helped General Winfield Scott achieve several important victories (figure 10.2).[8] Warren had a distinguished career as a military topographical engineer. His 1855–1856 survey of Sioux territory in the Black Hills gave the U.S. Army the knowledge it needed "of the proper routes

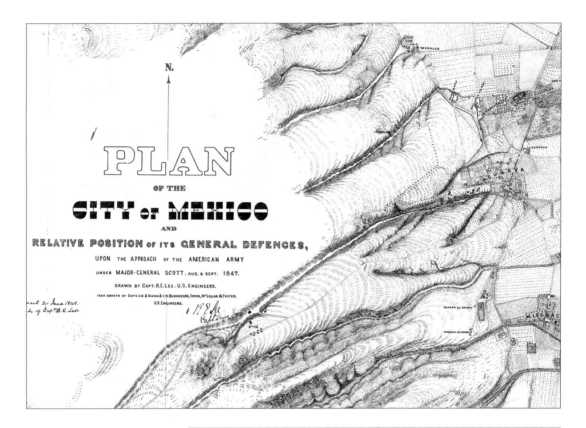

FIGURE 10.2

A young Captain Robert E. Lee led the U.S. military survey of Mexico City and its environs for General Winfield Scott during the Mexican–American War. Other young "topogs" involved in the survey included P. G. T. Beauregard and George B. McClellan, who went on to become generals in the Confederate and Union armies, respectively, in the Civil War.

RG77, Fort File Drawer 112, Sheet 55 (Cartographic Record), "Plan of the City of Mexico and Relative Position of Its General Defenses," drawn by Capt. R. E. Lee (1847), National Archives, College Park, Maryland.

by which to invade their country and conquer them."[9] Extant maps by both men in the National Archives show their mastery of triangular surveying and the impress of French-style technical drawing, though Warren's maps are far more accomplished than Lee's.[10]

Referring to the value of drawing animals in order to understand their physiognomy, the nineteenth-century geologist Louis Agassiz said, "a pencil is one of the best of eyes."[11] Topographical training and long years of practice in the field gave Lee and other "topogs" invaluable visual skills. Lee biographer Emory M. Thomas believes that Lee had an "extraordinary talent for 'reading' terrain. He seemed to understand the ground at a glance and to possess a sense of the relation between one terrain feature and another."[12] Federal commander Ulysses S. Grant, also an experienced topographer, was similarly said to have an intuitively brilliant grasp of the lay of the land and an ability to swiftly exploit advantageous positions.[13] By the time Grant was commanding Union forces in the western theater, his abilities were buttressed by the war's largest and most sophisticated field-mapping corps.[14] In the first two years of the war, however, cartographic resources and geographical knowledge of contested territory were meager on both sides.[15] Military surveys before the war had focused on aiding the improvement of commercial waterways, exploring the settlement frontier, and gathering intelligence for territorial conquest and subduing native resistance in the West. The familiar, long-settled lands of eastern states were relatively poorly mapped. Residents often possessed detailed knowledge of their home terrain, but few maps existed at the scale and with the accuracy that benefited military planning.

In their study of Civil War mapping, geographers Harold Gulley and Louis de Vorsey found "a fundamental lack of appreciation by both north and south of terrain intelligence and map production," which "led to strategic blunders and consequently numerous unnecessary deaths" in the eastern theater. For example, the maps produced for Union General George McClellan's assault on Virginia in the 1862 Peninsula campaign were so flawed that McClellan "lost faith" in maps and thereafter relied on oral reports from "scouts, prisoners, local residents, escaped slaves . . . deserters, reconnaissance patrols, road signs, and aerial observation. The chief weakness of these sources," the authors conclude, "was lack of scope." Confederate knowledge of eastern Virginia was little better; officers preferred much the same sources.[16] The great exception to the paucity of good Confederate maps in the early years was Jed Hotchkiss's map of the Shenandoah Valley. Hotchkiss, who served most prominently as cartographer to Confederate General Thomas J. "Stonewall" Jackson, poured into the map his personal knowledge of the valley as a local surveyor. Historians believe that the detailed field sketches that Hotchkiss made for Jackson significantly aided the general's quick maneuvers and his overall success in fighting federal forces up and down the Shenandoah.[17]

The lack of detailed topographic maps in 1861–1863 made a commanding officer's ability to assess terrain that much more important. The other kind of information that could be crucial for mounting a major attack or march was good intelligence from the field. The cavalry scouting and skirmish missions led by Major General J. E. B. Stuart were the lynchpin in Lee's successful operations in northern Virginia early in the war. As Lee began his bold march toward Pennsylvania in June 1863, Stuart was meant to keep him apprised of the disposition of Union troops between Washington, D.C., and southeastern Pennsylvania. Due to a series of logistical problems and errors in judgment, however, Stuart failed to send Lee a single dispatch. He did not reach the eventual site of engagement at Gettysburg until the second day of the battle.[18] Some students of the engagement believe that once Lee left the Shenandoah Valley, he was moving into hostile territory virtually blind.[19]

Although Lee had traveled to Carlisle, Pennsylvania, during his tenure as superintendent of West Point in 1855, neither he nor his generals possessed detailed knowledge of the region. Their best map for the area around Gettysburg may have been a mediocre map of Adams County that showed the location of households but lacked many of the roads and most of the topographical features that would have helped commanders plan the movement and positioning of their forces.[20] The Union army's intelligence was not much better. Meade's staff also had only the Adams County map as a local cartographic reference, although they traveled on familiar turnpikes from their encampments around the capital into Pennsylvania. Meade had no detailed information about the ground around Gettysburg until after the first day's fighting, when he rode out with topographical engineer William Henry Paine to view the battle lines as Paine sketched the topography around them (figure 10.3).[21] Lee reportedly considered the area around Gettysburg to be the likely meeting point of the two armies, but most historians believe that neither side specifically chose the site, nor did they know it well.[22]

Why did Lee lead approximately seventy-five thousand men into Pennsylvania without better geographical information?[23] Lee biographer Emory Thomas does not answer that question directly, though he argues that in seeking "a showdown battle in Pennsylvania," Lee intended to shock the Union into peace negotiations or at least cause president Abraham Lincoln to pull Union forces out of northern Virginia.[24] Lee had, of course, expected to gather information as his column moved north; Stuart's failure was not Lee's mistake. Lee also sent scouts on urgent reconnaissance missions to help him plan his strategy for the second day's battle.[25] Although anecdotal reports mention him consulting maps at Gettysburg, before that battle and others he rarely requested them and sometimes disregarded them.[26] That he was heading into some of the country's best, most thoroughly cultivated farm land may have bolstered Lee's hope for a quick victory as well. Wherever he encountered Union forces, at least the enormous Confederate train of marching men and horses would be well fed and watered in Pennsylvania.[27]

The limited geographical knowledge that each side's commanders brought to Gettysburg heightens the significance of the information they gleaned on the field. What were their lines of sight, their fields of vision? What could commanders

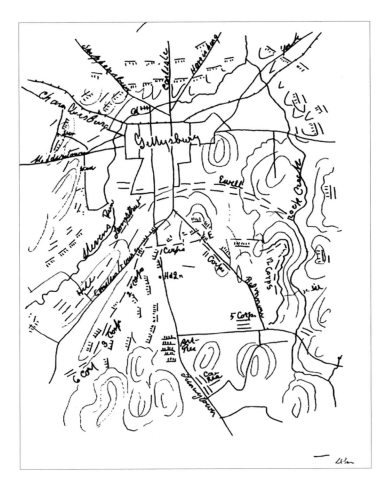

FIGURE 10.3

William H. Paine reportedly drew this sketch of the battlefield on horseback as he accompanied Major General George Meade in an evening reconnaissance on July 1. The map roughly records the location of hilltops and ridgelines, Rock Creek, and the roads converging on Gettysburg. Straight lines with hash mark indicate troop positions, along with the names of corps commanders.

William Paine, Gettysburg manuscript map (Cartographic Record), Paine Collection: A-7-19, National Archives, College Park, Maryland.

discern of the enemy's position and numbers? To answer these questions more comprehensively than one can by standing on the ground itself, we needed to create the best possible digital rendering of the battlefield terrain.

THE SEARCH FOR GOOD GROUND

As a military term, "good ground" means defensible terrain with a field of vision that minimizes the chance of being surprised by the enemy.[28] For the researchers involved in this project, it also came to mean geographical data that provides a good approximation of the battlefield landscape. The search for terrain data began in the office of Curtis Musselman, cartographer and GIS coordinator at Gettysburg National Military Park. Musselman generously shared with us the many GIS layers he and his colleagues had created over the years, including renderings of historic roads and lanes, fence lines, property boundaries, and buildings as they stood in 1863. He also provided a digital elevation model (DEM) developed for Adams County by a private firm in 1996 and a set of contour lines at five-foot intervals that had been interpolated from the DEM. The elevation data meets the U.S. Geological Survey's national map accuracy standards for 1:4,800-scale mapping, and the five-foot contours provide much more detail than the twenty-foot contours available for the area from the U.S. Geological Survey.[29] Detail mattered, because small differences in elevation were strategically important in the battle and in the views commanders had on foot and on horseback. The gentle swales over which the Confederates charged on the last day of battle, for example, were no more than eight and perhaps only six feet from bottom to top. The five-foot contours seemed a promising basis for analyses that would approximate commanders' actual fields of view.

To find out what parts of the battlefield would have been visible from a particular location, such as the top of the Lutheran Seminary, we had to convert the contour lines of elevation into a continuous digital surface that provided elevation values over the entire area of the battlefield. With GIS, we generated a triangulated irregular network, or TIN, from the five-foot contours. This process identifies lines of least distance between points along the digital contours to create a continuous net of triangles whose nodes hold elevation values (figure 10.4). The facets of the triangles

---

FIGURE 10.4   ▶

Detail of a triangulated irregular network (TIN) of the terrain of the battlefield area, derived from elevation contours created in 1996 for Adams County.

Elevation data courtesy of Adams County GIS Office, Gettysburg, Pennsylvania.

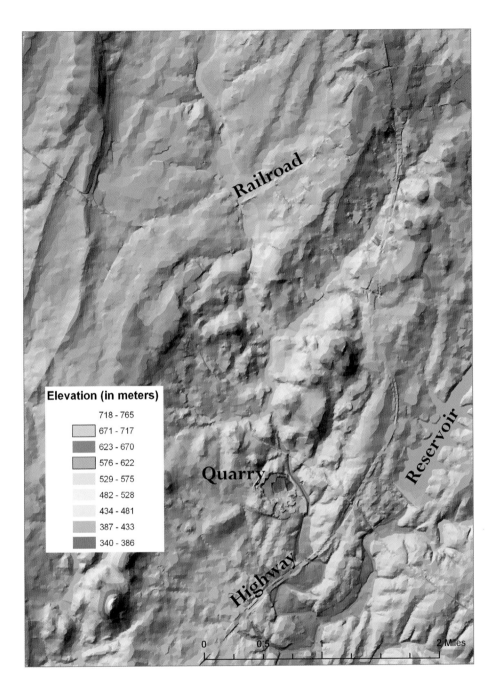

Elevation (in meters)

718 - 765
671 - 717
623 - 670
576 - 622
529 - 575
482 - 528
434 - 481
387 - 433
340 - 386

Railroad

Reservoir

Quarry

Highway

0   0.5   1   2 Miles

represent an approximation of the surface of the ground. We could then perform the visibility analysis to see the GIS program's estimate of which areas of the terrain surface would or would not be visible from specified viewpoints.

Like any human-made representation of the earth's surface, our TIN of the Gettysburg battlefield distorts reality.[30] The actual physical surface of the earth is not made of flat triangles. The TIN is bald of vegetation, whereas the battlefield was covered by various kinds of plants, from waist-high wheat to sixty-foot conifers. The TIN takes no account of diminished visibility at dawn or dusk, nor cloud-cover, nor the smoke of battle. It is a mathematical model, an abstraction generated from contours, which themselves were created by people using photogrammetric methods to interpolate continuous lines of elevation from spot heights and control points drawn on aerial photographs. In other words, the digital terrain is a highly reconstructed, simplified representation of reality. Its chief virtue is its comprehensiveness. It provides what Civil War commanders did not have: a synoptic view of a large area.

The Adams County five-foot contours and the digital terrain we produced from them have two significant short-comings for historical analysis. First, they represent the landscape of 1996, not the landscape as it existed at the time of the battle. The modern landscape includes a quarry, a reservoir, and a highway that skirts the boundary of the national park. They capture the terrain after 140 years of changing land use. Fields that have been continuously farmed since the Civil War may have gained or lost elevation over time due to the effects of mechanical plowing and erosion.[31] Second, the 1996 data contains numerous artifacts of computer calculation, such as the contours' unnaturally sharp corners and geometric shapes. While the 1996 contours probably represent elevation more accurately than any other source, they may not be the best representation of the shape of the battlefield's historical landscape.

Therefore, a second digital terrain model was created from historical maps produced by the U.S. Army Corps of Engineers, the post-Civil War successor to the topographical engineers. In 1868–1869, a crew of army topographers surveyed the Gettysburg battlefield in extraordinary detail. The manuscript map that the field director of the survey, First Lieutenant William H. Chase, produced under Warren's supervision depicts the battlefield at a scale of two hundred feet to the inch (1:2,400), with contours at four-foot intervals (figure 10.5). The entire manuscript map, which measures thirteen feet square, now exists in twenty sections that are kept in a vault at the National Archives with other national cartographic treasures. Between 1869 and 1874, the huge manuscript map was recompiled and reduced to a poster-sized scale of 1:12,000. The resulting engraved map was then rechecked and corrected by

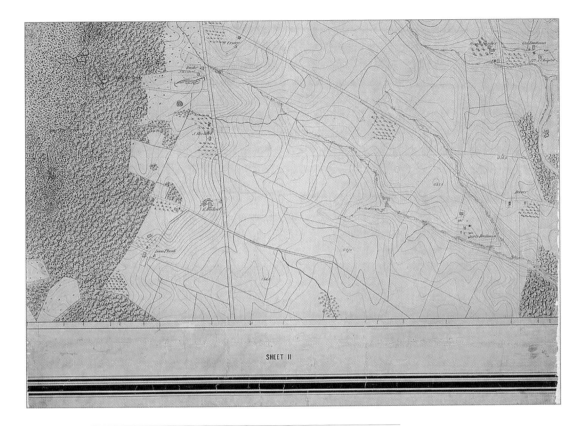

FIGURE 10.5

This detail of the 1868–1869 manuscript map of the battlefield shows the wooded
slope of Big Round Top, farm fields, buildings, and owners' names, creeks and roads,
and elevation as contours at four-foot intervals. The cartographers gave painstaking
attention to detail, as in their distinction between dense forest and orchards.

*RG77 CWMIF E81–2, 1 of 5, sheet II (Cartographic Record), "Map of the Battle Field of Gettysburg," Bvt. Maj. G. K.
Warren (1868–69), National Archives, College Park, Maryland. Photograph courtesy of Ronald Grim.*

a commercial surveyor and Army engineers. Proofs of the final engraved map were
sent for comment to dozens of former commanders who had fought at Gettysburg.[32]

What has come to be known as the Warren map[33] was one of many battlefield surveys
commissioned shortly after the war and paid for by congressional appropriations
and private donations.[34] Several of these surveys assumed a life beyond their initial

purpose of recording topography and troop positions. The military's desire to create an accurate historical record of key battles merged with a broader popular impulse to memorialize heroism and sacrifice.[35] Mapping where corps, brigades, units, and individuals fought became a way to immortalize their roles in famous battles. Mapping also served the interests of those eager to claim spots on the battlefield for military monuments, since determining the geographical location of battle lines and of a particular unit's moment of glory frequently raised arguments that only the authority of a map could settle. A New Hampshire artist and entrepreneur named John Bachelder seized the opportunity of immortalizing Gettysburg within days of the battle's conclusion. Bachelder interviewed hundreds of men who fought at Gettysburg. He established himself as the leading historian of the battle and eventually garnered $60,000 from Congress to map troop positions and record the battle's history. A map series that Bachelder published in 1876 remains the most widely used cartographic reference for the battle of Gettysburg.[36] The 1:12,000-scale map compiled from the Warren survey provided the topographical base for Bachelder's troop maps.

The uniquely detailed depiction of troop positions on the Bachelder maps (for which he claimed accuracy to within half an hour for some parts of the battle) reinforces the notion that Gettysburg was the most important battle of the Civil War. Few nineteenth-century topographical maps approach the final compilation map's masterful representation of landscape (figure 10.6). It was in its own way an impressive memorial to the battle.

Extant surveyor's notes show that the topographers meticulously surveyed the streams, noting every foot change in water depth, the slope and physical character of stream banks, and locations where a freshet could have drowned soldiers burdened with battle gear, as happened to some unfortunate Union soldiers when heavy rains inundated Gettysburg on July 4.[37] If similar care was expended in every aspect of the survey, the entire map may be accurate, though Musselman has found planimentric error of up to one hundred feet in some parts of the map. It is, in any case, the best historical source for reconstructing the terrain at the time of the battle.

FIGURE 10.6 ▶

"Battle Field of Gettysburg," 1874. This final proof of the map includes exceptionally fine shaded relief and hand-tinted vegetation over a buff background and crisp black lines that evoke the topography of the battlefield.

RG77 CWMF E105 (Cartographic Record), "Battle Field of Gettysburg," color proof, Bvt. Maj. Gen. A. A. Humphreys (ca. 1874), National Archives, College Park, Maryland.

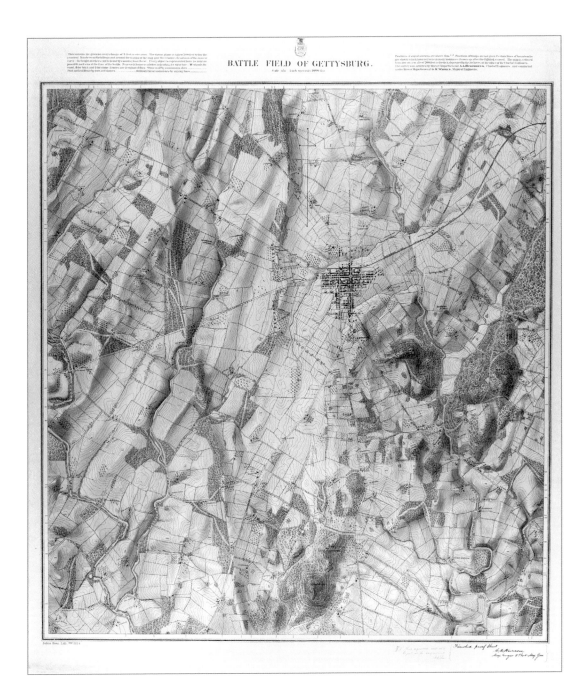

BATTLE FIELD OF GETTYSBURG.

Like the 1996 digital contours, the contours on the Warren map distort and simplify the ground. While they appear to show organic, realistic shapes for hills, valleys, and stream beds, the smoothly snaking lines reflect the aesthetic conventions of nineteenth-century topographical mapping. Having found few manuscript records of the survey, I could not determine how many contours were drawn based on estimated elevations or how carefully elevation was checked in the field. The only elevations marked on the reduced compilation or the manuscript map are spot heights on hilltops and the elevation of some contours where they cross streams or meet the outer frame of the map. One can assume that the attention the Army lavished on the map produced the most accurate elevations and rendering of the landscape that were possible with nineteenth-century mapping technologies.

Extracting contours from the Corps of Engineers map to use them in GIS analysis proved a daunting task. No scanning program could distinguish between the contour lines and the various lines and shapes representing fences, trees, boulders, and houses. The extraction process began with manual tracing of the four-foot contours from a good photocopy of a proof sheet of the engraved 1:12,000 map, using a light table, drafting pens, and Mylar sheets. While most of the map was traced at its original size, the steepest hills (Wolf Hill, Culp's Hill, Little Round Top, and Big Round Top) were enlarged to trace their tight contours. We scanned the Mylar tracings at high resolution, then used a program called ArcScan to separate lines that touched in steep areas and to ensure that lines had not been dropped during tracing and that contour lines connected across stream beds. Once the hills were patched in, each line was assigned elevation as recorded on the original map. The final step was the easy part: using GIS to generate a TIN from the final contours.

Like the contours on which it is based, the historic TIN of the battlefield has an appealing organic quality (figure 10.7). Valleys look more natural than in the blocky TIN from the modern data, and hills and ridgelines have the gradual, rounded slopes one associates with this part of Pennsylvania. If one excludes the small, deep quarry on the modern TIN, the range of elevations on the two surfaces differ by only twenty-two feet, though the historical map's elevations begin and most remain more than one hundred feet lower than the modern elevations.[38]

It was now possible to run viewshed analyses using the historical TIN. But the results could not be compared to viewsheds based on the 1996 data, nor would it be possible to combine the historical data with other GIS layers, until we assigned known geographical coordinates to the 1874 data. Without that, the historical

Tracing of historical contours   TIN from contours

FIGURE 10.7

Once the tracings of the hills were digitally joined to the rest of the historical contours (left) and each contour was assigned its elevation value, a TIN could be generated from them (right), providing a continuous surface that could be used for viewshed analysis.

Source data from RG77 CWMF E105–2 (Cartographic Record), "Battle Field of Gettysburg," Bvt. Maj. Gen. A. A. Humphreys (ca. 1874), National Archives, College Park, Maryland.

contours and TIN were simply lines and polygons with no known location on the earth. The GIS software could not display the historical and modern layers in the same view. It was as if the historical contours were out in the ocean somewhere, hundreds of miles from Gettysburg.

To place the contours in real geographical space, the first step was to add control points to the contour tracing. (This ideally should have been done while tracing the contours.) Control points are typically small buildings or road intersections that exist in the present-day and historical landscapes. Fortunately, many farmsteads shown on the 1874 map have been preserved and are clearly visible on high-resolution orthophotos (aerial photos that have been georectified, a process that removes the geographical distortions inherent in aerial photography). The farmsteads were added to the Mylar tracing. We then used a scan of the revised tracing to digitize the control points onto the digital contours. After a good deal of experimentation, we were able to match the control points to the location of the farm buildings on the orthophotos. Once the historical contours had real geographical location, it was possible to assign them the same projection as the 1996 data, so that the two could be overlaid for visual comparison.[39]

The results were not flawless. The location of specific landscape features in the two sets of contours varies significantly and in more than one direction. Hilltops and ridgelines are generally closely aligned, with displacement of less than fifty feet between the historical and modern contours for some landscape features, such as the peak of Little Round Top. Creek beds and more rolling terrain, however, differ by hundreds of feet in some locations. At the scale of the entire battlefield, viewsheds generated from the two datasets are remarkably similar. Figure 10.8 shows the outlines of two viewsheds taken from the crest of Little Round Top, with the 1996 data in red and the historical data in dark blue.

The two viewsheds show quite similar visible and invisible areas in the eastern half of the map but significantly different results in the western half. Some of the differences could be due to the many small errors introduced during the manual tracing of the contours and the subsequent manipulation of the historical data. It is also possible that some parts of the historical map were more carefully surveyed and drawn than others. A more systematic evaluation of the geometric accuracy of the historical data, perhaps including the precise measurement of spot heights with global positioning system (GPS) equipment, could enable more accurate georectification of the Warren map and its data for further historical analysis.

Given the relatively close match between the modern and historical elevation data for the parts of the battlefield we wanted to study, we decided to focus on viewsheds based on the historical data. Having found the Warren map to be reasonably accurate for the scale of the terrain analysis in mind, we could now confidently georectify a digital scan of the original and let the historical map serve as the background for the viewsheds, whose abstract quality in their native GIS form can make them difficult to read. It would also now be possible to add other GIS layers to help us visualize the landscape.

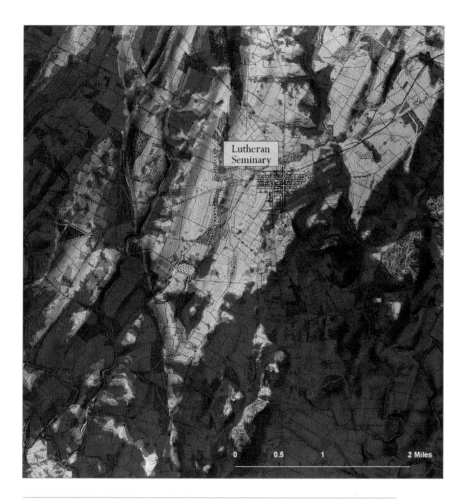

FIGURE 10.8

This image combines viewsheds taken from the top of the Lutheran Seminary cupola using the historical TIN and the 1996 elevation data. In this and other viewsheds, darkly colored areas are not visible, while areas where the historical map can be clearly seen are visible from the viewpoint. The two viewsheds overlap closely in some parts of the map but diverge in various directions in other areas.

Source data from RG77 CWMF E105–2 (Cartographic Record), "Battle Field of Gettysburg," Bvt. Maj. Gen. A. A. Humphreys (ca. 1874), National Archives, College Park, Maryland and courtesy of Adams County GIS Office, Gettysburg, Pennsylvania.

VISUALIZING THE BATTLEFIELD

What could Lee see during the second day of battle from his viewpoint in the cupola of the Lutheran Seminary? Historians have suggested that he had a good view of the ground within a half mile of the seminary, as well as Benner's Hill to the east, the nearest angle of the Union line on Cemetery Ridge, and the Union salient thrust forward by Major General Daniel E. Sickles near the Peach Orchard.[40] Viewshed analysis suggests that Lee may have been able to see considerably more than the rather limited areas that historians mention (figure 10.9). His view could have encompassed much of the northern half of the battlefield. It also may have provided

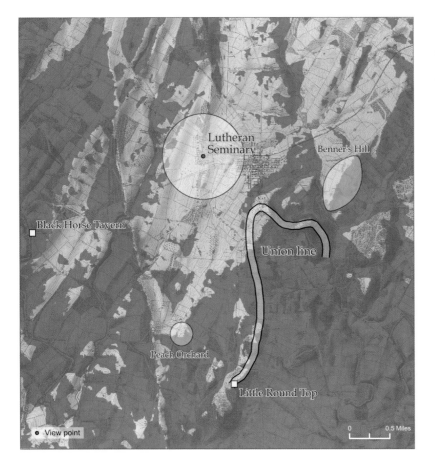

FIGURE 10.9

To generate a viewshed from the Lutheran Seminary cupola, we gave the viewpoint an "offset," or additional elevation above the terrain, of seventy-five feet, the distance from the ground to the cupola floor plus Lee's eye-level standing in his boots. The pale white ovals indicate areas historians say Lee could have seen from this vantage point. According to the viewshed analysis, all but the darker areas would have been visible.

Source data from RG77 CWMF E105–2 (Cartographic Record), "Battle Field of Gettysburg," Bvt. Maj. Gen. A. A. Humphreys (ca. 1874), National Archives, College Park, Maryland.

FIGURE 10.10

This viewshed approximates visibility from several closely situated view points, assuming Gouvernour Kemble Warren would have looked for enemy troops from several locations along the crest of Little Round Top. The red dots marking the viewpoints overlap on the map; on the ground they are spaced roughly twenty feet apart.

Source data from RG77 CWMF E105–2 (Cartographic Record), "Battle Field of Gettysburg," Bvt. Maj. Gen. A. A. Humphreys (ca. 1874), National Archives, College Park, Maryland.

a clear view of the rocky height of Little Round Top and the high ground along the Emmitsburg Road near the Peach Orchard, where Lee had intended for Longstreet's corps to enfilade the Union line with artillery fire.

One can be most confident about the areas the viewshed analysis indicates Lee would not have been able to see, which were precisely where the greatest threats to his army were accumulating: the area southeast of the Union's "fishhook" line, where reinforcements massed throughout the second day; the hotly contested ground between Little Round Top and the Peach Orchard; and large sections of the two valleys down which Longstreet marched and then countermarched Confederate forces before he eventually launched an assault on Little Round Top late that afternoon.

The second viewshed analysis was taken from the crest of Little Round Top (see figure 10.10). Union signalmen had been posted there to watch for Confederate movements, and it was there that Warren spied the approach of Longstreet's corps just in time to call forces into position to defend the Union line. The viewshed analysis suggests that the view from the promontory was generally excellent. It also specifically indicates that Longstreet's men would indeed have been visible as they marched over the ridge below the Black Horse Tavern. The alternate line of approach that Longstreet chose, following Willoughby Run behind the ridgeline closest to Little Round Top, does appear to be the better route for surprising the enemy.

Examining the view from Longstreet's perspective lends further justification for his decision. Lee had ordered Longsteet to attack the Union left flank on the morning of July 2. According to Longstreet, when the front of his marching line reached the ridge just beyond the Black Horse Tavern at about noon, they saw a Union signalman on Little Round Top and realized that the corps' advance would be dangerously

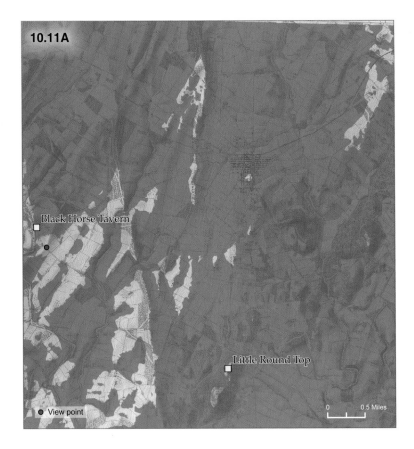

exposed. The viewshed from the road over the ridge confirms that the Round Tops were visible from Bream's Hill (figure 10.11A). A second analysis incorporates viewpoints from higher up the shoulder of the hill (figure 10.11B), where men studying the way ahead may well have walked for a better view. This viewshed shows even more exposed ground and more open fields beyond the second ridge to the east. Either of these views could well have led Longstreet to consider the planned route too risky. He may have moved his men too late and too slowly, but his decision to countermarch appears rational in light of the visual evidence.

The viewsheds thus far estimate visibility over a bare landscape, which is hardly what the battlefield was in 1863. Besides hills and ridgelines, woodlands most significantly obstructed commanders' lines of sight. One can very approximately gauge the

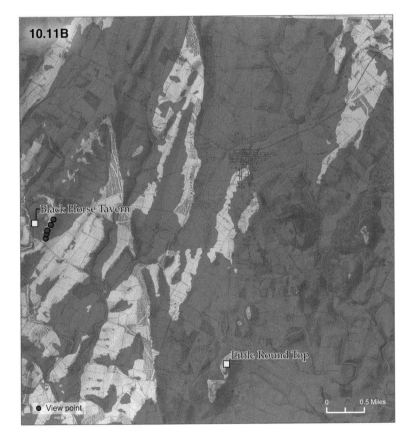

FIGURES 10.11A and B

Whether seen from the road (A) or farther up on Bream's Hill (B), the view toward Little Round Top appears dangerously exposed, according to viewshed analysis.

Source data from RG77 CWMF E105–2 (Cartographic Record), "Battle Field of Gettysburg," Bvt. Maj. Gen. A. A. Humphreys (ca. 1874), National Archives, College Park, Maryland.

extent to which trees increased visual obstruction by adding their average height to terrain elevation. Figure 10.12 shows the results of visibility analysis from the crest of Little Round Top using the terrain surface whose elevation values have been augmented in this way. The additional areas of invisibility cast a dusky shadow to the west of woodlands.[41]

While this technique may better approximate visibility, it is still a crude surrogate for the subtlety of human sight. As the 1874 map's symbols for vegetation suggest,

FIGURE 10.12

The view from Little Round Top looks far less clear when one adds the average height of hardwood forest to the terrain surface (compare with figure 10.10). The artificiality of the computer-generated viewshed is more readily apparent in this enlarged detail.

Source data from RG77 CWMF E105–2 (Cartographic Record), "Battle Field of Gettysburg," Bvt. Maj. Gen. A. A. Humphreys (ca. 1874), National Archives, College Park, Maryland. Tree heights courtesy of Curtis Musselman, Gettysburg National Military Park.

some woodlands had thick growth while others were patchy, shorter stands of second- or third-growth timber or regularly culled woodlots. All trees would have been in full leaf in early July, but approximating the density of vegetation would require simulation akin to the three-dimensional visualization used in computer animation.

Critics have expressed concern over the tendency of GIS users to reify accuracy and gee-whiz verisimilitude. They warn that we are wasting our time and deluding ourselves and the consumers of our images if GIS is mere eye candy or if we give credence to the specious accuracy of GIS images.[42] I could not agree more. One of the virtues of historical GIS (one of the headaches as well) is that it usually requires researchers to create their own data layers because so little historical evidence comes ready-made for use in GIS. In the process of constructing digital historical layers, one becomes intimately aware of the imprecision of the data, the compromises necessary to make it compatible with GIS formats, and how the data changes at each stage of digital manipulation. Historians traditionally discuss the gaps and biases in their sources as an important part of their interpretations. In the same spirit, any work of historical GIS should address the quality of sources and the kinds of uncertainty and error resulting from their use in spatial analysis.

CONCLUSION

In the margin of one of the final proof sheets of the Gettysburg battlefield map, Warren wrote, "As far as I am capable of judging this is the best representation of the ground I have seen and I cannot better it. Familiar with the topography as I am I don't know whether [it] satisfies the natural requirements, or the requirements of my own ideas."[43] Warren and the Army topographers who mapped the Gettysburg battlefield tried to depict that hallowed ground as realistically as they could.[44] The exquisite use of contours, color, shaded relief, and other cartographic symbols on the Warren map exceeds the verisimilitude that GIS can achieve, at least in our work here. In this study, GIS did not prove itself a superior method for re-creating the battlefield, though it did facilitate a new method for investigating a previously unexamined kind of evidence—namely, the evidence provided by the ground where a strategic battle was fought. Despite the technology's reputation for being either hyper-quantitative or hyper-realistic, it was most suggestive at an intuitive level. Some of the most interesting questions that emerged from this work related to individuals' emotional and psychological experiences during battle.

Lee had an excellent field of vision from the Lutheran Seminary on July 2, a bright summer day clouded only by gunsmoke. How did the panoramic view from the cupola affect Lee's perception of the day's events and his decision to launch one more attack the next day across the open fields before Cemetery Ridge? A massive monument to Lee stands near the spot where he is believed to have watched the final assault on July 3. The huge bronze statue depicts him several times life-size, mounted on his horse, Traveller. In fact, Lee had nothing like such an omniscient view. Standing with his field staff on the edge of a copse of woods near the center of the Confederate's line of attack, he would have had a fairly clear view across the undulating fields to his objective (figure 10.13).

Men might have dipped briefly out of view as they walked, then jogged and ran toward the Union line, but Lee would have seen many of them make the slow traverse and fall along the way. Like Batchelder's troop position maps, the GIS view-sheds help one imagine what might have gone through the minds of soldiers and commanders that fateful day. Applied to other battlefields and other wars, similar geographical analysis could provide many valuable insights into military strategy, the wisdom of command decisions, and the experience of war.

FIGURE 10.13 ▶

The viewshed from Lee's perspective during Longstreet's assault (Pickett's Charge) on July 3, 1863, estimates visibility of the ground. Soldiers would have been visible to varying degrees depending on their height, tree cover, and the terrain.

Source data from RG77 CWMF E105–2 (Cartographic Record), "Battle Field of Gettysburg," Bvt. Maj. Gen. A. A. Humphreys (ca. 1874), National Archives, College Park, Maryland.

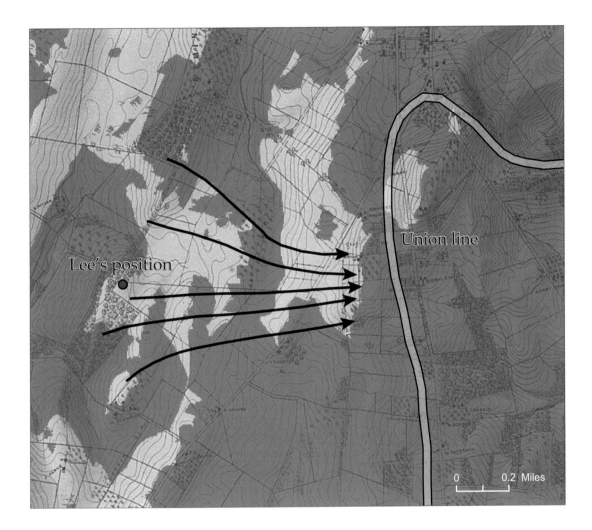

ACKNOWLEDGMENTS

Anne Kelly Knowles would like to thank the following people for their generous help with the Gettysburg research project: Curtis Musselman, cartographer and GIS coordinator at Gettysburg National Military Park; Col. Kavin Coughenour, U.S. Army Retired; Ronald E. Grim, curator of maps at the Norman B. Leventhal Map Center, Boston Public Library; Keith Kerr, archivist in the Cartographic Unit of the National Archives; Ralph E. Ehrenberg; Michael P. Conzen; Emory M. Thomas; and Richard Sewell, whose graduate seminar in Civil War history eventually culminated in this project. Bill Hegman provided GIS support throughout the project; Peter Dana intervened at key moments. The project was supported by faculty and student research grants from Middlebury College.

NOTES

1. The following accounts are based on descriptions of events in Edwin B. Coddington, *The Gettysburg Campaign: A Study in Command* (New York: Charles Scribner's Sons, 1968); James McPherson, *Battle Cry of Freedom: The Civil War Era* (New York: Oxford University Press, 1988) and *Hallowed Ground: A Walk at Gettysburg* (New York: Crown, 2003); and consultation with licensed battlefield guide Col. Kavin Coughenour, U.S. Army Retired, and Curtis Musselman, Cartographer and GIS Coordinator at Gettysburg National Military Park.

2. Twenty years ago, a bibliography of published works on Gettysburg included over two thousand entries; Curtis Musselman, Untitled graduate school research paper [Troop Position Mapping at Gettysburg] (University of Wisconsin Geography Department: Madison, Wis., circa 1985), typescript 40 pages. The trend shows no sign of abating.

3. Thousands of these documents are collected in *The War of the Rebellion: A Compilation of the Official Records of the Union and Confederate Armies,* 69 vols., prepared under the direction of the Secretary of War by Robert N. Scott (Washington, D.C.: Government Printing Office, 1880-1900) [Gettysburg: National Historical Society, 1971-1972].

4. *Final General Management Plan and Environmental Impact Statement,* Vol. 1: Gettysburg National Military Park, June 1999 (Washington, D.C.: National Park Service, 1999); interviews with Curtis Musselman and Col. Kavin Coughenour, U.S. Army Retired, February 2, 2003, Gettysburg National Military Park; Linda Wheeler, "Good Fences Make Good Battlefields: Military Volunteers Help to Restore Gettysburg Parkland to 1863 Conditions," *Washington Post,* May 8, 2003, section B3; Brian Black, *Contesting Gettysburg: Preserving a Sacred American Landscape* (Baltimore: Johns Hopkins University Press, in press).

5. Quoted in Emory M. Thomas, *Robert E. Lee: A Biography* (New York: W. W. Norton, 1995), 289.

6. Mark M. Smith, "Making Sense of Social History," *Journal of Social History* 37:1 (2003), 165-86.

7. Anne Marie Claire Godlewska, "Geography as Handmaiden to Power," in *Geography Unbound: French Geographic Science from Cassini to Humboldt* (Chicago: University of Chicago Press, 1999), 148-90; Peter

Michael Molloy, "Technical Education and the Young Republic: West Point as America's École Polytechnique, 1802-1833," unpublished PhD thesis (Brown University, 1975).

8. Thomas, *Robert E. Lee.*

9. David M. Jordan, *"Happiness Is Not My Companion": The Life of General G. K. Warren* (Bloomington: Indiana University Press, 2001); quotation from Warren's survey report, 30.

10. "Plan of the City of Mexico," Capt. R. E. Lee, 1846-1848, scale two inches to the mile (Cartographic Record), Record Group 77 (hereafter RG77), CWMF D112-55, and "Military Map of Nebraska and Dakota," G. K. Warren, 1855-1860 (Cartographic Record), RG77, CWMF Q-84-3, National Archives, College Park, Md.

11. Quoted in Samuel H. Scudder, "How Agassiz Taught Professor Scudder," in Lane Cooper, *Louis Agassiz as a Teacher* (Ithaca, N.Y.: Comstock Publishing, 1945), 58. Thanks to Robert J. O'Hara for introducing me to Agassiz's insight.

12. Thomas, *Robert E. Lee,* 140.

13. Earl B. McElfresh, *Maps and Mapmakers of the Civil War* (New York: Harry N. Abrams, 1999), 49.

14. Ibid., 244-45.

15. Ronald E. Grim, "Mapping the Battle of Gettysburg," unpublished typescript (n.d.), 16 pp.

16. Harold Gulley and Louis de Vorsey, "Lost in Battle," *The Geographical Magazine* 58: 6 (June 1986), 288-93, quotations on 288, 291; Thomas, *Robert E. Lee,* 235, 269, 282. Gulley and de Vorsey note that Confederate President Jefferson Davis's concern that "maps were a security risk" inhibited southern commanders from pressing for detailed surveys early in the war; "Lost in Battle," 289.

17. William J. Miller, *Mapping for Stonewall: The Civil War Service of Jed Hotchkiss* (Washington, D.C.: Elliott & Clark Publishing, 1993); Archie P. McDonald, ed., *Make Me a Map of the Valley: The Civil War Journal of Stonewall Jackson's Topographer* (Dallas: Southern Methodist University Press, 1973).

18. Emory M. Thomas, "Eggs, Aldie, Shepherdstown, and J. E. B. Stuart," in *The Gettysburg Nobody Knows,* ed. Gabor S. Boritt (New York: Oxford University Press, 1997), 101-21.

19. See, for example, Thomas, *Robert E. Lee,* 293, 298; McPherson, *Hallowed Ground,* 31, 36, 43; Earl B. McElfresh, "Blinded Giant: The Role of Maps in Robert E. Lee's Gettysburg Campaign," *Mercator's World* (May/June 2002), accessed online at http://www.mercatorsworld.com/ article.php3?i=74 on February 2, 2003.

20. Thomas, *Robert E. Lee,* 165. The county map is G. M. Hopkins, "Map of Adams Co., Pennsylvania," scale 1¼ inches to the mile (Philadelphia: M. S. & E. Converse, 1858). It shows only main roads, landowners' houses, and an inset plan of the town of Gettysburg. It shows no topographical features except a peach orchard that became the scene of much fighting on July 2, 1863.

21. McElfresh, *Maps and Mapmakers,* 248.

22. Thomas, *Robert E. Lee,* 292. Harold A. Winters argues it was the inevitable meeting point in "Terrains and Corridors: The American Civil War's Eastern Theater and World War I Verdun," in *Battling the Elements: Weather and Terrain in the Conduct of War* (Baltimore: Johns Hopkins University Press, 1998), 97-111.

23. The figure is derived from Coddington, *The Gettysburg Campaign,* 10, 15, 21-22, 23, 49, 51, 54-56.

24. Thomas, *Robert E. Lee,* 292-93, 302.

25. Harry W. Pfanz, *Gettysburg: The Second Day* (Chapel Hill, N.C.: University of North Carolina Press, 1987), 105-7.

26. Col. Birkett D. Fry to John Bachelder, December 27, 1877, reprinted in David L. and Audrey J. Ladd, eds., *The Bachelder Papers: Gettysburg in Their Own Words,* 3 vols. (Dayton, Ohio: Morningside, 1994), 518.

27. McElfresh, *Maps and Mapmakers,* 15–17 discusses the huge demands of Civil War armies for food, fodder, water, and shelter.

28. Personal communication, Col. Kavin Coughenour, U.S. Army Retired.

29. See U.S. Geological Survey, "United States National Map Accuracy Standards," available on the Web at http://rockyweb.cr.usgs.gov/nmpstds/nmas.html, checked on January 3, 2007. The contours were developed with photogrammetric methods from an aerial survey. Musselman tested them against one-foot contours developed at a scale of 1:1,200 for particular parts of Gettysburg National Military Park and found the elevations accurate to within one foot. Curtis Musselman, telephone interview, January 23, 2004; "Gettysburg, Pa.," scale 1:24,000, U.S. Geological Survey (1994).

30. Denis Wood, *The Power of Maps* (New York: Guilford Press, 1992).

31. Col. Kavin Coughenour, U.S. Army Retired, Gettysburg National Military Park tour, February 2, 2003.

32. The original manuscript map sections are in the National Archives, Cartographic Division, College Park Maryland; "Battle Field of Gettysburg," RG77, CWMF E-81. Proofs of the reduced compilation under the same title are cataloged under RG77, CWMF E105.

33. The manuscript map and its engraved offspring acknowledge G. K. Warren as supervisor of the project, but Warren's manuscript letters in the New York State Archives and his annotations on various proof sheets of the reduced map indicate that he did not personally supervise the field survey and exercised control only through his review of the manuscript map and subsequent proofs.

34. David A. Lilley, "Anticipating the *Atlas to Accompany the Official Records:* Post-war Mapping of Civil War Battlefields," *Lincoln Herald* 84:1 (Spring 1982), 37–42 and "The Antietam Battlefield Board and Its Atlas: Or The Genesis of the Carman-Cope Maps," *Lincoln Herald* 82:2 (Summer 1980), 380–387. Appropriations for the Gettysburg survey and related projects are recorded in S.exdoc.45 (40-3) 1360; S.exdoc.42 (45-2) 1781; S.misdoc.14 (45-3) 1833; and S.rp.694 (45-3) 1838.

35. Battlefield maps are collected in *The Official Atlas of the Civil War* (New York: Thomas Yoseloff, 1958). On memorialization, see, for example, Carol Reardon, *Pickett's Charge in History and Memory* (Chapel Hill, N.C.: University of North Carolina Press, 1997).

36. Senate documents, op. cit.; David L. and Audrey J. Ladd, eds., *The Bachelder Papers.* Morningside Press republished the complete set of twenty-eight Bachelder maps in 1999.

37. Roll 43, Rock Creek, Sheet No. 5, G. K. Warren Papers, New York State Library and Archives.

38. The Warren map notes "the datum plane beginning 500 feet below the cemetery." More research is required before we can determine just how the plane-table survey was conducted in the Civil War era and why the resulting elevations differ so greatly from the modern data, though the use of a different datum is probably part of the answer.

39. The first round of spatial adjustment produced mediocre results, with the historical and modern contours as much as four hundred feet apart for key locations on the battlefield. A second round of spatial adjustment brought key landscape features into much closer alignment. The TIN used for the historical viewsheds in this chapter was derived from the second spatial adjustment.

40. Pfanz, *Gettysburg,* 104–5.

41.The additional elevation was derived by assigning the average height of hardwood trees, estimated by GNMP personnel at forty feet, to areas of circa 1863 woodland, and then using a tool called Raster Calculator in ArcGIS to add that height to the elevations of the areas on the Adams County 1996 DEM that overlapped the woodlands layer. The slight offset visible in the outline of the shaded areas as compared to the boundaries of forested areas hints at the imperfect alignment of the historical and modern datasets. The woodland layer was used by permission of Curtis Musselman, GNMP, who developed it from a variety of historical maps and other sources.

42. Critiques of geographers' obsessive focus on issues of accuracy include Derek Gregory, *Geographical Imaginations* (Cambridge, Mass.: Blackwell, 1994); Michael Curry, *Digital Places: Living with Geographic Information Systems* (London: Routledge, 1998); and John Pickles, "Arguments, Debates, and Dialogs: The GIS-Social Theory Debate and the Concern for Alternatives," in *Geographical Information Systems,* 2nd ed., vol. 1, ed. Paul A. Longley, Michael F. Goodchild, David J. Maguire, and David W. Rhind (New York: John Wiley& Sons, Inc., 1999), 49-60.

43. Marginal notes signed by G. K. Warren on "Battle Field of Gettysburg," NARA RG77, CWMF E105a-4.

44. The phrase comes from Abraham Lincoln's "Gettysburg Address," delivered at the ceremony dedicating part of the battlefield as a national cemetery on November 19, 1863: ". . . we can not dedicate—we can not consecrate—we can not hallow—this ground. The brave men, living and dead, who struggled here, have consecrated it . . ." Many historians later applied the phrase to Gettysburg, most recently in the title of *Hallowed Ground,* a recent book by leading Civil War historian James McPherson.

CONCLUSION: AN AGENDA FOR HISTORICAL GIS

Anne Kelly Knowles, Amy Hillier, and Roberta Balstad

Historical GIS scholarship has made great progress during the past six years. Since publication of *Past Time, Past Place* in 2002, we have many more published examples of HGIS, including the award-winning *On the Great Plains* by Geoff Cunfer and *The Great Meadow* by Brian Donahue. Opportunities for history scholars to learn about GIS have expanded through special conferences, panels at history meetings, workshops, and classes. It is no longer a complete surprise to see historians using maps, spatial data, and some kind of GIS analysis in their scholarship. The growth of HGIS signals increasing recognition among historians that space should be considered in historical analysis.

Its promise, however, is far from fully realized. As David Bodenhamer points out in his essay, some historians remain skeptical of the intellectual merits of GIS or uninterested in what geographical methods have to offer. Others lack the computer skills, data, hardware, and software necessary to join the ranks of enthusiasts represented by the contributors to this volume. Historical GIS as a whole lacks the institutional infrastructure necessary to support and maintain the digital data resources that will be created as the use of HGIS expands. These circumstances must be considered in any plan for moving HGIS scholarship forward. For HGIS to become a significant branch of historical and geographical scholarship, we must address head-on the many challenges that have limited its development as an interdisciplinary movement. Like any subfield of lasting importance, historical GIS requires a strong intellectual foundation and common practices to sustain more and deeper scholarship in the future. Individual scholars, colleges and universities, the funding community, and the software industry all have important contributions to make in this endeavor.

Much of the work ahead will require taking a hard look at how we conceptualize HGIS. Colleagues in feminist geography and critical GIS have much to offer here. Feminist geographers have challenged the strict dichotomy that many draw between quantitative and qualitative scholarship, a divide that typically puts GIS on the quantitative side.[1] Technically, the scanned Peutinger Map on the cover of this book is a grid of numbered pixels, each one corresponding to a particular color, but who would argue that that rich representation is quantitative data? Richard Talbert and Tom Elliott's quantitative analysis of the Peutinger Map is deeply informed by their qualitative understanding of historical sources, as was Anne Kelly Knowles's analysis of the battlefield of Gettysburg. Constructing historical geospatial databases often involves translating textual information into numbers, but as Brian Donahue shows in his study of land use in colonial New England, such translation requires as much care and awareness of historical context and nuance as any other historical method.

Historical GIS should be conceptualized as both quantitative and qualitative. Over-emphasizing the quantitative aspects of HGIS unnecessarily distances the majority of historians who have neither the inclination nor the training to quantify what they study. A broad conceptualization also clarifies the ways in which HGIS connects the humanities and the social sciences through the common recognition that space has been a fundamental aspect of individual and social thought and behavior throughout history. HGIS has greatest meaning as it relates to multiple disciplines, which means that those who are most adept with geospatial technologies should make greater efforts to share their knowledge. Small interdisciplinary conferences, such as the conference at the Newberry Library that gave rise to this book and the "Geography and the Humanities Symposium" sponsored by the Association of American Geographers, University of Virginia, and the American Council of Learned Societies in June 2007, offer ideal opportunities for scholars to share expertise and challenge one another's assumptions. As these conferences demonstrated, bringing people together to discuss intellectual issues of broad interest generates heat and light. At larger history conferences, experienced HGIS scholars need to build relationships with newcomers in fields where geospatial methods are particularly promising, such as migration, economic, military, and urban history. Conference panels and paper sessions need to mix GIS and non-GIS users. Where HGIS is the topic for the session, scholars who do not use GIS should be invited as discussants. We should not be content with preaching to the converted.

In addition to feminist geography, HGIS practitioners can learn from critical GIS by focusing on analysis and the creation of knowledge rather than distribution and visual display of information.[2] GIS will add little to our understanding of history if it is relegated to being a clever device for creating illustrations that show what we already know. The contributors to this book use GIS to generate new knowledge, whether by mapping distributions inherent in historical data or deriving new geographic information through spatial or statistical analysis. Critical GIS also calls for careful scrutiny of data sources (something familiar to historians) and asks scholars to be aware of the power dynamics implicit in creating and representing data. With an expanding pool of HGIS users, these cautions become that much more important. Developments in GIScience and quantitative methods also point toward new challenges for HGIS. Ian Gregory urges HGIS scholars to expand the set of spatial analytical techniques they use to include spatial statistics. Michael

Goodchild argues that historical scholars should learn to use newer forms of GIS, such as object-oriented GIS, that are better suited to historical analysis than older forms of the technology that are rooted in the conceptualization of spatial phenomena as points, lines, and polygons on a static map. The dynamism that now animates GIScience should inspire HGIS as well.

The best way to keep HGIS focused on analysis is to encourage question-driven research. As Knowles suggests in her introductory chapter, HGIS scholarship is most compelling when spatial questions are central to the research, rather then afterthoughts that produce a map or two at the end of a project. Tremendous opportunities await historical researchers because relatively few historical subjects have been examined from a geographical perspective. The Holocaust offers one example. It has been studied intensively by scholars in many fields, but little Holocaust scholarship to date has been explicitly geographical. In August 2007, an interdisciplinary workshop at the Center for Advanced Holocaust Studies in Washington, D.C., considered how new research could be stimulated by asking spatial questions. For example, the Nazis created a vast, unprecedented geography of exclusion and containment in the form of ghettos as well as concentration, labor, and death camps. How, when, and why did these places develop? To what extent was their intended purpose reflected in the distinctive morphology of each type of place and the exercise of spatial control within its bounds? What might we learn from a close examination of the shifting regional and local volume of camp transports, their destinations, which groups of people were being transported, and the geography of survival? GIS will likely play a crucial role in answering these questions.

We also need comparative studies. Much of the HGIS work published to date consists of single-site case studies. What would a comparative GIS study of ancient cities reveal? What can we learn by looking at the geographical patterns of internal migration and immigration in multiple U.S. cities? To be most effective, comparative studies will require common data standards, units of analysis, and thematic layers of historical information. Research projects based in the United States and Europe are currently creating geospatial databases of railroad construction in the nineteenth and twentieth centuries. Were thematic digital infrastructure layers available for studying the history of transportation, urban growth, land use, and land cover, more scholars might undertake historical GIS, and their work could much more readily be made comparable across space, time, and scale. Although researchers are now trying to avoid duplicating one another's labor-intensive efforts in building GIS infrastructure, it remains difficult to choose between project-specific investments in base layers versus building geospatial datasets for use by the larger scholarly community.

The need for better data-sharing mechanisms is one of several issues related to institutional support for HGIS. As more historical research involves GIS and other geographical methods, students, professors, and history professionals outside academia need more opportunities for learning geospatial methods and adapting existing technologies to their purposes. We need more and better GIS teaching and training for history. The course in urban studies that Amy Hillier describes in her chapter and the graduate program at the University of Idaho mentioned in Knowles's introduction are exceptions. While most colleges and universities offer GIS courses, few of them are designed for historians. New GIS courses might feature a partnership between historians and other faculty or graduate students with the skill to teach GIS software. Semester-long courses provide the best opportunity for students to learn enough GIS to apply it successfully in an independent project such as a thesis or dissertation, but fitting a whole new course into the curriculum can be impractical. In these cases, integrating lessons on content-specific GIS techniques into a historical course may make more sense. For example, one could include instruction in georectifying historical maps in an undergraduate research seminar to enable students to use GIS to study change over time. The digital supplement offers examples of these types of lessons, with presentations for lecture use as well as free ArcExplorer Java Edition for Education software and map layers for exploring in lab sessions.

Faculty who wish to learn how to use GIS on their own can avail themselves of a number of resources. The National Science Foundation–funded Spatial Perspectives for Analysis in Curriculum Enhancement program (SPACE) was designed to teach instructors how to introduce spatial methodologies into undergraduate courses in anthropology, archaeology, history, economics, political science, sociology, criminology, demography, and urban studies.[3] One- and two-week workshops have been used to show instructors how to use spatial software and develop lectures and labs. The former Center for Educational Technology (CET) and the National Institute for Technology and Liberal Education (NITLE) offered similar introductory and intermediate workshops in GIS. Online GIS training courses provide an additional resource, but courses focused on GIS applications in history have yet to be developed.

In short, there is a rapidly growing need for improved GIS infrastructure for historical scholarship. The creation of GIS databases adds further complexity to research that has the already difficult goal of reconstructing and reinterpreting the past. It is impractical to assume that all historians practicing HGIS will have the time or the resources to collect their own geospatial data and create their own GIS databases. For this reason, it is essential that shared infrastructure enable large-scale GIS data collection, the preservation and maintenance of geospatial databases, and access to historical geospatial data via Internet-based resources.

Building large-scale HGIS data collections is expensive and time-consuming. It will remain a cottage industry until there is a means of creating economies of scale for historians by allowing them to pool their data resources and use data produced by others. For HGIS to succeed, we must continue to cultivate an ethic of sharing data and develop metadata standards, data formats, and more online digital collections that make sharing practical. This is as critical for teaching as for research. Historians will need access to data both in their own area of training and in other specialties if we are to encourage comparative studies. Some data sharing can take place on a small scale, with scholars contributing their data and documentation to sites like the Electronic Cultural Atlas Initiative. But there is a need for more large-scale data projects like the national historical GIS projects discussed in chapter 1 and for digital map collections like those at the Library of Congress and Harvard University.

The creation of an institutional infrastructure for HGIS will require significant financial resources. Major humanities funding organizations such as the American Council of Learned Societies, National Endowment for the Humanities, and Institute for Museum and Library Services provided crucial support for digital history projects during the past decade. We now need funding sources to dedicate sustained support for an evolving and expanding HGIS infrastructure. The private sector will likely continue to make advances in the software and even to provide seed money for research projects. For historical GIS databases to be preserved and made accessible to all students and scholars, however, we need support for new types of institutions that will foster the development of common documentation or metadata standards for historical geospatial data and provide long-term access to digital collections. These institutions should probably be funded by government agencies or foundations because their primary goal should be advancing scholarship rather than profiting from any particular project.

In addition to money, developing geospatial data infrastructure for history requires collaboration between institutions that hold primary historical source material. The Philadelphia Area Consortium of Special Collections (PACSCL), made up of museums, libraries, colleges, and universities in Philadelphia, provides one model. The consortium collaborated to secure funding to create the GeoHistory Network and explore possibilities of georeferencing and sharing data across collections. PACSCL members also provide support for projects initiated by individual member institutions. The Columbia University Libraries provide a model that retains and preserves GIS databases created by faculty, much as many universities have established institutional repositories for their faculty's published articles. The Inter-University Consortium for Political and Social Research (ICPSR) is another institution that is reexamining its capacity to provide more resources for those who use geospatial data.

Finally, we need new GIS tools suited to the skills of historical scholars and to the questions they want to ask. We need software companies and programmers to develop new programs or extensions to existing packages that do the following:

1. Provide options for representing uncertainty, perhaps similar to color palettes and symbol sets, to help nonexpert cartographers wisely choose colors and symbols appropriate for representing varying degrees of certainty. Such options should draw on existing cartographic methods, such as using dashed lines, hollow symbols, and degrees of transparency. But we also need more scholars to think creatively about how to code and describe the many kinds of uncertainty found in historical documents so that we can effectively analyze and visualize it.

2. Make it easier and more intuitive to document sources and track their use through the stages of iterative GIS analysis. Existing GIS and relational database functionality could be adapted to facilitate source documentation that is more akin to adding footnotes or endnotes. Then GIS programs could generate more familiar forms of documentation than the current extremely technical metadata forms. Historians would particularly like a tool that automatically creates data source notes for maps as easily as GIS software now creates legends.

3. Calculate and represent change over time more easily. This would include tools for working with longitudinal data for area units that change, as when one uses area interpolation, as well as animation tools.

Maintaining a technical staff with these skills and capacities is expensive. Institutions will need to invest in equipment and training upgrades at regular and frequent intervals. Moreover, well-trained employees are in great demand, and turnover could be rapid. All this suggests that, while it should not be impossible to maintain HGIS facilities, it could cost considerably more than historical research support has cost in the past.

What will HGIS look like in five or ten years? There is no question that GIS-based historical scholarship will yield new discoveries. Whole chapters of history will need to be rewritten or revised. Historical scholarship will gain insight and context from more explicitly identifying where and how geography shaped events. We will have more nuanced stories and more confidence in our interpretations.

History will be better, but so will GIS and the GISciences. The intellectual rigor, analytical depth, and standards for documentation that we advocate here are relevant to all fields that employ GIS. In the coming years, GIS will continue to work its way into our daily lives, helping us to make sense of the enormous amount of information available to us. We want students and scholars in history and all fields to be critical consumers of geographic information, whether they are analyzing historical data or live satellite images. Because historical GIS forces us to include time in geographical analysis, it promises to provide valuable new perspectives to the GISciences. A decade from now, we will be talking not only about how GIS has changed history, but how historical scholarship has changed GIS.

NOTES

1. Mei-Po Kwan, "Feminist Visualization: Re-Envisioning GIS as a Method in Feminist Geographic Research," *Annals of the Association of American Geographers* 92 (2002): 645–61; Stephen A. Matthews, James E. Detwiler, and Linda M. Burton, "Geo-Ethnography: Coupling Geographic Information Analysis Techniques with Ethnographic Methods in Urban Research," *Cartographica* 40:4 (2005): 75–90; Sara McLafferty, "Women and GIS: Geospatial Technologies and Feminist Geographies," *Cartographica* 40:4 (2005): 37–45.

2. Peter J. Taylor and Ronald J. Johnston, "GIS and Geography," in *Ground Truth: The Social Implications of Geographic Information Systems,* ed. John Pickles (New York: Guildford Press, 1995), 51–67; Eric Sheppard, "Knowledge Production through Critical GIS: Geneology and Prospects," *Cartographica* 40:4 (2005): 5–21.; Francis Harvey, Mei-Po Kwan, Marianna Pavlovskaya, "Introduction: Critical GIS," *Cartographica* 40:4 (2005): 1–4.

3. http://www.csiss.org/SPACE/.

CHAPTER INTRODUCTION CREDITS

Chapter 1: Detail from map of Lycia in Richard J. A. Talbert, editor, *The Barrington Atlas of the Greek and Roman World*. © 2000 Princeton University Press. Reprinted by permission of Princeton University Press.

Chapter 2: Huizhou Fuzhi 惠州 府志 (1595 ed.).

Chapter 3: Courtesy of University of Pennsylvania Archives.

Chapter 4: National Oceanic and Atmospheric Administration. Coast and Geodetic Survey Historic Image Collection, National Oceanic and Atmospheric Administration Central Library.

Chapter 5: Outline of country from Great Britain Historical GIS.

Chapter 6: Map created by Brian Donahue. An earlier version appeared in *The Great Meadow* by Brian Donahue, published by Yale University Press.

Chapter 7: Etiene-Jules Marey, *La Méthode Graphique* (Paris: G. Masson, 1885), fig. 37. Courtesy of Rare Books Collection, University of Chicago Library, Special Collections Research Center.

Chapter 8: Original map by the authors. Topographic base developed from GTOPO30 DEM. Peutinger Map feature locations interpolated from materials compiled by the Classical Atlas Project and the Ancient World Mapping Center.

Chapter 9: Map and data courtesy ESRI. Courtesy Photodisc-Education 1/Getty Images

Chapter 10: RG77 CWMF E105 (Cartographic Record), "Battle Field of Gettysburg," color proof, But. Maj. Gen. A. A. Humphreys (ca. 1874), National Archives, College Park, Maryland.

BIBLIOGRAPHY

Albu, Emily. "Imperial Geography and the Medieval Peutinger Map." *Imago Mundi* 57 (2005): 136–48.

Alderman, Ellen, and Caroline Kennedy. *The Right to Privacy.* New York: Knopf, 1995.

Allen, K. M. S., S. W. Green, and E. B. W. Zubrow. *Interpreting Space: GIS and Archaeology.* London: Taylor & Francis, 1990.

Amelung, I. "New Maps for the Modernizing State: Western Cartographical Knowledge in Late 19th Century China." In *Graphics and Text in the Production of Technical Knowledge in China: The Warp and the Weft*, edited by F. Bray, V. Dorofeeva-Lichtmann, and G. Métailié. Leiden: Brill, forthcoming.

Anselin, Luc. "Local Indicators of Spatial Association—LISA." *Geographical Analysis* 27 (1995): 93–115.

Arctur, David, and Michael Zeiler. *Designing Geodatabases: Case Studies in GIS Data Modeling.* Redlands, Calif.: ESRI Press, 2004.

Ayers, Edward L., and Anne S. Rubin. *Valley of the Shadow: Two Communities in the American Civil War.* New York: W. W. Norton & Co., 2000.

Bailey, Trevor C., and Anthony C. Gatrell. *Interactive Spatial Data Analysis.* Harlow: Longman, 1995.

Baker, Alan R. H. *Geography and History: Bridging the Divide.* Cambridge: Cambridge University Press, 2003.

Baker, Alan R. H., and Mark Billinge, eds. *Geographies of England: The North-South Divide, Imagined and Material.* Cambridge: Cambridge University Press, 2004.

Baker, Christopher W. *Scientific Visualization: The New Eyes of Science.* Brookfield, Conn.: Millbrook Press, 2000.

Beauregard, Robert A. "Federal Policy and Postwar Urban Decline: A Case of Government Complicity." *Housing Policy Debate* 12: 1 (2001): 129–51.

Berman, Merrick Lex. "Boundaries or Networks in Historical GIS: Concepts of Measuring Space." *Historical Gegoraphy* 33 (2005): 118–33.

———. "Persistence and Scale in Historical Gazetteers." Paper presented at Electronic Cultural Atlas Initiative and Pacific Neighborhood Consortium, Honolulu, November 2005. http://www.fas.harvard.edu/~chgis/.

Bescoby, D. J. "Detecting Roman Land Boundaries in Aerial Photographs Using Radon Transforms." *Journal of Archaeological Science* 33 (2006): 735–43.

Bidwell, Percy W. "The Agricultural Revolution in New England." *American Historical Review* 26 (1921): 683–702.

Bielenstein, H. "Chinese Historical Demography, A.D. 2–1982." *Bulletin of the Museum of Far Eastern Antiquities* 59 (1987): 1–288.

Black, Brian. *Contesting Gettysburg: Preserving a Sacred American Landscape.* Baltimore: Johns Hopkins University Press, in press.

Blancke, Shirley. "Survey of Pre-Contact Sites and Collections in Concord." Report for Massachusetts Historical Commission Survey and Planning Project, 1980.

Bol, Peter K. "The Rise of Local History: History, Geography, and Culture in Southern Song and Yuan Wuzhou." *Harvard Journal of Asiatic Studies* 61:1 (2001): 37–76.

———. *"This Culture of Ours"—Intellectual Transitions in T'ang and Sung China.* Stanford: Stanford University Press, 1992.

Bol, Peter K., and Jianxiong Ge. "China Historical GIS." *Historical Geography* 33 (2005): 150–2.

Booch, Grady, James Rumbaugh, and Ivar Jacobson. *The Unified Modeling Language User Guide.* Upper Saddle River, N.J.: Addison-Wesley, 2005.

Bradshaw, Roy, and Robert J. Abrahart. "Widening Participation in Historical GIS: The Case of Digital Derby 1841." RGS-IBG Annual International Conference, London, September 1, 2005.

Bragdon, Kathleen J. *Native People of Southern New England, 1500-1650.* Norman, Okla.: University of Oklahoma Press, 1996.

Braudel, Fernand. *The Mediterranean and the Mediterranean World in the Age of Philip II.* Translated by Siân Reynolds. Berkeley, Calif.: University of California Press, 1992.

Brin, David. *The Transparent Society.* Reading, Mass.: Addison-Wesley, 1998.

Brody, Hugh. *Maps and Dreams: Indians and the British Columbia Frontier.* New York: Knopf, 1981.

Brook, T. "Mapping Knowledge in the Sixteenth Century: The Gazetteer Cartography of Ye Chunji." *The [Princeton University, Gest] East Asian Library Journal* 7:2 (1994): 5–32.

Burgess, Ernest W., and Robert E. Park. *The City.* Chicago: University of Chicago Press, 1925.

Burrough, Peter A., and Andrew U. Frank, eds. *Geographic Objects with Indeterminate Boundaries.* London: Taylor & Francis, 1996.

Bushman, Richard. *From Puritan to Yankee: Character and the Social Order in Connecticut, 1690-1765.* New York: W.W. Norton, 1967.

Campbell, Bruce M. S. *English Seigniorial Agriculture 1250-1450.* Cambridge: Cambridge University Press, 2000.

Campbell, Bruce M. S., and Ken Bartley. *England on the Eve of the Black Death: An Atlas of Lay Lordship, Land and Wealth, 1300-49.* Manchester: Manchester University Press, 2006.

Cao Wanru 曹婉如, et al., eds. *Zhongguo gudai ditu ji* 中國古代地圖集. 3 vols. Beijing, Wenwu chuban she, 1990–94.

Carlyle, Thomas. "On History." In *The Varieties of History: From Voltaire to the Present,* edited by Fritz Stern, 95. New York: Vintage Books, 1997.

Carman, Harry J., ed. *American Husbandry.* New York: Columbia University Press, 1939.

Carr, Edward Hallett. *What Is History?* New York: Random House, 1961.

Carter, Paul. *The Road to Botany Bay: An Essay in Spatial History.* London: Faber & Faber, 1987.

Chaffee, J.W. *The Thorny Gates Learning in Sung China: A Social History of Examinations.* Cambridge: Cambridge University Press, 1985.

Changery, M. J. "A Dust Climatology of the Western United States," NUREG/CR-3211 Asheville, North Carolina: National Climatic Data Center, 1983.

Chrisman, Nicholas. *Exploring Geographic Information Systems,* 2d ed. New York: John Wiley & Sons, Inc., 2002.

Cliff, Andrew D. and J. K. Ord. *Spatial Autocorrelation.* London: Pion, 1973.

Coddington, Edwin B. *The Gettysburg Campaign: A Study in Command.* New York: Charles Scribner's Sons, 1968.

Cohen, Daniel J., and Roy Rosenzweig. *Digital History: A Guide to Gathering, Preserving, and Presenting the Past on the Web.* Philadelphia: University of Pennsylvania Press, 2006.

Cox, Gary W., and Jonathan N. Katz. *Elbridge Gerry's Salamander: The Electoral Consequences of the Reapportionment Revolution.* Cambridge: Cambridge University Press, 2002.

Crampton, Jeremy. *The Political Mapping of Cyberspace.* Chicago: University of Chicago Press, 2003.

Cresswell, Tim. *On the Move: Mobility in the Modern Western World.* New York: Routledge, 2006.

———. *The Tramp in America.* London: Reaktion Books, 2001.

Cronon, William. *Changes in the Land: Indians, Colonists, and the Ecology of New England.* New York: Hill and Wang, 1983.

———. "A Place for Stories: Nature, History, and Narrative." *Journal of American History* 78 (March 1992): 1347-76.

Cunfer, Geoff. "Causes of the Dust Bowl." In *Past Time, Past Place: GIS for History,* edited by Anne Kelly Knowles. Redlands, Calif.: ESRI Press, 2002: 93-104.

———. *On the Great Plains: Agriculture and Environment.* College Station: Texas A&M University Press, 2005.

Curry, Michael R. "The Digital Individual in the Private Realm." *Annals of the Association of American Geographers* 87 (1997): 681-99.

———. *Digital Places: Living with Geographic Information Systems.* London: Routledge, 1998.

———. "Rethinking Privacy in a Geocoded World." In *Geographic Information Systems: Principles and Applications,* 2nd ed., edited by Paul A. Longley, Michael F. Goodchild, David J. Maguire, and David W. Rhind, 757-66. New York: John Wiley & Sons, Inc., 1998.

Curtis, S., and I. Rees Jones. "Is There a Place for Geography in the Analysis of Health Inequality?" *Sociology of Health & Illness* 20 (1998): 645-72.

Darby, H. Clifford. *Domesday England.* New York: Cambridge University Press, 1977.

Date, C. J. *An Introduction to Database Systems.* Reading, Mass.: Addison-Wesley, 2000.

David Rumsey Map Collection. http://www.davidrumsey.com.

DenBoer, Gordon. *Wisconsin, Atlas of Historical County Boundaries,* edited by John H. Long. New York: Charles Scribner's Sons, 1997, 238-42.

Dennis, J. "Between Lineage and State: Extended Family and Gazetteer Compilation in Xinchang County." *Ming Studies* 45-46 (2001): 69-113.

Doel, Ronald E., and Pamela M. Henson. "Reading Photographs: Photographs as Evidence in Writing the History of Recent Science." In *Writing Recent Science,* edited by Ronald E. Doel and Thomas Söderqvist. London: Routledge, 2006: 201-36.

Donahue, Brian. *The Great Meadow: Farmers and the Land in Colonial Concord.* New Haven, Conn.: Yale University Press, 2004.

Dorling, Daniel. *Area Cartograms: Their Use and Creation. Concepts and Techniques in Modern Geography,* 59. Norwich: University of East Anglia, Environmental Publications, 1996.

Dorofeeva-Lichtmann, V. "Geographical Treatises in Chinese Dynastic Histories: 'No Man's Land' Between Sinology and History of Science." Proceedings of the XXI International Congress of History of Science, Mexico City, 2001.

Du Bois, W. E. B. *The Philadelphia Negro: A Social Study.* Philadelphia: University of Pennsylvania Press, 1899.

Du Yongtao. "Translocality, Place Making, and Cultural Formation: Huizhou Merchants in Late Imperial China, 1500-1800." PhD diss., University of Illinois, Urbana-Champagne, 2005.

Dwight, Timothy. *Travels in New England and New York.* Vol. 1. Cambridge, Mass.: Harvard University Press, 1969.

Earle, Carville. *Geographical Inquiry and American Historical Problems.* Stanford: Stanford University Press, 1992.

Eberhard, W. "Temple Building Activities in Medieval and Modern China: An Experimental Study." *Monumenta Serica.* 23 (1964): 264-318.

Edney, Matthew H. "Reconsidering Enlightenment Geography and Map Making: Reconnaissance, Mapping, Archive." In *Geography and Enlightenment,* edited by David N. Livingstone and Charles W. J. Withers. Chicago: University of Chicago Press, 1999: 165-98.

Eliot, T. S. *Complete Poems and Plays, 1909-1950.* New York: Harcourt, 1952.

Ell, Paul S., and Ian N. Gregory. "Demography, Depopulation, and Devastation: Exploring the Geography of the Irish Potato Famine." *Historical Geography* 33 (2005): 54-77.

Elliott, Tom, and Richard Talbert. "Mapping the Ancient World." In *Past Time, Past Place: GIS for History,* edited by Anne Kelly Knowles. Redlands, Calif.: ESRI Press, 2002: 145-62.

Etzioni, Amitai. *The Limits of Privacy.* New York: Basic Books, 1999.

Evans, I. S. "The Selection of Class Intervals." *Transactions of the Institute of British Geographers* 2 (1977): 98-124.

Fang Xuanling 房玄齡. *Jin shu* 晉書. *Scripta Sinica* ed. Beijing: Zhonghua shuju, 1974.

Faure, D. "What Weber Did Not Know: Towns and Economic Development in Ming and Qing China." In *Town and Country in China: Identity and Perception,* edited by D. Faure and T. T. Liu. Houndsmills: Palgrave, 2002: 58-84.

Favro, Diane. "Wagging the Dog in the Digital Age: The Impact of Computer Modeling on Architectural History." Paper presented at The Computer Symposium: The Once and Future Medium for the Social Sciences and the Humanities, Brock University, Toronto, May 30, 2006.

Final General Management Plan and Environmental Impact Statement. Vol. 1: Gettysburg National Military Park, June 1999. Washington, D.C.: National Park Service, 1999.

Fischer, Douglas T., Stephen V. Smith, and Robert R. Churchill. "Simulation of a Century of Runoff across the Tomales Watershed, Marin County, California." *Journal of Hydrology* 186 (1996): 253-73.

Fisher, David Hackett. *Historian's Fallacies: Toward a Logic of Historical Thought.* New York: Harper & Row, 1970.

Fitch, Catherine A., and Steven Ruggles. "Building the National Historical Geographic Information System." *Historical Methods* 36:1 (Winter 2003): 41-51.

Flowerdew, Robin, A. Geddes, and M. Green. "Behaviour of Regression Models under Random Aggregation." In *Modelling Scale in Geographical Information Science,* edited by N. J. Tate and P. M. Atkinson, 89-104. Chichester: John Wiley & Sons, Inc., 2001.

Forer, P., and D. Unwin. "Enabling Progress in GIS and Education." In *Geographical Information Systems,* edited by Paul A. Longley, Michael F. Goodchild, David J. Maguire, and David W. Rhind, 747-56. New York: John Wiley & Sons, Inc., 1999.

Foresman, Timothy W., ed. *The History of Geographic Information Systems: Perspectives from the Pioneers.* Upper Saddle River, N.J.: Prentice Hall, 1998.

Foster, David R. "Thoreau's Country: A Historical-Ecological Perspective on Conservation in the New England Landscape." *Journal of Biogeography* 29 (2002): 1537–56.

Fotheringham, A. Stewart. "Trends in Quantitative Methods I: Stressing the Local." *Progress in Human Geography* 21 (1997): 88–96.

Fotheringham, A. Stewart, Chris Brunsdon, and Martin Charlton. *Geographically Weighted Regression: The Analysis of Spatially Varying Relationships.* Chichester: John Wiley & Sons, Inc., 2002.

———. *Quantitative Geography: Perspectives on Spatial Data Analysis.* London: Sage, 2000.

Fotheringham, A. Stewart, and D. W. Wong. "The Modifiable Areal Unit Problem in Multi-Variate Statistical Analysis." *Environment and Planning A* 23 (1991): 1025–44.

Gaddis, John Lewis. *The Landscape of History: How Historians Map the Past.* New York: Oxford University Press, 2002.

Ganzel, Bill. *Dust Bowl Descent.* Lincoln: University of Nebraska Press, 1984.

Gao Congming 高聰明. *Songdai huobi yu huobi liutong yanjiu* 宋代貨幣與貨幣流通研究. Baoding, Hebei daxue chubanshe, 1999.

Gastner, M. T., and M. E. J. Newman. "Diffusion-Based Method for Producing Density Equalizing Maps." *Proceedings of the National Academy of Sciences* 101 (2004): 7499–503.

Gatrell, Anthony C. "Any Space for Spatial Analysis?" In *The Future of Geography,* edited by Ronald J. Johnston, 190–208. London: Methuen, 1985.

———. *Geographies of Health.* London: John Wiley & Sons, Inc., 2002.

Gautier Dalché, Patrick. "La trasmissione medievale e rinascimentale della *Tabula Peutingeriana.*" In *Tabula Peutingeriana: Le Antiche Vie del Mondo,* edited by Francesco Prontera, 43–52. Florence: Olschki, 2003.

Getis, A., and J. K. Ord. "The Analysis of Spatial Association by Use of Distance Statistics." *Geographical Analysis* 24 (1992): 189–206.

Gilliland, Jason. "Imag(in)ing London's Past into the Future with Historical GIS." Paper presented at the Annual Association of Canadian Geographers, Toronto, June 1, 2006.

Gillings, Mark, and David Wheatley. *Spatial Technology and Archaeology: The Archaeological Applications of GIS.* London: Taylor & Francis, 2002.

"GIS: Tool or Science?" Forum, *Annals of the Association of American Geographers* 87: 2 (1997): 346–73.

Godlewska, Anne Marie Claire. *Geography Unbound: French Geographic Science from Cassini to Humboldt.* Chicago: University of Chicago Press, 1999.

Goldewijk, Kees Klein, and Navin Ramankutty. "Land Cover Change over the Last Three Centuries Due to Human Activities: The Availability of New Global Data Sets." *GeoJournal* 61 (2004): 335–44.

Goodchild, Michael F. *Introduction to Spatial Autocorrelation. Concepts and Techniques in Modern Geography,* 47. Norwich: GeoAbstracts, 1987.

Goodchild, Michael F., Luke Anselin, and U. Deichmann. "A Framework for the Areal Interpolation of Socioeconomic Data." *Environment and Planning A* 25 (1993): 383–97.

Goodchild, Michael F., and Donald G. Janelle, eds. *Spatially Integrated Social Science.* Oxford: Oxford University Press, 2004.

Goodchild, Michael F., and N. S.-N. Lam. "Areal Interpolation: A Variant of the Traditional Spatial Problem." *Geo-Processing* 1 (1980): 297–312.

Goudie, A. S. "Dust Storms in Space and Time." *Progress in Physical Geography* 7 (1983): 502–30.

Goudie, A. S., and N. J. Middleton. "The Changing Frequency of Dust Storms through Time," *Climatic Change* 20 (March 1992): 197–225.

Gregory, Derek. *Geographical Imaginations.* Cambridge, Mass.: Blackwell, 1994.

Gregory, Ian N. "The Accuracy of Areal Interpolation Techniques: Standardising 19th- and 20th-Century Census Data to Allow Long-Term Comparisons." *Computers Environment and Urban Systems* 26 (2002): 293–314.

——. *A Place in History: A Guide to Using GIS in Historical Research.* Oxford: Oxbow Books, 2003.

——. "Time-variant GIS Databases of Changing Historical Administrative Boundaries: A European Comparison," *Transactions in GIS* 6: 2 (2002): 161–78.

Gregory, Ian N., C. Bennett, V. L. Gilbam, and H. R. Southall. "The Great Britain Historical GIS Project: From Maps to Changing Human Geography." *Cartographic Journal* 39:1 (2002): 37–49.

Gregory, Ian N., and Paul S. Ell. "Analyzing Spatio-Temporal Change Using National Historical GISs: Population Change during and after the Great Irish Famine." *Historical Methods* 38 (2005): 149–67.

——. "Breaking the Boundaries: Integrating 200 Years of the Census Using GIS." *Journal of the Royal Statistical Society, Series A* 168 (2005): 419–37.

——. "Error Sensitive Historical GIS: Identifying Areal Interpolation Errors in Time-Series Data." *International Journal of Geographical Information Science* 20 (2006): 135–52.

——. *Historical GIS: Technologies, Methodologies, and Scholarship.* Cambridge: Cambridge University Press, in press.

Gregory, Ian N., Karen Kemp, and Ruth Mostern. "Geographical Information and Historical Research: Current Progress and Future Directions." *History and Computing* 13 (2001): 7–22.

Greven, Philip J. *Four Generations: Population, Land, and Family in Colonial Andover, Massachusetts.* Ithaca, N.Y.: Cornell University Press, 1970.

Gross, Robert. *The Minutemen and Their World.* New York: Hill and Wang, 1976.

Gulley, Harold, and Louis de Vorsey. "Lost in Battle." *The Geographical Magazine* 58: 6 (June 1986): 288–93.

Guo Zhengzhong 郭正中. *Liang Song chengxiang shangpin huobi jingji kaolue* 兩宋城鄉商品貨幣經濟考略. Beijing, Jingli guangli chuban she, 1997.

Gutmann, Myron P., and Geoff Cunfer. "A New Look at the Causes of the Dust Bowl." Pub. no. 99-1. Lubbock, Texas: International Center for Arid and Semiarid Land Studies, 1999.

Hägerstrand, Torsten. "What about People in Regional Science?" *Papers of the Regional Science Association* 24 (1970): 7–21.

Hall, Stephen S. *Mapping the Next Millennium.* New York: Random House, 1992.

Hammett, Julia E. "Ethnohistory of Aboriginal Landscapes in the Southeastern United States." In *Biodiversity and Native America,* edited by Paul E. Minnis and Wayne J. Elisens, 249–93. Norman: University of Oklahoma Press, 2000.

Hansen, V. *Changing Gods in Medieval China,* 1127–1276. Princeton: Princeton University Press, 1990.

Hansen, Wallace R. *Geology and Mineral Resources of the Hudson and Maynard Quadrangles Massachusetts.* Washington, D.C.: USGS Geological Survey Bulletin 1038, 1956.

Hare, Timothy S. "Using Measures of Cost Distance in the Estimation of Polity Boundaries in the Postclassic Yautepec Valley, Mexico." *Journal of Archaeological Science* 31 (2004): 799-814.

Hargett, James M. "Song Dynasty Local Gazetteers and Their Place in the History of Difangzhi Writing," *Harvard Journal of Asiatic Studies* 56:2 (1996): 405-42.

Harley, J. Brian. "Deconstructing the Map." *Cartographica* 26 (1989): 1-20.

———. "Maps, Knowledge, and Power." In *The Iconography of Landscape*, edited by Denis Cosgrove and Stephen Daniels, 277-312. Cambridge: Cambridge University Press, 1988.

———. *The New Nature of Maps*, edited by Paul Laxton. Baltimore: Johns Hopkins University Press, 2001.

Harris, Trevor M. "GIS in Archaeology." In *Past Time, Past Place: GIS for History*, edited by Anne Kelly Knowles, 131-43. Redlands, Calif.: ESRI Press, 2002.

Harrison, H. "Village Identity in Rural North China: A Sense of Place in the Diary of Liu Dapeng." In *Town and Country in China: Identity and Perception*, edited by D. Faure and T.T. Liu, 85-106. Houndsmills: Palgrave, 2002.

Harrower, Mark. "Representing Uncertainty: Does It Help People Make Better Decisions?" White paper prepared for the UCGIS Workshop: Geospatial Visualization and Knowledge Discovery Workshop, National Conference Center, Landsdowne, Virginia, November 18-20, 2003.

Hartwell, R. "Demographic, Political, and Social Transformation of China, 750-1550." *Harvard Journal of Asiatic Studies* 42:2 (1982): 365-442.

Harvey, Francis, Mei-Po Kwan, and Marianna Pavlovskaya. "Introduction: Critical GIS." *Cartographica* 40:4 (2005): 1-4.

Healey, Richard G. *The Pennsylvanian Anthracite Coal Industry, 1860-1902: Economic Cycles, Business Decision-Making, and Regional Dynamics.* Scranton, Pa.: University of Scranton Press, 2007.

Healey, Richard G., and Trem R. Stamp. "Historical GIS as a Foundation for the Analysis of Regional Economic Growth: Theoretical, Methodological, and Practical Issues." *Social Science History* 24:3 (2000): 575-612.

Heasley, Lynne. "Shifting Boundaries on a Wisconsin Landscape: Can GIS Help Historians Tell a Complicated Story?" *Human Ecology* 31:2 (2003): 183-211.

Hill, Linda. *Georeferencing: The Geographic Associations of Information.* Cambridge, Mass.: MIT Press, 2006.

Hillier, Amy. "Redlining and the Home Owners' Loan Corporation." *Journal of Urban History* 29: 4 (2003): 394-420.

History and Computing 13: 1 (2001, published 2003). Guest editors Ian N. Gregory and Paul S. Ell.

Hofstadter, Douglas R. *Le Ton beau de Marot: In Praise of the Music of Languages.* New York: Basic Books, 1997.

Hsu, Mei-ling. "The Qin Maps: A Clue to Later Chinese Cartographic Development." *Imago Mundi* 45 (1993): 90-100.

Hu Bangbo. "Cartography in a Chinese Gazetteer of 1268, The Gazetteer of Linan Prefecture." *Middle States Geographer* 32 (1999): 61-70.

———. "Maps and Political Power: A Cultural Interpretation of the Maps in *The Gazetteer of Jiankang Prefecture.*" *Journal of the North American Cartographic Information Society* 34 (1999): 9-22.

Huang Jinsheng 黃金聲, ed. *Jinhua xianzhi* 金華縣志. 10 *juan.* 1823.

Huang Minzhi 黃敏枝. *Songdai fojiao shehui jingjishi lunji* 宋代佛教社會經濟史論集. Taibei, Xuesheng shuju, 1989.

Hucker, Charles O. *Dictionary of Official Titles in Imperial China*. Stanford: Stanford University Press, 1985.

Hull House residents. *Hull House Maps and Papers*. New York: T.Y. Crowell & Co., 1895.

Hymes, R. P. *Statesmen and Gentlemen: The Elite of Fu-Chou, Chiang-hsi, in Northern and Southern Sung*. Cambridge: Cambridge University Press, 1986.

Jackson, Kenneth. *Crabgrass Frontier: The Suburbanization of the United States*. New York: Oxford University Press, 1985.

Jaffee, David. *People of the Wachusett: Greater New England in History and Memory, 1630–1860*. Ithaca, N.Y.: Cornell University Press, 1999.

Jessop, Martyn. "The Visualization of Spatial Data in the Humanities." *Literary and Linguistic Computing, 19* (2004), 335–50.

Jiaqing Chongxiu Da Qing yitong zhi 嘉慶重修大清一統志. Shanghai, Shang wu yin shu guan, 1934.

Johnson, David. *The Medieval Chinese Oligarchy*. Boulder: Westview Press, 1977.

Johnston, Ronald J. *Philosophy and Human Geography: An Introduction to Contemporary Approaches*. London: Edward Arnold, 1983.

Jones, William. "A Topographical Description of the Town of Concord, August 20th, 1792." *Collections of the Massachusetts Historical Society, 1792, vol. 1, 237*.

Jordan, David M. *"Happiness Is Not My Companion": The Life of General G. K. Warren*. Bloomington: Indiana University Press, 2001.

Karlgren, Bernard. "The Book of Documents: Yu gong (Tribute of Yu)." *Bulletin of the Museum of Far Eastern Antiquities* 22 (1950): 12–18.

Kennedy, Liam, Paul S. Ell, E. M. Crawford, and L. A. Clarkson. *Mapping the Great Irish Famine: A Survey of the Famine Decades*. Dublin: Four Courts Press, 1999.

Knowles, Anne Kelly. "A Case for Teaching Geographic Visualization without GIS." *Cartographic Perspectives* 36 (Spring 2000): 24–37.

———. "Introduction to the Special Issue: Historical GIS: The Spatial Turn in Social Science History." *Social Science History* 24:3 (2000): 451–67.

———, ed. *Past Time, Past Place: GIS for History*. Redlands, Calif.: ESRI Press, 2002.

———, ed. "Reports on National Historical GIS Projects." *Emerging Trends in Historical GIS, Historical Geography* 33 (2005): 134–58.

Knowles, Anne Kelly, and Richard G. Healey. "Geography, Timing, and Technology: A GIS-Based Analysis of Pennsylvania's Iron Industry, 1825–1875." *Journal of Economic History* 66:3 (2006): 608–34.

Koteff, Carl. *Surficial Geology of the Concord Quadrangle, Massachusetts*. Washington, D.C.: USGS Map GQ-331, 1964.

Krygier, John B. "Envisioning the American West: Maps, the Representational Barage of 19th Century Expedition Reports, and the Production of Scientific Knowledge." *Cartography and Geographic Information Systems* 24:1 (1997): 27–50.

Kwan, Mei-Po. "Feminist Visualization: Re-envisioning GIS as a Method in Feminist Geographic Research." *Annals of the Association of American Geographers* 92 (2002): 645–61.

Kwan, Mei-Po, and J. Lee, "Geo-Visualization of Human Activity Patterns Using 3-D GIS: A Time-Geographic Approach." In *Spatially Integrated Social Science*, edited by Michael F. Goodchild and Donald G. Janelle, 48–66. New York: Oxford University Press, 2004.

Ladd, David L., and Audrey J. Ladd, eds. *The Bachelder Papers: Gettysburg in Their Own Words,* 3 vols. Dayton, Ohio: Morningside, 1994.

Ladurie, Emmanuel Le Roy. *Love, Death, and Money in the Pays d'Oc.* Translated by Alan Sheridan. New York: Braziller, 1982.

———. *The Peasants of Languedoc.* Translated by John Day. Urbana: University of Illinois Press, 1974.

Lake, M. W., P. E. Woodman, and S. J. Mithen. "Tailoring GIS Software for Archaeological Applications: An Example Concerning Viewshed Analysis." *Journal of Archaeological Science* 25 (1998): 27-38.

Lamouroux, C. "Geography and Politics: The Song-Liao Border Dispute of 1074/75." *China and Her Neighbours: Borders, Visions of the Other, Foreign Policy, 10th to 19th Century,* edited by S. Dabribghaus and R. Ptak, 1-28. Weisbaden: Harrassowitz Verlag, 1997.

Lancaster, Lewis R., and David J. Bodenhamer. "The Electronic Cultural Atlas Initiative and the North American Religion Atlas." In *Past Time, Past Place: GIS for History,* edited by Anne Kelly Knowles, 163-77. Redlands, Calif.: ESRI Press, 2002.

Langran, Gail. *Time in Geographic Information Systems.* London: Taylor & Francis, 1992.

Leeming, F. "Official Landscapes in Traditional China." *Journal of the Economic and Social History of the Orient* 23, parts 1-2 (1980): 153-204.

Li Jifu 李吉甫 and He Cijun 賀次君. *Yuanhe jun xian tu zhi* 元和郡縣圖志. Beijing, Zhonghua shu ju, 1983.

Li Ruwei 李汝為, ed. *Yongkang xianzhi* 永康縣志. 16 *juan.* 1892.

Lilley, David A. "Anticipating the *Atlas to Accompany the Official Records:* Post-War Mapping of Civil War Battlefields." *Lincoln Herald* 84: 1 (Spring 1982): 37-42.

———. "The Antietam Battlefield Board and Its Atlas: Or the Genesis of the Carman-Cope Maps." *Lincoln Herald* 82: 2 (Summer 1980): 380-7.

Lilley, Keith, Chris Lloyd, and Steven Trick. *Mapping the Medieval Urban Landscape: Edward I's New Towns of England and Wales.* http://www.qub.ac.uk/urban_mapping.

Llobera, Marcos. "Building Past Landscape Perception with GIS: Understanding Topographic Prominence." *Journal of Archaeological Science* 28 (2001): 1005-14.

Long, John H. "The Case for Historical Cartographic Data Files." Unpublished conference paper, American Historical Association, Dallas, Texas, December 1977.

———. "The Nature of Research into Past County Boundaries and Its Implications for Historical GIS Infrastructure." Unpublished conference paper, Social Science History Association, St. Louis, Missouri, October 2002.

Longley, Paul A., Michael F. Goodchild, David J. Maguire, and David W. Rhind, eds. *Geographic Information Systems and Science.* New York: John Wiley & Sons, Inc., 2001.

Maantay, J. "Zoning, Equity, and Public Health." *American Journal of Public Health* 91:7 (2001): 1033-41.

MacDonald, Bertrum H., and Fiona A. Black. "Using GIS for Spatial and Temporal Analyses in Print Culture Studies: Some Opportunities and Challenges." *Social Science History* 24:3 (2000): 505-36.

MacEachren, Alan M. "Visualization Quality and the Representation of Uncertainty." In *Some Truth with Maps: A Primer on Symbolization & Design.* Washington, D.C.: Association of American Geographers, 1994.

MacEachren, Alan M., and Fraser Taylor. *Visualization in Modern Cartography.* London: Elsevier, 1994.

Malin, James C. "Dust Storms, 1850-1900." *Kansas Historical Quarterly* 14 (May, August, November 1946): 129-44, 265-96, 391-413.

Maling, D. H. *Measurements from Maps: Principles and Methods of Cartometry.* New York: Pergamon, 1989.

Mann, Charles. *1491: New Revelations of the Americas before Columbus.* New York: Alfred A. Knopf, 2005.

Massey, Doreen. *For Space.* London: Sage, 2005.

———. "Space-Time, 'Science,' and the Relationship between Physical Geography and Human Geography." *Transactions of the Institute of British Geographers: New Series* 24 (1999): 261-76.

Matthews, Stephen A., James E. Detwiler, and Linda M. Burton. "Geo-Ethnography: Coupling Geographic Information Analysis Techniques with Ethnographic Methods in Urban Research." *Cartographica* 40:4 (2005): 75-90.

Maya Mapping Project. *Maya Atlas: The Struggle to Preserve Maya Land in Southern Belize.* Berkeley: North Atlantic Books, 1997.

McCormick, Michael. *Origins of the European Economy: Communications and Commerce,* A.D. 300-900. Cambridge: Cambridge University Press, 2001.

McDonald, Archie P., ed. *Make Me a Map of the Valley: The Civil War Journal of Stonewall Jackson's Topographer.* Dallas: Southern Methodist University Press, 1973.

McElfresh, Earl B. "Blinded Giant: The Role of Maps in Robert E. Lee's Gettysburg Campaign." *Mercator's World* (May/June 2002). http://www.mercatorsworld.com/article.php3?i=74 (accessed on February 2, 2003).

———. *Maps and Mapmakers of the Civil War.* New York: Harry N. Abrams, 1999.

McKinney-Whetstone, Diane. *Tumbling.* New York: Morrow, 1996.

McLafferty, Sara. "Women and GIS: Geospatial Technologies and Feminist Geographies." *Cartographica* 40:4 (2005): 37-45.

McPherson, James. *Battle Cry of Freedom: The Civil War Era.* New York: Oxford University Press, 1988.

———. *Hallowed Ground: A Walk at Gettysburg.* New York: Crown, 2003.

Meinig, Donald W. *The Shaping of America: A Geographical Perspective on 500 Years of History,* 4 vols. New Haven: Yale University Press, 1986-2004.

Merchant, Carolyn. *Ecological Revolutions: Nature, Gender and Science in New England.* Chapel Hill, N.C.: University of North Carolina Press, 1989.

Metraux, Stephen. "Waiting for the Wrecking Ball: Skid Row in Postindustrial Philadelphia." *Journal of Urban History* 25: 5 (1999): 691-716.

Meuhrcke, Phillip C. "The Logic of Map Design." In *Cartographic Design: Theoretical and Practical Perspectives,* edited by Clifford H. Wood and C. Peter Keller, 271-8. New York: John Wiley & Sons, Inc., 1996.

Miller, Konrad, *Itineraria Romana: Römische Reisewege an der Hand der Tabula Peutingeriana dargestellt.* Stuttgart: Strecker und Schröder, 1916.

Miller, William J. *Mapping for Stonewall: The Civil War Service of Jed Hotchkiss.* Washington, D.C.: Elliott & Clark Publishing, 1993.

Mitchell, Don. *The Right to the City: Social Justice and the Fight for Public Space.* New York: Guilford Press, 2003.

Mohl, Raymond. "Planned Destruction: The Interstates and Central City Housing." In *From Tenements to the Taylor Homes,* edited by J. F. Bauman, R. Biles, and K. M. Szylvian, 226-45. University Park, Penn.: Pennsylvania State University Press, 1985.

Mokyr, Joel. *Why Ireland Starved: A Quantitative and Analytical History of the Irish Economy, 1800-1850.* London: Harper Collins, 1983.

Molloy, Peter Michael. "Technical Education and the Young Republic: West Point as America's École Polytechnique, 1802-1833." PhD thesis, Brown University, 1975.

Monmonier, Mark. *Bushmanders and Bullwinkles: How Politicians Manipulate Electronic Maps and Census Data to Win Elections.* Chicago: University of Chicago Press, 2001.

———. *Drawing the Line.* New York: Henry Holt, 1995.

———. *Spying with Maps.* Chicago: University of Chicago Press, 2002.

Muir, Diana. *Reflections in Bullough's Pond: Economy and Ecosystem in New England.* Hanover, N.H.: University Press of New England, 2000.

Murphy, Alexander B. "Geography's Place in Higher Education in the United States." *Journal of Geography in Higher Education* 31:1 (2007): 121-41.

Needham, Joseph. *Science and Civilisation in China,* vol. 3. Cambridge: Cambridge University Press, 1959: 497-590.

Nelson, Arthur E. *Surficial Geologic Map of the Natick Quadrangle, Middlesex and Norfolk Counties, Massachusetts.* Washington, D.C.: USGS Map GQ-1151, 1974.

Norris, Tim. "Review of *Maya Atlas: The Struggle to Preserve Maya Land in Southern Belize by the Maya Mapping Project.*" *Natural History* (April 1998): 10.

Novak, Peter. *That Noble Dream: The "Objectivity" Question and the American Historical Profession.* Cambridge: Cambridge University Press, 1988.

Office for National Statistics. *National Statistics Online website.* 2005. http://www.statistics.gov.uk/StatBase/Expodata/Spreadsheets/D6803.xls (accessed on August 22, 2005).

The Official Atlas of the Civil War. New York: Thomas Yoseloff, 1958.

Ogburn, Dennis E. "Assessing the Level of Visibility of Cultural Objects in Past Landscapes." *Journal of Archaeological Science* 33 (2006): 405-13.

Openshaw, Stanley. *The Modifiable Areal Unit Problem. Concepts and Techniques in Modern Geography,* 38. Norwich: Geobooks, 1984.

O'Sullivan, David, and David Unwin. *Geographic Information Analysis.* Chichester: John Wiley & Sons, Inc., 2003.

Ouyang Min 歐陽忞. *Yudi guangji* 興地廣記. Chengdu: Sichuan da xue chu ban she, 2003.

Owen, J. B., and Laura Woodworth-Ney. "Envisioning a Master's Degree Program in Geographically Integrated History." *Journal of the Association for History and Computing* 8:2 (2005): n.p.

Padrón, Ricardo. *The Spacious Word: Cartography, Literature, and Empire in Early Modern Spain.* Chicago: University of Chicago Press, 2004.

Palamidese, Patrizia. *Scientific Visualization: Advanced Software Techniques.* New York: Ellis Horwood, 1993.

Park, Robert E., and Ernest W. Burgess. *The City.* Chicago: University of Chicago Press, 1925.

Patterson, William A., and Kenneth E. Sassaman. "Indian Fires in the Prehistory of New England." In *Holocene Human Ecology in Northeastern North America,* edited by George P. Nicholas. New York: Plenum Press, 1988: 107-35.

Paxman, Jeremy. *The English: A Portrait of a People.* London: Penguin, 1999.

Pearson, Alastair W., and Peter Collier. "Agricultural History with GIS." In *Past Time, Past Place: GIS for History,* edited by Anne Kelly Knowles, 105-16. Redlands, Calif.: ESRI Press, 2002.

Peterson, C.A. "Court and Province in Mid- and Late T'ang." In *The Cambridge History of China,* vol. 3: *Sui and T'ang China, 589–906,* edited by D. Twitchett, 464–550. Cambridge: Cambridge University Press, 1979.

Peuquet, Donna J. *Representations of Space and Time.* New York: Guilford, 2002.

Pfanz, Harry W. *Gettysburg: The Second Day.* Chapel Hill, N.C.: University of North Carolina Press, 1987.

Pickles, John. "Arguments, Debates, and Dialogues: The GIS-Social Theory Debate and the Concern for Alternatives." In *Geographic Information Systems,* edited by Paul A. Longley, Michael F. Goodchild, David J. Maguire, and David W. Rhind, 49–60. New York: John Wiley & Sons, Inc., 1999.

———, ed. *Ground Truth: The Social Implications of Geographic Information Systems.* New York: Guilford Press, 1995.

———. "Representations in an Electronic Age: Geography, GIS, and Democracy." In *Ground Truth: The Social Implications of Geographic Information Systems,* edited by John Pickles, 1–50. New York: Guilford Press, 1995.

Pickover, Clifford A., and Stuart K. Tewsbury, eds. *Frontiers of Scientific Visualization.* New York: John Wiley & Sons, Inc., 1994.

Plewe, Brandon. "The Nature of Uncertainty in Historical Geographic Information." *Transactions in GIS* 6:4 (2002): 431–56.

Powell, Sumner Chilton. *Puritan Village: The Formation of a New England Town.* Middletown, Conn.: Wesleyan University Press, 1963.

Ramankutty, Navin, and Jonathan A. Foley. "Characterizing Patterns of Global Land Use: An Analysis of Global Croplands Data." *Global Biogeochemical Cycles* 12 (1998): 667–85.

———. "Estimating Historical Changes in Global Land Cover: Croplands from 1700 to 1992." *Global Biogeochemical Cycles* 13 (1999): 997–1027.

Raper, Jonathan. *Multidimensional Geographic Information Science: Extending GIS in Space and Time.* New York: Taylor & Francis, 2000.

Ray, Benjamin C. "Teaching the Salem Witch Trials." In *Past Time, Past Place: GIS for History,* edited by Anne Kelly Knowles, 19–33. Redlands, Calif.: ESRI Press, 2002.

Reardon, Carol. *Pickett's Charge in History and Memory.* Chapel Hill, N.C.: University of North Carolina Press, 1997.

"Reports on National Historical GIS Projects" (various authors). *Historical Geography* 33 (2005): 134–58.

Robinson, Arthur H. *The Look of Maps.* Madison, Wis.: University of Wisconsin Press, 1952.

Robinson, Arthur H., and Barbara Bartz Petchenik. *The Nature of Maps: Essays toward Understanding Maps and Mapping.* Chicago: University of Chicago Press, 1976.

Robinson, Arthur. H., Joel L. Morrison, Phillip C. Muehrke, A. J. Kimerling, and S. C. Guptill. *Elements of Cartography,* 6th ed. Chichester: John Wiley & Sons, Inc., 1995.

Rogerson, Peter A. *Statistical Methods for Geographers.* London: Sage, 2001.

Rosenfeld, Gavriel. "Why Do We Ask 'What If?' Reflections on the Function of Alternative History." *History and Theory* 41 (December 2002): 90–103.

Rumsey, David, and Edith M. Punt. *Cartographica Extraordinaire: The Historical Map Transformed.* Redlands, Calif.: ESRI Press, 2004.

Rumsey, David, and Meredith Williams. "Historical Maps in GIS." In *Past Time, Past Place: GIS for History,* edited by Anne Kelly Knowles, 1–18. Redlands, Calif.: ESRI Press, 2002.

Rush, Mark E. "Teaching Reapportionment Using GIS." Paper presented at the Associated College of the South GIS symposium. Georgetown, Tex., February 2003.

Rush, Mark, and John Blackburn. "Political Science: Redistricting for Justice and Power." In *Understanding Place: GIS and Mapping across the Curriculum,* edited by Diana Stuart Sinton and Jennifer J. Lund, 128–39. Redlands, Calif.: ESRI Press, 2007.

Salway, Benet. "The Nature and Genesis of the Peutinger Map." *Imago Mundi* 57 (2005): 119–35.

———. "Travel, *Itineraria* and *Tabellaria*." In *Travel and Geography in the Roman Empire,* edited by Colin Adams and Ray Laurence, 22–66. London and New York: Routledge, 2001.

Schama, Simon. *Landscape and Memory.* New York: Random House, 1996.

Seaman, David. "GIS and the Frontier of Digital Access: Applications of GIS Technology in the Research Library." Paper presented at Future Foundations: Mapping the Past—Building the Greater Philadelphia GeoHistory Network, held at the Chemical Heritage Foundation, Philadelphia, organized by The Philadelphia Area Consortium of Special Collections Libraries, December 3, 2005.

Shaw, Clifford R., and Henry D. McKay. *Juvenile Delinquents and Urban Areas.* Chicago: University of Chicago Press, 1942.

Shaw, Gareth, and Dennis Wheeler. *Statistical Techniques in Geographical Analysis.* London: David Fulton, 1994.

Sheehan-Dean, Aaron C. "Similarity and Difference in the Antebellum North and South." In *Past Time, Past Place: GIS for History,* edited by Anne Kelly Knowles, 35–49. Redlands, Calif.: ESRI Press, 2002.

Sheppard, Eric. "Knowledge Production through Critical GIS: Genealogy and Prospects." *Cartographica* 40:4 (2005): 5–21.

Shiba Yoshinobu. "Ningpo and Its Hinterland." In *The City in Late Imperial China,* edited by G. W. Skinner, 391–440. Stanford: Stanford University Press, 1977.

——— 斯波義信. "Sōdai no toshika wo kangaeru 宋代の都市化を考える." *Tōbōgaku* 東方學 102 (2001): 1–19.

Shui Anli 税安禮. *Lidai dili zhizhang tu* 歴代地理抵掌圖. Shanghai, Shanghai guji chuban she, 1989 reprint.

Siebert, Loren. "Rail Names as Indicators of Enduring Influence of Old Provinces in Modern Japan." *Geographical Review of Japan,* ser. B, 73:1 (2002): 1–26.

———. "Urbanization Transition Types and Zones in Tokyo and Kanagawa Prefectures." *Geographical Review of Japan,* ser. B, 73:2 (2000): 207–24.

———. "Using GIS to Document, Visualize, and Interpret Tokyo's Spatial History." *Social Science History* 24:3 (2000): 537–74.

———. "Using GIS to Map Rail Network History." *Journal of Transport History* 25:1 (2004): 84–104.

Sinton, Diana S., and Jennifer J. Lund. *Understanding Place: GIS and Mapping across the Curriculum.* Redlands, Calif.: ESRI Press, 2007.

Skinner, G. William. "Cities and the Hierarchy of Local Systems." In *The City in Late Imperial China,* edited by G. W. Skinner, 275–354. Stanford: Stanford University Press, 1977.

———. "Introduction: Urban Development in Imperial China." In *The City in Late Imperial China,* edited by G. W. Skinner, 3–32. Stanford: Stanford University Press, 1977.

———. "Marketing and Social Structure in Rural China." *Journal of Asian Studies* 24:1–3 (1964–1965): 3–43, 195–228, 363–399.

———. "The Structure of Chinese History." *Journal of Asian Studies* 44:2 (1985): 271–92.

Skinner, G. William, M. Henderson, and Jianhua Yuan. "China's Fertility Transition through Regional Space: Using GIS and Census Data for a Spatial Analysis of Historical Demography." *Social Science History* 24:3 (2000): 613–48.

Smith, Mark M. "Making Sense of Social History." *Journal of Social History* 37:1 (2003): 165–86.

Smith, Neil. "Real Wars, Theory Wars." *Progress in Human Geography* 16 (1992): 257–71.

Snow, Dean R. *The Archaeology of New England.* New York: Academic Press, 1980.

"Soils and Their Interpretation for Various Land Uses, Town of Concord, Massachusetts." Washington, D.C.: Soil Conservation Service, USDA, 1966.

Solnit, Rebecca. *Hollow City: The Siege of San Francisco and the Crisis of American Urbanism.* New York: Verso, 2000.

*Song shi*宋史 *(Scripta Sinica ed.),* www.sinica.edu.tw.

Stafford, Barbara Maria. *Good Looking: Essays on the Virtue of Images.* Cambridge, Mass.: MIT Press, 1996.

Staley, David J. *Computers, Visualization, and History: How New Technology Will Transform Our Understanding of the Past.* Armonk, N.Y.: M.E. Sharpe, 2003.

Stern, Fritz, ed. *The Varieties of History: From Voltaire to the Present.* New York: Vintage Books, 1972.

Stone, Michael. "Map or Be Mapped." *Whole Earth* (Fall 1998): 54.

Sui, Daniel Z. "GIS, Cartography, and the 'Third Culture': Geographic Imaginations in the Computer Age." *Professional Geographer* 56 (2004): 62–72.

Summerby-Murray, Robert. "Analysing Heritage Landscapes with Historical GIS: Contributions from Problem-Based Inquiry and Constructivist Pedagogy." *Journal of Geography in Higher Education* 25:1 (2001): 37–52.

———. "Historical Geography: Mapping Our Architectural Heritage." In *Understanding Place: GIS and Mapping Across the Curriculum,* edited by Diana Sinton and Jennifer Lund, 237–47. Redlands, Calif.: ESRI Press, 2007.

Talbert, Richard J. A., ed., in collaboration with Roger S. Bagnall, et al., map editors Mary E. Downs and M. Joann McDaniel. *Barrington Atlas of the Greek and Roman World.* Princeton, N. J.: Princeton University Press, 2000.

Talbert, Richard. "Cartography and Taste in Peutinger's Roman Map." In *Space in the Roman World: Its Perception and Presentation,* edited by Richard Talbert and Kai Brodersen, 113–41. Münster: LIT, 2004.

Talbert, Richard. "Konrad Miller, Roman Cartography, and the Lost Western End of the Peutinger Map." In *Historische Geographie der Alten Welt. Grundlagen, Erträge, Perspektiven: Festgabe für Eckart Olshausen aus Anlass seiner Emeritierung,* edited by Ulrich Fellmeth, Peter Guyot, and Holger Sonnabend, 353–66. Hildesheim: Olms, 2007.

Talbert, Richard. "Rome's Provinces as Framework for World-View." In *Roman Rule and Civic Life: Local and Regional Perspectives,* edited by Luuk De Ligt, et al, 21–37. Amsterdam: Gieben, 2004.

Tan Qixiang 谭其骧, ed. *Zhongguo lishi ditu ji* 中國歷史地圖集. Shanghai, Ditu chubanshe, 1982.

Tang Rensen 唐壬森, ed. *Lanxi xianzhi* 蘭溪縣志. 8 *juan.* 1888.

Taylor, Peter J., and Ronald J. Johnston. "GIS and Geography." In *Ground Truth: The Social Implications of Geographic Information Systems,* edited by John Pickles. New York: Guilford Press, 1995: 51–67.

Ter Haar, B. "Local Society and the Organization of Cults in Early Modern China: A Preliminary Study." *Studies in Central and East Asian Religions* 8 (1995): 1–43.

Thogersen, S., and S. Clausen. "New Reflections on the Mirror: Local Chinese Gazetteers *(difangzhi)* in the 1980s." *Australian Journal of Chinese Affairs* 27 (1992): 1–24.

Thomas, Emory M. "Eggs, Aldie, Shepherdstown, and J. E. B. Stuart." In *The Gettysburg Nobody Knows*, edited by Gabor S. Boritt. New York: Oxford University Press, 1997: 101–21.

———. *Robert E. Lee: A Biography*. New York: W. W. Norton, 1995.

Thomas, Peter A. "Contrasting Subsistence Strategies and Land Use as Factors for Understanding Indian-White Relations in New England." *Ethnohistory* 23 (1976): 1–18.

Thomas, William G. III, and Edward L. Ayers. "An Overview: The Differences Slavery Made: A Close Analysis of Two American Communities." *American Historical Review* 108 (2003): 1299–1308.

Tice, Jim, Erik Steiner, et al. *The Interactive Nolli Website.* http://nolli.uoregon.edu.

Tufte, Edward R. *The Visual Display of Quantitative Information.* Cheshire, Conn.: Graphics Press, 1986.

Tukey, John W. *Exploratory Data Analysis.* Reading, Mass.: Addison-Wesley, 1977.

Twain, Mark. *Life on the Mississippi.* New York: Bantam, 1983.

Twitchett, Denis C. *Financial Administration under the T'ang Dynasty.* Cambridge: Cambridge University Press, 1963.

von Glahn, Richard. "Towns and Temples: Urban Growth and Decline in the Yangzi Delta, 1100–1400." In *The Song-Yuan-Ming Transition in Chinese History*, edited by P. J. Smith and R. V. Glahn, 176–211. Cambridge: Harvard University Asia Center, 2003.

Wang Cun 王存, ed. *Yuanfeng jiuyu zhi* 元豐九域志. 1784.

Wang Cun 王存, ed. *Yuanfeng jiuyu zhi* 元豐九域志. Beijing, Zhonghua shuju, 1984.

Wang Maode 王懋德, ed. *Jinhua fuzhi* 金華府志. 30 *juan.* 1578.

Wang, S. J.-S. "Out of Control: The Place of Shanshui (Mountains and Rivers) in the Geographical Discourse of Early Imperial China." PhD thesis, Ann Arbor, University of Michigan, 1999.

Wang Zhuo 王倬 and Zhang Mao 章懋, eds. *Lanxi xianzhi* 蘭溪縣志. 5 *juan.* 1510; 1614 reprint.

The War of the Rebellion: A Compilation of the Official Records of the Union and Confederate Armies, 69 vols., prepared under the direction of the Secretary of War by Robert N. Scott. Washington, D.C.: Government Printing Office, 1880–1900.

Weber, Ekkehard. *Tabula Peutingeriana: Codex Vindobonensis 324.* Graz: Akademische Druck-u. Verlagsanstalt, 1976.

Wei Zheng 魏徵, and Linghu Defen 令狐德棻. *Sui shu* 隋書. *Scripta Sinica* ed. Beijing: Zhonghua shuju, 1973.

Wheatley, Paul. *The Pivot of the Four Quarters: A Preliminary Enquiry into the Origins and Character of the Ancient Chinese City.* Chicago: Aldine, 1971.

Wheeler, Michael. "Topography, Politics, and the Erie Canal." Paper presented at the Association of American Geographers annual meeting, Chicago, March 9, 2006.

Whitney, Gordon G., and William C. Davis, "Thoreau and the Forest History of Concord, Massachusetts." *Forest History* 30 (1986): 70–81.

Wilkinson, E. P. *Chinese History: A Manual.* Cambridge, Mass.: Harvard University Asia Center for the Harvard-Yenching Institute, distributed by Harvard University Press, 2000.

Williams, Terry Tempest. *Refuge: An Unnatural History of Family and Place.* New York: Vintage, 1992.

Winchester, Simon. *The Map that Changed the World: William Smith and the Birth of Modern Geology.* New York: HarperCollins, 2001.

Winters, Harold A. *Battling the Elements: Weather and Terrain in the Conduct of War.* Baltimore: Johns Hopkins University Press, 1998.

Wood, Denis. *The Power of Maps.* New York: Guilford Press, 1992.

Wood, Joseph S. *The New England Village.* Baltimore: Johns Hopkins Press, 1997.

Woodward, David, et al., eds. *The History of Cartography,* vol. 1 and vol. 2, books 1, 2, 3. Chicago: University of Chicago Press, 1987-1998.

Worster, Donald. *Dust Bowl: The Southern Plains in the 1930s.* New York: Oxford University Press, 1979.

Xue Dingming 薛鼎銘, ed. *Pujiang xianzhi* 浦江縣志. 20 *juan.* 1779.

Yee, Cordell D. K. "Cartography in China." In *The History of Cartography: Cartography in the Traditional East and Southeast Asian Societies,* vol. 2, book 2, edited by J. B. Harley and D. Woodward, 35-202, 228-31. Chicago: University of Chicago Press, 1994.

Yue Shi 樂史. *Taiping huan yu ji* 太平寰宇記. Taibei, Taiwan shang wu yin shu guan 臺灣商務印書館, 1983 reprint.

Zhang, Jingxiong, and Michael F. Goodchild. *Uncertainty in Geographical Information.* London, New York: Taylor & Francis, 2002.

Zhang Minggeng 张明庚 and Zhang Mingju 张明聚, eds. *Zhongguo lidai xingzheng quhua: gongyuan qian 211 nian—gongyuan 1991 nian* 中国历代行政区划: 公元前211年—公元1991年. Beijing 北京, Zhongguo Huaqiao chuban she 中国华侨出版社, 1996.

Zheng Qiao 鄭樵. *Tong zhi* 通志. Beijing, Zhonghua shuju, 1987.

Zhou Shiying 周士英, ed. *Yiwu xianzhi* 義烏縣志. 20 *juan.* 1596; 1640 reprint.

Zhou xian tigang 州縣提綱 (*Congshu jicheng* ed.).

Zhou Yinghe 周應合. *Jingding Jiankangzhi* 景定建康志. 1809.

Zhou Zongzhi 周宗智, ed. *Jinhua fuzhi* 金華府志. 20 *juan.* 1480.

Zou Zhenhuan 鄒振環. *Wan Qing xifang dili xue zai Zhongguo: yi 1815 zhi 1911 nian xifang dilixue yizhu de zhuanbo yu yingxiang wei zhongxi* 晚清西方地理學在中國: 1815 至1911年西方地理譯著的轉播與影響為中心. Shanghai, Shanghai guji chuban she, 2000.

ABOUT THE AUTHORS

Roberta Balstad (PhD in history, 1973, University of Minnesota) is senior research scientist at Columbia University and a Senior Fellow with the Center for International Earth Science Information Network (CIESIN), where she served as director from 1998 to 2005. Her prior executive positions include director of the Division of Social and Economic Science at the National Science Foundation. She also taught at colleges and universities, including Catholic University and University of Michigan. Her publications include *City and Hinterland: A Case Study of Urban Growth and Regional Development* (Greenwood Press 1979) and more recent essays on science and society, crises in the social sciences, and remote sensing and GIS.

David J. Bodenhamer (PhD in American history, 1977, Indiana University) is professor of history and executive director of The Polis Center at Indiana University-Purdue University, Indianapolis. His extensive publications include *The Bill of Rights in Modern America: After 200 Years* (Indiana University Press 1993) and *Fair Trial: Rights of the Accused in American History* (Oxford University Press 1992). He is North American team director for ECAI, the Electronic Cultural Atlas Initiative. His online atlas of religion in North America (www.religionatlas.org) is one of the first large historical GIS to be completed and made accessible to the general public on the Internet.

Peter K. Bol (PhD in East Asian studies, 1982, Princeton University) is Charles H. Carswell Professor of Chinese History and chair of the Department of East Asian Languages and Civilizations at Harvard University. He is also founding director of the Center for Geographic Analysis at Harvard. Since 1998 he has been director of the National Resource Center for East Asia. He currently directs the China Historical GIS project based at the Harvard Yenching Institute. He has published dozens of articles and five books, most recently *Ways with Words: Writing about Reading Texts from Early China* (Stanford University Press 2000).

Robert Churchill (PhD in geography, 1979, The University of Iowa) was professor of geography at Middlebury College, where he made his career as a teacher and mentor and introduced the teaching of GIS. His wide-ranging publications include studies of the geography of suicide, ice in the Great Lakes, flood hazards in Sri Lanka, and cartographic techniques. Dr. Churchill was an experienced educator who organized a series of innovative GIS institutes at Middlebury. He was a physical geographer and cartographer by training but learned GIS in the context of his teaching and research interests in social and cultural geography.

Geoff Cunfer (PhD in history, 1999, University of Texas-Austin) is associate professor of history at the University of Saskatchewan. Before moving to Saskatchewan, he was director of the Center for Rural and Regional Studies at Southwest Minnesota State University. His publications include *On the Great Plains: Agriculture and Environment* (Texas A&M University Press 2005), which won the President's Award for best first book from the Social Science History Association. Currently he is developing a historical GIS that uses physical geographical data, such as meteorological and soils data, to provide a clearer picture of the course and social consequences of agricultural disaster.

Brian Donahue (PhD in history, 1995, Brandeis University) is associate professor of American Studies in the Environmental Studies Program at Brandeis University. He formerly was director of education at The Land Institute in Salina, Kansas, and was the recipient of a National Endowment of the Humanities Independent Scholar Fellowship in 1997. His book *The Great Meadow: Farmers and the Land in Colonial Concord* (Yale University Press 2004), which won the George Perkins Marsh Award from the American Society for Environmental History and the Theodore Saloutos Prize from the Agricultural History Society, is based on GIS analysis of historical sources. He also wrote *Reclaiming the Commons: Community Farming and Forestry in a New England Town* (Yale University Press 1999).

Tom Elliott (PhD in ancient history, 2004, University of North Carolina at Chapel Hill) is director of the Ancient World Mapping Center at the University of North Carolina at Chapel Hill. He is an interdisciplinary scholar, having approached his graduate studies in ancient history from a background in computer science. His dissertation examines the history of Roman imperial boundary disputes. He constructed and manages the historical GIS at the heart of the Ancient World Mapping project, the ongoing digitization and expansion of the spatial information published in the *Barrington Atlas of the Greek and Roman World* (Princeton 2000).

Michael F. Goodchild (PhD in geography, 1969, McMaster University) is professor of geography at the University of California, Santa Barbara; chair of the executive committee, National Center for Geographic Information and Analysis (NCGIA); associate director of the Alexandria Digital Library Project; and director of NCGIA's Center for Spatially Integrated Social Science. He is a member of the National Academy of Sciences and of the American Academy of Arts and Sciences. The most recent of his many honors and awards are induction into the GIS Hall of Fame of the Urban and Regional Information Systems Association, the Lifetime Achievement

Award of the Geospatial Information and Technology Association, and the Prix Vautrin Lud of the Festival International de Géographie (all 2007). He was editor of the Methods, Models, and Geographic Information Sciences section of the *Annals of the Association of the American Geographers* from 2000 to 2006. He has written or coauthored some fifteen books and over four hundred scientific papers.

Ian N. Gregory (PhD in geography, 2001, University of London) is a Senior Lecturer in Digital Humanities at Lancaster University. He has published extensively on the use of GIS in historical research, including *Historical GIS: Technologies, Methodologies and Scholarship* (Cambridge 2007, coauthored by Paul S. Ell) and *A Place in History: A Guide to Using GIS in Historical Research* (Oxbow 2003). He was architect of the Great Britain Historical GIS, and most of his work focuses on the creation and use of historical GIS databases. More recently, he has become interested in using GIS in other humanities desciplines such as English literature.

Amy Hillier (PhD in social welfare, 2001, University of Pennsylvania) is assistant professor in the Department of City and Regional Planning, University of Pennsylvania. A series of recent and forthcoming articles explore her dissertation and postdoctoral research on redlining in Philadelphia, in which she used GIS-based spatial analysis to test long-standing assumptions about the extent and characteristics of discriminatory lending. She has also researched neighborhood-level determinants of preterm birth, physical activity, and obesity under grants from the National Institutes of Health, Center for Disease Control and Prevention, and Robert Wood Johnson Foundation.

Anne Kelly Knowles (PhD in geography, 1993, University of Wisconsin, Madison) is associate professor in the Department of Geography at Middlebury College. She has edited three previous volumes of essays on historical GIS, including *Past Time, Past Place: GIS for History* (ESRI Press 2002). Her research on early nineteenth-century immigration and industrialization appears in *Calvinists Incorporated: Welsh Immigrants on Ohio's Industrial Frontier* (University of Chicago Press 1997) and many articles. The book she is writing on the American iron industry, 1800–1868, has been supported by fellowships from the American Council of Learned Societies and the National Endowment for the Humanities.

Richard Talbert (PhD in classics, 1972; Litt.D., 2003, Cambridge University) is William Rand Kenan, Jr. Professor of History at the University of North Carolina at Chapel Hill. Dr. Talbert's distinguished career in the study of the classics and classical history has yielded several important books, including *The Senate of Imperial Rome* (Princeton University Press), which won the American Philological Association's Award of Merit and two editions of *Plutarch on Sparta* (Penguin 1988, 2005). He has an extensive record as an editor of journals, monograph series, and reference works. Several of his publications treat the world-views and map consciousness of the ancient Greeks and Romans, and he is no less concerned with the revival of cartographic study in contemporary classical research. His comprehensive *Barrington Atlas of the Greek and Roman World* appeared from Princeton in 2000. Recently, he has worked to establish a permanent Ancient World Mapping Center at UNC-Chapel Hill to expand and diversify the achievement of the *Barrington Atlas,* in part through the development of relevant historical GIS.

    Richard White (PhD in history, University of Washington) is the Margaret Byrne Professor of American History at Stanford University and codirector of the Bill Lane Center for the North American West. He is the author of many books and articles, among them *The Organic Machine* (1995), *The Middle Ground* (1991), and *"Its Your Misfortune and None of My Own": A New History of the American West* (1991). He is a recipient of an Andrew Mellon Distinguished Achievement Award that is funding a new project on Spatial History at Stanford.

INDEX

database management systems, development of, 182

datasets
 analyzing, 134
 representing spatial aspects of, 124

Davidson, Amelie, 84

de Vorsey, Louis, 241

deciles, splitting data into, 139

Declaration of Independence, 69

demographic data, treatment of, 64. *See also* geodemographic firms

density analysis, applying in CHGIS, 46

dependent variables, estimating values of, 141

di li zhi, translation of, 38

"The Differences Slavery Made," 6

digital boundary files, creating, 78-79

digital Derby, building of, 10

digital gazetteers, emergence of, 229. *See also* gazetteers

digital history, 5-6

digital resource, application of, 6

Dirty Thirties, dust storms in, 111

Domesday England, 8

Donahue, Brian, xv, 8, 151, 267-268, 294

Dorofeeva-Lichtmann, Vera, 38-39

drought, relationship to dust storms, 108-109

Dust Bowl. *See also* plains climates
 causes of, 96-97, 109
 limited information about, 117
 relationship to New Deal policies, 117
 study of, 102

Dust Bowl: The Southern Plains in the 1930s, 97-100, 102

dust storms
 before big plow-up (1854-1896), 109-114
 causes of, 100
 common occurrence of, 110-111
 comparing reports of, 116
 descriptions of, 111-112
 documentation of, 110-111
 and drought, 108-109
 exacerbation of, 118
 mapping, 112
 occurrences by county, 116
 and plowed land, 106-107
 shifting spatial and temporal scales for study of, 109-110

dynamic data, analysis of, 196

Eagle (Wichita, Kansas), 117

ecological fallacy, 128

Edinburgh University (Great Britain Historical GIS), 15

Edo-Tokyo, spatial history of, 10

education, impact of GIS on, 63

Edwardian England, infant mortality in, 129

Electronic Cultural Atlas Initiative (ECAI), 16, 271

Eliot, T. S., 221

Ell, Paul S., 132

Elliott, Tom, xiv, 13, 199, 207-208, 267, 294

Emerson, Ralph Waldo, 153

England and Wales, north-south divide in, 129, 136

Enlarged Terrestrial Atlas (1553), 42

Enlightenment, view of maps during, 67

environmental history and GIS, 8-9, 16, 96-118, 152-175

error, 131-132, 212-215

ethical questions, raising, 67

Eurasian landmass, map of, 42

Europe (AD 300-900) study, 9-10

Europe and Eurasia, historical GIS projects in (2005), 15

exploratory approaches, applying spatial statistics in, 128

expressway construction
 impact on Philadelphia's Skid Row, 80-82
 impact on South Street in Philadelphia, 84

expressway projects, examples of, 78

faculty, GIS resources available to, 270

Farrell, Lucas, 235

Favro, Diane, 10-11

feature locations, plotting in thematic maps, 125

Feinberg, Andrew, 235

figures. *See also* historical maps; maps
 areal weighting, 131
 "Boundary Map of Boluo County," Guangdong, 43
 Concord East Quarter land use (1749), 170-171
 Concord East Quarter settlement, 163
 Concord First Division (circa 1652), 159
 Concord landownership patterns, 164-167
 Concord native landscape (1600), 157
 Concord surficial geology, 154-155

quantitative history, ix, 2, 103-109, 124-146, 267-268

Queen's University, Belfast study, 10

racial concentrations (1935), mapping, 77

rain shortfalls, relationship to dust storm locations, 109

rainfall deficits, mapping for southern plains, 108

raster GIS maps versus polygons, 87

Ray, Benjamin C., 6

Ready Charts of Geography through the Ages, 34

reapportionment process, scrutiny of, 69

Record of the Best Sights of the Realm, 48

redistricting process, interpreting, 69-70

redlining example, 87-90

Refuge, 71

regions, components of, 194

registers, treatment in CHGIS, 41

relational database management systems
    applying to map content, 183
    development of, 182
    dissatisfaction with, 195

religion history, future application of, 230

religious networks, treatment in CHGIS, 51-52

research questions, formulation of, 72, 80, 82, 84-87

residential patterns, comparing over time, 76

residential security maps, creation of, 75

The Road to Botany Bay: An Essay in Spatial History, 4-5

Roman Empire, geography of, 13. *See also* Peutinger Map

Rothstein, Arthur, 97

Roush, Will, 235

Rumsey, David, 12, 76, 229

Rush, Mark, 71

Salem Witch Trials Archive, 5-6

Salina, Kansas publications, reports of dust storms in, 109

scale, and geographical analysis, 9, 101-102, 103-110, 118

Schama, Simon, 67

scholarly practice, historical GIS as, 8-17

Scott, Winfield, 240

Second Division grants, reflecting in Concord study, 160-162

Seibert, Loren, 10

senses, history of, 239

Shaw, Clifford, 82

Shenandoah Valley, map of, 241-242

Shun and Yu, story of, 29

Sioux territory (1855-1856), survey of, 240-241

Skinner, William G., 47

slavery, relationship to "modernity," 6

slope term, use with predictor variable, 141

Smith, Neil, 67

Smith, William (atlas of 1874), 16-17, 223

Snow, John, 223

social class, W. E. B. Du Bois's map of, 74-75

social issues, engaging students in, 67-68

social science research. *See also* quantitative history
    historical GIS applied to, 2, 14

software programs, needs for, 272

Soja, Edward, ix

Song dynasty, transition of Tang dynasty to, 47

source zones versus target zones, 130

South Korean HGIS, 15

southern plains
    progress of plow-up in, 105-106
    rainfall shortages in, 108

space
    importance of, 126-127
    including in analysis, 128
    relationship to analytical thinking, 86-90
    relationship to historical geography, 126-127
    relationship to places, 127
    relationship to time, 127
    and spatial statistics, 126-128
    treatment as cultural marker, 229

SPACE (Spatial Perspectives for Analysis in Curriculum Enhancement) program, objective of, 270

spatial analysis
    capabilities of, x, 146
    limitation of, 126-127

spatial analysis research topics
    Great Irish Famine, 129
    infant mortality in England and Wales, 129

spatial autocorrelation, measuring, 134

spatial data
    finding, 74, 79-80
    linking with attribute data, 126

spatial economy and land use, history of, 8-10

DATA LICENSE AGREEMENT

Important: Read carefully before opening the sealed media package

Environmental Systems Research Institute, Inc. (ESRI), is willing to license the enclosed data and related materials to you only upon the condition that you accept all of the terms and conditions contained in this license agreement. Software provided with the data and related materials may be subject to a separate click-through license. Please read the terms and conditions carefully before opening the sealed media package. By opening the sealed media package, you are indicating your acceptance of the ESRI License Agreement. If you do not agree to the terms and conditions as stated, then ESRI is unwilling to license the data and related materials to you. In such event, you should return the media package with the seal unbroken and all other components to ESRI.

ESRI LICENSE AGREEMENT

This is a license agreement, and not an agreement for sale, between you (Licensee) and Environmental Systems Research Institute, Inc. (ESRI). This ESRI License Agreement (Agreement) gives Licensee certain limited rights to use the data and related materials (Data and Related Materials). All rights not specifically granted in this Agreement are reserved to ESRI and its Licensors.

Reservation of Ownership and Grant of License: ESRI and its Licensors retain exclusive rights, title, and ownership to the copy of the Data and Related Materials licensed under this Agreement and, hereby, grant to Licensee a personal, nonexclusive, nontransferable, royalty-free, worldwide license to use the Data and Related Materials based on the terms and conditions of this Agreement. Licensee agrees to use reasonable effort to protect the Data and Related Materials from unauthorized use, reproduction, distribution, or publication.

Proprietary Rights and Copyright: Licensee acknowledges that the Data and Related Materials are proprietary and confidential property of ESRI and its Licensors and are protected by United States copyright laws and applicable international copyright treaties and/or conventions.

Permitted Uses: Licensee may install the Data and Related Materials onto permanent storage device(s) for Licensee's own internal use.

Licensee may make only one (1) copy of the original Data and Related Materials for archival purposes during the term of this Agreement unless the right to make additional copies is granted to Licensee in writing by ESRI.

Licensee may internally use the Data and Related Materials provided by ESRI for the stated purpose of GIS training and education.

Uses Not Permitted: Licensee shall not sell, rent, lease, sublicense, lend, assign, time-share, or transfer, in whole or in part, or provide unlicensed Third Parties access to the Data and Related Materials or portions of the Data and Related Materials, any updates, or Licensee's rights under this Agreement.

Licensee shall not remove or obscure any copyright or trademark notices of ESRI or its Licensors.

Term and Termination: The license granted to Licensee by this Agreement shall commence upon the acceptance of this Agreement and shall continue until such time that Licensee elects in writing to discontinue use of the Data or Related Materials and terminates this Agreement. The Agreement shall automatically terminate without notice if Licensee fails to comply with any provision of this Agreement. Licensee shall then return to ESRI the Data and Related Materials. The parties hereby agree that all provisions that operate to protect the rights of ESRI and its Licensors shall remain in force should breach occur.

Disclaimer of Warranty: The Data and Related Materials contained herein are provided "as-is," without warranty of any kind, either express or implied, including, but not limited to, the implied warranties of merchantability, fitness for a particular purpose, or noninfringement. ESRI does not warrant that the Data and Related Materials will meet Licensee's needs or expectations, that the use of the Data and Related Materials will be uninterrupted, or that all nonconformities, defects, or errors can or will be corrected. ESRI is not inviting reliance on the Data or Related Materials for commercial planning or analysis purposes, and Licensee should always check actual data.

Data Disclaimer: The Data used herein has been derived from actual spatial or tabular information. In some cases, ESRI has manipulated and applied certain assumptions, analyses, and opinions to the Data solely for educational training purposes. Assumptions, analyses, opinions applied, and actual outcomes may vary. Again, ESRI is not inviting reliance on this Data, and the Licensee should always verify actual Data and exercise their own professional judgment when interpreting any outcomes.

Limitation of Liability: ESRI shall not be liable for direct, indirect, special, incidental, or consequential damages related to Licensee's use of the Data and Related Materials, even if ESRI is advised of the possibility of such damage.

No Implied Waivers: No failure or delay by ESRI or its Licensors in enforcing any right or remedy under this Agreement shall be construed as a waiver of any future or other exercise of such right or remedy by ESRI or its Licensors.

Order for Precedence: Any conflict between the terms of this Agreement and any FAR, DFAR, purchase order, or other terms shall be resolved in favor of the terms expressed in this Agreement, subject to the government's minimum rights unless agreed otherwise.

Export Regulation: Licensee acknowledges that this Agreement and the performance thereof are subject to compliance with any and all applicable United States laws, regulations, or orders relating to the export of data thereto. Licensee agrees to comply with all laws, regulations, and orders of the United States in regard to any export of such technical data.

Severability: If any provision(s) of this Agreement shall be held to be invalid, illegal, or unenforceable by a court or other tribunal of competent jurisdiction, the validity, legality, and enforceability of the remaining provisions shall not in any way be affected or impaired thereby.

Governing Law: This Agreement, entered into in the County of San Bernardino, shall be construed and enforced in accordance with and be governed by the laws of the United States of America and the State of California without reference to conflict of laws principles. The parties hereby consent to the personal jurisdiction of the courts of this county and waive their rights to change venue.

Entire Agreement: The parties agree that this Agreement constitutes the sole and entire agreement of the parties as to the matter set forth herein and supersedes any previous agreements, understandings, and arrangements between the parties relating hereto.

Related titles from ESRI Press

Past Time, Past Place: GIS for History
ISBN 978-1-58948-032-2

Understanding Place: GIS and Mapping
across the Curriculum
ISBN 978-1-58948-149-7

Mapping the Future of America's
National Parks: Stewardship through
Geographic Information Systems
ISBN 978-1-58948-080-3

Charting the Unknown: How Computer
Mapping at Harvard Became GIS
ISBN 978-1-58948-118-3

ESRI Press publishes books about the science, application, and technology of GIS. Ask for these titles at your local bookstore or order by calling 1-800-447-9778. You can also read book descriptions, read reviews, and shop online at www.esri.com/esripress. Outside the United States, contact your local ESRI distributor.